EVANGELISTIC PREACHING

EVANGELISTIC PREACHING

CHARLES GRESHAM & KEITH KEERAN

COLLEGE PRESS PUBLISHING COMPANY
Joplin, Missouri

Library of Congress Catalog Card Number: 90-86282
International Standard Book Number: 0-89900-392-3

TABLE OF CONTENTS

PART III: Evangelistic Sermons from the Present

Foreword

What does the average person sitting in America's pews expect from listening to an evangelist of the Gospel of Christ? The truth! But not cold, hard imperatives stated in dogmatic terms. Rather, the old, familiar themes adorned with flesh and bones — truth encapsulated in a warm, feeling human being who can, by all the skill of the narrator's craft, bring that truth to the heart, not only to the mind.

I do not come to be astounded at the knowledge acquired through years of studying at the seminary or from reading Pulpit Digest. I do not come to listen to some new-fangled theory that applies to only a select few. I come to hear about God's love for me from a man who is personally acquainted with that love of God.

I do not come to be part of an audience as theater patrons are. I don't want to have my emotions played with lightly or my thinking trifled with. I don't want to be entertained or amused and neither do I want to be challenged to a theological debate nor to get ammunition so that I can debate others.

I come to be stirred to action. I want to feel what the Gospel writers felt. I want to feel what the speaker feels so that I can feel it too, and believe it too. I do not come to match wits with a clever speech-maker. I come to be challenged to living a better and much fuller life than I ever knew possible. I need to hear words of encouragement that I can share with others who, like me, may be floundering in a world mostly devoid of unselfish love. I come to see an evangelist emotionally involved in the message and filled with conviction.

I come to see Jesus.

Dr. Robert Migneault

General Introduction

Evangelism and Church Growth are concepts on the lips of many evangelicals in this present age. Such terms no longer appear to be antiquated, nor are they considered what Michael Green calls "dirty words." The word evangelism no longer has the connotation of "proselytizing about it, of big meetings and famous but perhaps simplistic and slick preachers." Whereas, this term suggested "illicit psychological pressure" and "mass hysteria," it now is seen within its original New Testament context as spreading the good news. Michael Green suggests that if evangelism is basically a matter of truth — truth about God's grace seen in Jesus of Nazareth and his reconciliation of sinful man — then "it is churlish to keep it to yourself. If you see the need others have of it, then you are likely to give yourself to enabling them to discover it." (Preface in David Watson, *I Believe in Evangelism*, Wm. B. Eerdmans, 1976, p. 7).

Going along with this renewed emphasis upon evangelism is the recognition that evangelism is the very heart of the Church, the Christian community, and that every member of the Body of Christ is involved in ministry which ought to be directed toward the Church's growth both externally and internally. The call then is to all to be involved in some way with the evangelistic efforts that local churches, both at home and abroad, are making. Not only is there a general ministry, a priesthood of all believers, but each minister or priest should be a witness of Christ and point, by work and word, toward the Good News in Him.

One of the important factors that seem to be significant in the growing, evangelistic church is a body of dynamic, witnessing members. Dr. Tetsunao Yamamori who has studied and written extensively in this area says that "a church likely to grow is made up of numerous dynamic witnessing members in actual and frequent contact with non-Christians in the community." (In Elmer L. Towns, *The Complete Book of Church Growth*, Tyndale House, 1982, p. 316). Other specialists agree with Dr. Yamamori. This is not only what careful study demonstrates but is a reinforcement of Biblical principles.

But, at the same time the "principle of witnessing members" is recognized as essential to a vibrant, evangelistic, growing church, the same experts who are studying growth patterns in American Churches are aware that a dedicated servant/leader (or pastor, as the term is frequently used to refer to this leader) is even more essential.

C. Peter Wagner writes out of his study and observation: "I have found that a pastor who is willing and able to lead his church in growth is the first vital sign of a healthy church." He adds: "to be perfectly frank, many churches are not growing because their pastor does not want them to grow." (In Towns, ibid., p. 280).

But, this is more than an attitude that such leaders must have and share. It is more than interpersonal relationships that encourage witnessing and evangelistic outreach. The servant/leader must recognize that his preaching is essential to a growing church. Elmer Towns, in a recent study, writes:

> It has become apparent that the major tool in building church attendance is the Sunday morning preaching service. Obviously, it must be supported by the Sunday school, counseling, evangelistic outreach, and other services of the church. Since the preaching service is the major tool in building the service, pastors will have to give more attention than ever before to the preparation and delivery of their messages. (Towns, ibid., p. 24).

This principle has been recognized within the Restoration Movement of recent years. The late Ira North, minister of the great Madison Church of Christ in Madison, Tennessee, authored a small book on Church Growth not long before his death. In this work, *Balance: A Tried and Tested Formula for Church Growth*, Dr. North sets this forth as the first basic principle: "A strong, solid, positive, sensible pulpit is essential." He writes:

> So much depends upon the pulpit. If the education program is to be strong and vibrant, it must have encouragement from the pulpit. If members are to grow spiritually

11

and be inspired and uplifted in their worship, they need to hear a message from the pulpit calculated to that end. A weak, or hostile, or insensitive pulpit can destroy more in a matter of minutes than can be built up with many hours of dedicated labor (Gospel Advocate Co., 1983, p. 13).

He adds:

> I have observed over a period of many years that congregations that grow have a strong pulpit.... There is no substitute for a strong, loyal, faithful, solid, sensible pulpit if the congregation is to grow (Ibid., p. 17).

This is one of the reasons for setting forth this book on evangelistic preaching. Preachers — servant/leaders of congregations of Christ — need to know what evangelism and evangelistic preaching is. They need to see such preaching within Christian history and within the Restoration Movement.They need to understand the current needs that pulpits must meet in this century and the next.

Every preacher will preach evangelistically at some time or other. In fact, whether in a special series of evangelistic services or Sunday after Sunday from his own pulpit, the preacher should always have the evangelistic motive in mind. The sermon may be pastoral, inspirational, judgmental, when needed, but behind every sermon there should be the evangelistic heart. Every sermon — whatever its specific theme — must in some way serve the evangel. It may center in the evangel for the benefit of those who need to make initial decisions, or it may spell out the implications of the evangel (gospel) for those who are maturing in the Christian faith. The evangel is the touchstone of all effective preaching.

Included in this volume are not only principles of preparation and delivery but a presentation of evangelistic messages from the past and present. The editors have chosen these to demonstrate not only historical and cultural factors that always arise in any kind of preaching but to show that the evangel remains constant within such change. These sermons may also help younger preachers see how great preaching has been done and is continuing to be practiced. We pray that this volume will be helpful in encouraging evangelistic preaching.

Charles R. Gresham and
Keith Keeran

EVANGELISM AND EVANGELISTIC PREACHING: PAST, PRESENT, AND FUTURE

1

The Nature of Evangelism and Evangelistic Preaching

CHARLES R. GRESHAM

Before one can say anything significant about evangelistic preaching, he must give attention to that term that is the heart of evangelistic preaching — evangelism. This is the crucial question: What is evangelism? Anyone aware of recent thought will not see the answer to this question simplistically. There rages a controversy within ecumenical Christianity between evangelism as some kind of humanization or political and social liberation and evangelism seen in more traditional terms as producing individual conversion. Other questions also come to the fore. What is the gospel? How is evangelism related to the Church? Are evangelistic results only personal or are they not also corporate?

These questions may not be answered to the satisfaction of everyone, but there must be some consideration given to them. Perhaps the best approach (and, perhaps, the only approach) is to move back into that group of documents produced in the very heart of that first community of faith and by those first evangelists and examine these questions from that context. If indeed these new covenant Scriptures were written by those claiming direct guidance by the Living Lord through His Spirit, then it would follow that they should reflect the Divine Will.

With these documents as our source, let us view evangelism, etymologically (that is, as to the exact meaning of those words used to refer to or describe this entity); historically (as the early church developed in the apostolic age); and practically, that is, by making application of what is found in this source to our present understanding.

Evangelism Viewed Etymologically

The term evangelism comes from the Greek word *euangelion* meaning "gospel" or "good news". This term originally denoted a reward for good tidings but the idea of reward dropped out and the word stood for the good news itself.[1]

Within the four Gospels the term is used most frequently with the phrase "of the Kingdom". In both Matthew and Mark, Jesus is referred to as coming in to Galilee "proclaiming the gospel of the kingdom" (Mt. 4:23, Mk. 1:14). Mark is even more specific as he points out that Jesus preached the "gospel of God", saying, "The time is fulfilled and the kingdom of God is at hand, repent and believe in the gospel" (Mk. 1:14,15).[2] Luke records that visit that Jesus made to the synagogue in his hometown of Nazareth. Here he is allowed to speak to the congregation gathered and does so using Isaiah 61:1-2 as his text. That Messianic passage reads: "The Spirit of the Lord is upon me, because he anointed me to preach the Gospel to the poor. He sent me to proclaim release to the captives, and recovery of sight to the blind, to set free those who are down trodden, to proclaim the favorable year of the Lord" (Lk. 4:16-19). Having finished reading this text, Jesus sat down to speak and startled his audience by saying: "Today, this Scripture has been fulfilled in your hearing" (Lk. 4:21).

In the Acts of the Apostles, the term *euangelion*, gospel, is used but with a more specific meaning. Peter, speaking for the conference at Jerusalem where the question of circumcision is being probed by representatives of the Jerusalem and Antioch churches, says: "Brethren you know that in the early days God made a choice among you, that by my mouth the Gentiles should hear of the gospel and believe" (Acts 15:7). When one looks back into chapter ten to see what Peter had announced to those first Gentiles at Caesarea, he is aware that "gospel" centered in the work of Jesus of Nazareth. Later, Paul will tell the Ephesian elders that he did not consider his life so dear as to keep him from fulfilling his God-given ministry "to testify solemnly of the gospel of the grace of God" (Acts 20:24).

In Paul's letters the term gospel is used very frequently and accompanied by varying phrases or put into different contexts so that there is no question about what is meant. In Romans one it is the "gospel of God" to which Paul is set apart, good news "concerning His Son who was born of the seed of David according to the flesh, who was declared with power to be the Son of God by the resurrection from the dead..." (Rom. 1:1-4). This gospel is "the power of God for salvation to every one who believes, to the Jew first and also to the Greek" (Rom. 1:16). In Galatians one, Paul is surprised that the Galatians were deserting Christ for "a different gospel." There is no other Gospel, he affirms; there are only "distortions" of the gospels of Christ. He then speaks almost vehemently: "But even though we or an angel from heaven, should preach to you a gospel contrary to that which we have preached to you, let him be accursed" (Gal. 1:6-8).

It is undoubtedly in the first Corinthian letter that Paul spells out the nature of the *euangelion*, gospel, the best. In introducing that section on the reality of the resurrection of all believers, Paul says:

> Now I made know to you, brethren, the gospel which I preached to you, which also you received, in which also you stand by which also you are saved, if you hold fast the work which I preached to you, unless you believed in vain. For I delivered unto you as of first importance what I also received, that Christ died for our sins according to the Scriptures, and that He was buried, and that He was raised on the third day according to the Scriptures... (I Cor. 15:1-3).

Closely connected with the noun, *euangelion*, "gospel," is the verb *euangelizo*, "to preach the gospel." This verb is used several times in the Gospels, but in these instances (except for Mk. 16:16)[3] the gospel preached or proclaimed is the good news of the coming Kingdom. In the Acts of the Apostles and the remainder of the New

Testament this verb denoted the proclamation of Jesus as Christ, Savior, and Lord. Acts 5:42 speaks of both teaching and preaching the gospel as the continued activity of the early church. In this passage a form of *euangelizo* is used, followed by a direct object, Jesus Christ.

But not only is this verbal used extensively but other verbals are also found with the term, "gospel." The verb *kerusso*, "to preach or proclaim," is frequently found with *euangelion*, "gospel" as its object (Mt. 4:23; Gal. 2:3). *Laleo*, "to speak" is also used (I Thess. 2:2), as is *diamarturomai*, "to testify thoroughly," (Acts 20:24) and *katangello*, "to proclaim" (I Cor. 9:14). These all emphasize that evangelism is the proclamation of good news about Jesus Christ, His person, and His gracious work.

From the same root as *euangelion* "gospel" and *euangelizo* "to preach the gospel" comes another significant New Testament word, *euangelistes*, "the evangelist" or "gospel preacher." This term is used only three times in the New Testament. In Acts 21:8, Luke records that Paul and his party were shown hospitality by Philip, the "evangelist," in Caesarea. Luke had previously noted Philip's evangelistic efforts in Samaria and in connection with the Ethiopian official who was returning home from a pilgrimage to Jerusalem (Acts 8:5ff). In Samaria Philip was "proclaiming Christ" (8:5) and "preaching the gospel (*euangilizomeno*) of the Kingdom of God and the name of Jesus Christ" (8:12). He was also "preaching the gospel" (*euangelizonto*) to many other Samaritan villages (8:25). From such an evangelistic campaign he was directed by the Spirit towards the South, encountering the Ethiopian official. From that significant passage in Isaiah 53, which the official was reading aloud as he rode along,

Philip "preached Jesus (*euangelizato*) to him" (8:35). Philip's role in the early church was as an evangelist, a preacher of the Gospel. He "kept preaching the gospel to all the cities," Luke will say in summarizing his activity (Acts 8:40).

In Paul's second letter to Timothy that tremendous charge and challenge is given to this young man whom Paul knew as his son in the Gospel. He is not only to "preach the word...reprove, rebuke, exhort with great patience and instruction" (II Tim. 4:2), he is also to "do the work of an evangelist (*euangelistes*)" (4:5). One can preach without evangelizing, but to evangelize means to bring the message of Christ to those who have not yet responded to Him. Timothy as he works with Christians in Ephesus, must never overlook this important function.

That function is clearly seen in Ephesians 4 where Paul speaks of those "gifts" which the ascended Lord gave to His Church so that "the saints" may be equipped for the "work of service" (Eph. 4:7-12). The foundational gifts are apostles and prophets with their Spirit-inspired message for God's people. Then, there is the evangelistic gift (*hoi euangelistai* — "some to be evangelists"), by which that message of good news in Christ is to be carried to all. Finally, there are the pastoral and didactic gifts ("some pastors-teachers") by which God's flock, the Church, may be shepherded and fed spiritually. These last three functions are carried out by individuals who recognize their gift (the apostles and prophets have fulfilled their function and no longer exist except through the inspired Word).

What, then, is evangelism? From this brief word study it is apparent that it is the proclamation of that good news that centers in Jesus Christ carried out by anyone who will share such glad tidings with one who is in need.

Evangelism Viewed Historically

It is not sufficient to understand evangelism from the standpoint of a New Testament word study, it must also be seen within the historical context of the Apostolic age. When Jesus came into the world "in the fullness of time...in order that He might redeem those who were under the Law, that we might receive the adoption as sons" (Gal. 4:4-5), He Himself was the Gospel, the good news. He knew what He would accomplish by His obedience to His Father, so He preaches, and sends His followers to preach, good news of the coming Kingdom. This is the new Age to be inaugurated by the outpoured Spirit, even as Joel predicted and Peter proclaimed on that Pentecost following Jesus' resurrection.

In those documents that we call Gospels, the "beginning of the gospel of Jesus Christ, the Son of God" (Mk. 1:1) is set out. They speak of the life, and ministry of this One who had been sent by His Father to redeem all mankind. These accounts set out what was "accomplished among us" (Lk. 1:1); what Jesus "began to do and teach" (Acts 1:1). Emphasis is upon what He did; not only that "He went about doing good" (Acts 10:38), but that at Jerusalem he was crucified and arose from the dead. The details of His passion (as that final week will be called, Acts 1:3) are given profusely in all four of these accounts. One of them, Luke, will report that Jesus even discussed "His departure which He was about to accomplish at Jerusalem" with Moses and Elijah on the mountain of

Transfiguration (Lk. 9:31). The Kingdom had come in Jesus; the content of the good news of this Kingdom was provided by His life and work, a work culminating in shameful death on His part, but a glorious resurrection and exaltation supplied by His Father (see Phil. 2:5-11).

In Luke's second volume, which we know as the Acts of the Apostles, evangelism is seen in reality. "Go and make disciples, baptizing them..." Jesus had commanded the Apostles (Mt. 28:19-20). "Repentance for forgiveness of sins" is to "be proclaimed in His name to all the nations — beginning from Jerusalem," Luke reports the risen Jesus as saying to the Apostles in that upper room at Jerusalem (Lk. 24:47). In Acts these commands are carried out as the Spirit given by Jesus directs these special envoys. The Apostles are eyewitnesses (Acts 1:8; 5:32; Heb. 2:3-4, etc.); they could not "stop speaking what" they had seen and heard (Acts 4:20). Hence, it is important that a successor to Judas be chosen from among those men "who have accompanied us all the time that the Lord Jesus went in and out among us — beginning with the baptism of John, until the day that He was taken up from us" (Acts 1:21-22).

As the Book of Acts unfolds, these witnesses, particularly Peter, John, and Paul, are proclaiming this basic content. That first sermon delivered on Pentecost by Peter centered in "Jesus the Nazarene, a man attested by God with miracles and wonders and signs" (Acts 2:22). This man was delivered up, "nailed to a cross by the hands of godless men and put to death" (Acts 2:23). But, this was no accident or unforeseen action viewed from heavenly perspective, for it was done according to the "foreknowledge of God" and by His "predetermined plan" (Acts

2:23). "And God raised Him up again, putting an end to the agony of death, since it was impossible for Him to be held in its power" (Acts 2:24). But there is more, says Peter; for not only has God raised up this Jesus (of which we are all witnesses), He has also "exalted Him to the right hand of God" (Acts 2:32-33). Therefore, all of Israel is given assurance and certainty that this same Jesus whom they crucified "God has made both Lord and Christ" (Acts 2:36).

Though the particulars of the kerygma (the preaching) may vary, depending upon audiences and circumstances, the essential items of Jesus' life, death, burial, resurrection, and exaltation are the heart of that proclaimed (See Acts 3:12-21; 4:8-12; 5:29-32; 13:17-32; 17:30-31). Salvation depends upon the reception of this message centering in Jesus as Messiah for, as Peter said before the Sanhedrin, "there is salvation in no one else; for there is no other name under heaven that has been given among men, by which we must be saved" (Acts 4:12). C.H. Dodd, in his work, *The Apostolic Preaching and Its Development* (1936), summarized the preaching of the apostolic age under the following topics:[4]

First, the age of fulfillment has dawned. "This is what was spoken by the prophet Joel" (Acts 2:16). "But what God foretold by the mouth of all the prophets...he thus fulfilled" (Acts 3:18). "And all the prophets who have spoken, from Samuel and those who came afterwards, also proclaimed these days" (Acts 3:24). The apostles declared that the messianic age has dawned.

Second, this has taken place through the ministry, death, and resurrection of Jesus, of which a brief account is given, with proof from the Scriptures that all took place "according to the definite plan and foreknowledge of God" (Acts 2:23).

Third, by virtue of the resurrection, Jesus has been exalted at the right hand of God as messianic head of the new Israel (Acts 2:33-36; 3:13).

Fourth, the Holy Spirit in the church is the sign of Christ's present power and glory. "Being therefore exalted at the right hand of God, and having received from the Father the promise of the Holy Spirit, he has poured out this which you see and hear" (Acts 2:33).

Fifth, the messianic age will shortly reach its consummation in the return of Christ. "That he may send the Christ appointed for you, Jesus, whom heaven must receive until the time for establishing all that God spoke by the mouth of his holy prophets from of old" (Acts 3:21).

Finally, the kerygma always closes with an appeal for repentance, the offer of forgiveness and of the Holy Spirit, and the promise of salvation, that is, of the life of the Age to Come to those who enter the community. "Repent, and be baptized every one of you in the name of Jesus Christ for the forgiveness of your sins; and you shall receive the gift of the Holy Spirit. For the promise is to you and to your children and to all that are far off, every one whom the Lord our God calls to him" (Acts 2:38-39).

In the Epistles, Gospel preaching is frequently mentioned both historically and theologically. Paul reminds the Corinthians that though they may have "countless tutors in Christ" yet they had only one father; for, he says, "I became your father through the gospel" (I Cor. 4:15). In the first of his letters to Thessalonica he refers to how he had come to them, after much suffering and mistreatment at Philippi, with "boldness in our God to speak to you the gospel of God amid much opposition" (I Thess. 2:2).

The theological or didactical implications of the Gospel are no less pronounced than such historical references. In fact, the whole of the Roman letter may be considered nothing more than what the Gospel implies. Many believe that that great affirmation of Paul in Romans 1:16 is the theme of the letter. "I am not ashamed of the gospel, for it is the power of God for salvation to every one who believes, to the Jew first and also to the Greek," says Paul. He adds: "For in it (that is, in the gospel) the righteousness of God is revealed from faith to faith; as it is written, 'But the righteous man shall live by faith'" (Rom. 1:17). This righteousness of God, thus revealed, becomes the theme of the epistle. It is a righteousness needed because of man's sinfulness (Rom. 1:18-3:21); it is a righteousness made possible by Jesus' propitiatory sacrifice (Rom. 3:24-26); and it is a righteousness appropriated by faith rather than earned by keeping the Law (3:28-5:11). Such righteousness appropriated by faith must be lived out in faith so that sin may be conquered and overcome (Rom. 6:1-23). But this will not be accomplished by human will alone but by the presence and power of the Holy Spirit given to those who obey Christ (Rom. 8:9-28).

Evangelism Viewed Practically

A summary is now in order. Evangelism is Gospel preaching. The good news proclaimed is that salvation has been offered to all. This salvation is focused in Jesus who was sent into the world as God's deliverer. His life, death, resurrection, and exaltation to Lordship are the particulars of this good news, for all this was accomplished in behalf of mankind. These great events, these Divine Facts, are the historical basis and foundation of evangelism.

But evangelism is Gospel preaching, and, in the Book of Acts, the parameters of that preaching are set. The preaching was directed toward decision; it was persuasion. To the question, "What must we do?" the Spirit-directed apostles replied "Repent and be baptized" (Acts 2:37-38). The gospel must be received and it is so received by initial faith, a faith that believes the testimony given (Rom. 10:17), a faith that causes a change of heart and life to result (repentance) and a faith that is sealed and made complete in immersion into the triune name of the Godhead (Mt. 28:19-20). The invitation was given and response was made, culminating in baptism (Acts 2:41; 22:16f; etc.).

But gospel preaching brought continuing results. Upon obedient response, those first converts were promised "remission of sins and the gift of the Holy Spirit" (Acts 2:38). They were also incorporated ("added") into that original nucleus, which was the Church (Acts 2:41,47). Within this "fellowship," they continually served their new-found Master and Lord, guided by the Apostles' teaching, reminded of their Master's sacrifice in "the breaking of bread" and continuing instant in prayer (Acts 2:42). But, they also were reproducing themselves as they "went about preaching the word" (Acts 8:4). So that early church grew and multiplied as more and more were evangelized, responded and were added to their number.

In light of this summary of New Testament truth, one

could hardly improve upon that comprehensive definition of evangelism that was set out in 1918 by the Anglican Archbishop's Committee of Inquiry on the Evangelistic work of the Church:

> To evangelize is so to present Jesus Christ in the power of the Holy Spirit, that men shall come to put their trust in God through Him, accept Him as their Savior, and serve Him as their King in the fellowship of His Church.[5]

Evangelistic preaching, then, is identical to evangelizing. Methodologically, it is as broad and varied as that evangelizing seen in the apostolic age. There we see evangelistic preaching directed to large multitudes. Peter at Pentecost (Acts 2) and in Solomon's porch (Acts 3), and Paul in the Areopagus (Acts 17); both illustrate such mass evangelism. But more frequently, the Apostolic records reveal evangelistic preaching directed towards much smaller groups. A group of women by the riverside (Acts 16), various households or families (Cornelius, Acts 10; the Philippian jailer, Acts 16), small groups gathered in marketplaces (Acts 17) or in houses (Acts 18:7-8), were all audiences of evangelistic preaching. In one instance, evangelistic preaching was in a one-to-one situation (Acts 8:26-39).

But preaching, understood in the Biblical sense, is essential to evangelism. It is God's instrument in saving men. Paul could say in his first letter to the Corinthians that "God was well pleased through the foolishness of the message preached (the kerygma, the preaching) to save those who believe" (I Cor. 1:12). In the same connection Paul says, "but we preach Christ crucified, to Jews a stumbling-block, and to Gentiles foolishness, but to those who are called, both Jews and Greeks, Christ the power of God and the wisdom of God" (I Cor. 1:23-24). In the Roman letter, Paul, with inexorable logic, moves from the salvation granted to those calling upon God to the preacher and the necessity of such preachers being sent (Rom. 10:13-14). For, if "faith comes from hearing and hearing by the word of Christ" (Rom. 10:17), then the one bringing glad tidings of Christ is essential to the response of faith. No wonder Paul exclaims by quoting that beautiful passage in Isaiah: "How beautiful are the feet of those who bring glad tidings of good things!" (Isa. 52:7 quoted in Rom. 10:15). Evangelistic preaching is not a method it is a message; it is not a mere process it is an all-consuming passion. Such Biblical truth must be our standard and must guide our methodology and practice.

NOTES

1. W.E. Vine, *An Expository Dictionary of New Testament Words*, Vol. II, p. 167.

2. All Scripture quotations will be from the New American Standard Version.

3. Here, in this longer ending of Mark which is probably a scribal addition, the gospel preached is that which brings salvation if it is responded to in faith and baptism.

4. This summary is from G.E. Ladd, *A Theology of the New Testament*, (Grand Rapids: Wm. B. Eerdmans, 1974), p. 329.

5. *Toward the Conversion of England*, (Toronto: J.M. Dent and Sons, 1946), p.1.

2

Evangelistic Preaching In Christian History

CHARLES R. GRESHAM

What is seen in the Apostolic Age as witnessed in the New Testament Scriptures continued to be carried out in the following centuries. Itinerant evangelists (or "prophets") were circulating among the churches preaching the redeeming message. The *Didache*, or Teaching of the Twelve (a second-century work) is concerned to set out standards by which these itinerants' ministries would be evaluated. After all, "drifting from place to place and trading on the hospitality of the local Christian congregations was a temptation for some" (Max Warren, *I Believe in the Great Commission*, Eerdmans, 1976, p. 78). The credentials demanded by this significant document were Christlike lives, messages that correspond to New Testament reality, and spiritual fruits resulting from their ministry.

But, not only is evangelistic preaching carried out by such itinerants, it was the heart of located ministries. Whatever may be made of Ignatius' claim to being a bishop in the monarchical sense, there can be little doubt concerning his evangelistic fervor as bishop of Antioch. Other bishops such as Gregory in Pontus, Iraneus in Gaul, Cyprian of Carthage were all active in evangelism and they were typical of these first three centuries, not exceptional. The growth of the Christian community during these centuries, in spite of Roman persecution and the opposition of heathen philosophy, is clear evidence of a tremendous evangelistic thrust.

The Apologists of these early centuries were evangelists. Their writings, often directed toward heathen opponents or Roman officials, were pre-evangelistic in nature. They were concerned about eliminating misunderstanding about the Christian community, but they were also concerned in showing positively how Christian thought and life was superior to that seen in the contemporary culture. Later Apologists, such as Clement and Origen of Alexandria, would use the forms of Greek thought, dominant in that day, to convey the Gospel. Such a comprehensive task was fraught with great peril but was seen as a necessity if Christianity was to be seen as a reasonable faith.

The Bible itself was an evangelist during those early centuries. As in the Apostolic Age, the Bible was central, not just the Old Testament but the apostolic writings as well.

Aristides, one of the earliest Apologists, writing not to Jews but to pagans, urged them after reading his letter, to turn to the Bible and read it for themselves (Apology, p. 16), while Chrysostom argued that a man could find in the Bible all that he needed to understand the faith. It seems beyond dispute that the early Christian preachers and writers constantly used the Scriptures as a means of persuading non-Christians to accept the faith. The Bible was the regular tool of evangelism (A.M. Chirgwin, *The Bible in World Evangelism*, SCM Press, 1954).

Events proved that this literary method was effective. The Bible did win converts. In fact, this became so effective that a view was widely held in the early church that "the regular way to become a convinced Christian was to read the Holy Scriptures" (A. Harnack, *Bible Reading in the Early Church*, p. 42). So, according to their own testimonies, Justin, Tatian, Theophilus, became Christians. Later Augustine's conversion demonstrates the power of the Scriptures to convert.

Such evangelistic power displayed in the reading of Scripture led to the translation of the Scriptures into various languages. The motive was evangelistic. These early translators were concerned with the spread of the Gospel. Within 100 years of the close of the first century, Scriptures, in whole or part, were translated into Syrian, Latin, and Coptic. In the next two centuries, parts of the Bible were available in Ethiopic, Armenian, Gothic, Georgian and one or two other languages.

Along with the translation of Scripture and the evangelistic results from individual reading, there developed the reading aloud of Scripture (frequently with comments — hence, homilies) in public or semi-public places. Originally, this practice aimed at providing illiterate people, who had no Bible of their own, opportunity to hear the Word of God. This practice became the basis for the development of the lectionaries of a later time with the parallel development of preaching from one of the passages chosen for that particular Lord's Day.

Yet there were certain forces at work within the post-apostolic church which would tend to mar the simplicity and fullness of the Gospel and, therefore, tend to throttle gospel proclamation. One of these was the influence Greek philosophy had in subtly changing the Christian message from emphasis upon the centrality and factuality of the incarnate Son for salvation to dependence upon knowledge, Greek definition, and good works. This gave rise to a new sacerdotalism, in which a clerical priesthood became dominant, and to a mechanical sacramentarianism, often seen as mystical and magical, which tended to emphasize sign and symbol, not the spiritual reality giving the symbol meaning.

Then, too, the development of the concept of original sin as hereditary with its consequent corollary, infant baptism, tended to undermine the necessity of a voluntary faith-commitment to salvation and entrance into the Church as Christ's Body. This coupled with the Constantinian "state church" concept was disastrous to the continuation of evangelistic outreach as seen in the apostolic age. As Kierkegaard will later state (within the context of the Danish state church), "When everyone is Christian, Christianity no longer exists." If baptism as the conscious response to the Gospel, the seal of salvation and the reception of Spirit, is no longer the voluntary act of a believer, has it not become a mere empty form? There is, then, no longer a place for evangelistic preaching that is directed toward an initial heart-felt, voluntary response.

Within the Middle Ages evangelism and evangelistic preaching as reflected in the New Testament is almost completely absent. There are, however, preachers who are instrumental in spiritual revival. There is undoubtedly some question as to whether those "revived" were genuinely Christian. Again, the state church with its sacramental system considered many to be "Christian" who were never regenerated by the Spirit. Many of these were undoubtedly brought to a saving knowledge of Christ (however faulty). In that sense, the initiation of such revival may well be termed evangelistic preaching of a sort.

An example of such a "revivalist" was Bernard of Clairvaux (1091-1165) who was, perhaps, the mightiest preacher of the Middle Ages. Most of his preaching was directed toward the monks in various monasteries. His message was centered in justification by faith and forgiveness by grace. He itinerated from place to place, in country after country, preaching to all who would listen.

Another significant personage of the Middle Ages who was a true evangelist of God's grace was Francis of Assisi (1182-1126). He was the son of a wealthy merchant who lived a rather loose, pleasure-filled life prior to his conversion. "One day, however, while listening to the story of the sending out of the disciples as recorded in Matthew 10, Francis accepted the call to follow Christ, and gave himself to a life of poverty and itinerant preaching." (Paulus Scharpff, *History of Evangelism*, Eerdmans, 1966, p. 6). In addition, he gathered students around him out of which developed a religious order (the Franciscans). By 1219, this order numbered 5,000; and by 1264 there were some 200,000 Franciscans in 8,000 cloisters scattered throughout central Europe. This order, following the lead of their founder, stimulated a great revival within the existing Church. Some believe that the religious awakening produced by the Franciscans was as widespread in their day as was the Wesleyan revival at a later date.

Berthold von Regensburg (d. 1272) is an excellent example of this Franciscan awakening. He toured extensively, preaching to large crowds. When church buildings were too small to hold those who came, he simply preached out of doors. Vividly setting forth the love of Christ, he called the masses to repentance, attempting to kindle a responding love in the hearts of his hearers.

Dominicus of Spain (1170-1221), a contemporary of Francis, established an order similar to the Franciscan order. The Dominicans became great preachers and concentrated their efforts upon the monasteries whereas the Franciscans were more concerned with the general populace. Out of the Dominican order came such great pulpiteers as Johann Tauler (1300-1361) of Strasbourgh, and (Meister) Eckhart (1260-1327) of Cologne.

Not only was there accepted revival within the Roman Church of the Middle Ages, there were also attempts to reform which were met with ecclesiastical opposition. In Lyons, France, Peter Waldo (1179-1218) founded a lay-preaching order, translating the Bible into the common language so that these lay preachers could use such in their preaching of repentance. Their distribution of the Bible in the vulgar language, along with their zeal, aroused official displeasure and, eventually, open persecution. Despite this persecution, they continued their activity and moved to other countries. The Waldensians, as they are now known, continue to this present day.

One example of this evangelistic thrust is seen among the Celts. Celtic monasticism (if it can be called monasticism) was rather loosely organized on a more familial structure. There was no enforced celibacy; some of the members were married, others were not. As they moved through wide areas in thinly populated countries (beginning in Ireland, through the Islands, and finally to the Continent), they adapted themselves to the societal structures that they found. They spread the Faith by both preaching and contagious life-style. Dr. Stephen Neill, historian of the Christian Missionary enterprise writes:

> One of the most notable of these 'wanderers for Christ' was the younger Columba, often called Columban to distinguish him from his more famous namesake (550-615). Columban was already forty years old when he set out on his travels. His first scene of labor was eastern France, where he founded the monastery of Luxeil. Twenty years later Columban incurred the hostility of the Bergundian court because of the boldness with which he rebuked the immorality of the ruler. Expelled from Luxeil with his Celtic monks, he set out again to preach the Gospel to the still pagan peoples whom he found in the neighborhood of Lake Constance. Driven out yet once more by the spread of the Bergundian power, he retired to die in another of his foundations, the monastery of Bobbio in northern Italy (A History of Christian Mission, (Eerdmans, 1965), p. 72).

A little later, Ramon Lull (?-1315) was motivated to preach Christ to the Muslim world. In trying to carry out this mission, he traveled across North Africa, the Middle East and reached the borders of India. In 1276 he founded a college at Miramar for the study of Arabic. He saw clearly that the Crusaders were not the answer to Christian conquest. "In a prayer of meditation," writes Max Warren, he pointed out a better way — 'It appears to me, O Lord, that the conquest of that sacred land will not be achieved...save by love and prayer and the shedding of tears as well as blood...Let the knights become religious, let them be adorned with the sign of the Cross and filled with the grace of the Holy Spirit, and let them go among the infidels to preach truth concerning thy passion.' (op. cit., p. 89).

Such sweetness in the bitter record of the medieval Church's approach to Islam is but a small foretaste of what could have happened had the medieval Church responded.

Twice in the late thirteenth century Kublai Khan, ruler of the Mongols, sent messengers to the Pope requesting missionaries — 'send me one hundred men skilled in your religion — ...And so I shall be baptized, and then all my barons and great men, and then their subjects. And so there shall be more Christians here than there in your parts.' Only two Dominicans were sent and they, unworthy members of a great missionary order, got as far as Armenia and then feared to go further (Ibid., p. 90).

As a result, most of the Mongols became Muslims and provided that great surge and impetus that finally triumphed at Constantinople in 1453.

But in the late medieval period there were other men — Reformers before the Reformation — who were even more representative of the evangelistic preachers of that earlier apostolic age. John Wycliffe (1320-1384), professor of theology at Oxford University in England, was not only an opponent of several features of Romanism which would later be termed "Popery," he was also one who saw the great need of renewing the religious level of the common people. He translated portions of the Scripture into the vernacular to make it accessible to others than scholars. He also gathered about him a group of conscientious students of the Word and sent them out to preach in the vernacular from the translated Word. Called Lollards, these simple preachers soon met with opposition from clerics and prelates of the Church, but were welcomed by the common folk and were instruments of evangelistic renewal within the Anglican Catholic Church.

John Hus (c.1369-1415), was a professor of theology at the University of Prague and a popular preacher. He was an acknowledged disciple of Wycliffe, having become acquainted with his writings while a student at the University. Later he would say: "I confess that members of this University and myself have possessed and read his works for 20 years and more." Hus wholeheartedly adopted Wycliffe's views on the authority of the Scriptures, the corruption of the Church and its need for renewal. As popular preacher, these themes became prominent and a groundswell of revival was felt throughout Bohemia. Even after his condemnation and martyrdom, these Bohemian Brethren (or Unitas Fratrum, Unity of the Brethren, as they preferred to call themselves) continued to grow and spread, particularly when persecuted by the established Roman Church. Within a century, this movement stemming from John Hus, had three to four hundred churches with a total membership of perhaps 100,000. They had spread throughout central Europe and were involved in evangelistic work in Turkey, Asia Minor, Syria, Palestine and Egypt.

A new impetus was given this movement when a large number settled upon the estates of Count Nicholas von

Zinzendorf, a Lutheran Pietist, much interested in evangelistic and missionary outreach. Under his organizational genius these Moravian Brethren (Zinzendorf's estate was in the area of Moravia) were soon involved in mission work throughout the new world, Greenland, Iceland, and elsewhere. Their pietistic and evangelistic zeal were to be quite influential in triggering the Evangelical Awakening associated with the Wesleys in the eighteenth century.

Another "Reformer before the Reformation" that should be noted was Girolamo Savonarola (1452-1498). As prior of St. Marco in Florence, Italy, he became much concerned about the spiritual condition of his people and began calling them to repentance. He was concerned that they read and understand the Scriptures, for "the Scriptures," he said, "point and lead only to Christ, and not to Mary or the saints" (Scharpff, p. 9). He also preached that without believing faith in the forgiveness of Christ, the priest's absolution meant nothing. It was unfortunate that Savonarola became entangled in politics. His opposition to the famous Medici family led eventually to his death at the stake in 1498. Luther was but fifteen years old when this fiery reformer exclaimed: "The Church will be renewed, but first it will be disciplined, and that shortly" (Scharpff, p. 9).

Although the sixteenth century Reformers — Luther, Zwingli, Calvin, etc. — could not be called evangelists in the technical, New Testament sense, yet they set the stage for the recovery of New Testament evangelism. By declaring the Bible to be sole authority and by emphasizing the primacy of faith they were setting forth the basic foundation for a continuation of evangelism and evangelistic preaching.

Most of the gains that the Protestant Reformers made were from those who were already nominal members of the state churches of medieval times. Hence, the preaching of Luther and Calvin was directed toward renewal among those claiming to be Christian. There was little recognition by any of these classic Reformers that the Great Commission obligated all Christians to evangelism.

William Richey Hogg writes:

> One searches in vain in the Works of Martin Luther for any exposition of Matthew 28:19-20 or Mark 16:15 that would hint at the Church's responsibility to move beyond Christendom. This silence is in notable contrast to expressed papal understanding of the Great Commission.
>
> Similarly, one searches John Calvin's Institutes and commentaries without finding any positive recognition of a theology of missions. Examination of Zwingli, Bucer, John Knox and Melancthon produces the same negative report. To be sure Luther's doctrine of salvation and of the priesthood of all believers, and Calvin's theology with its' inherent activism, concern for the extension of the kingdom, and emphasis upon the responsibility of the elect for humanity and society, have missionary implications (and were later appealed to), but the Reformers did not link these with missionary obligation. ("Rise of Protestant Missionary Concern, 1517-1914," in Gerald H. Anderson, ed., *The Theology of the Christian Mission*, Abingdon Press, 1961, pp. 98-99).

Of course, Luther and Calvin, and their colleagues, were men of their times. They accepted the state church pattern of medievalism with infant baptism and other of its accompaniments. They did not see the necessity, as did the Anabaptists, for the establishing of churches of believers entered only by those who had voluntarily responded to the Gospel. They did, however, lay the groundwork for evangelistic conquest through their recovery of theological insights in the New Testament and through their insistence that the Scriptures should be read by all. Luther, particularly, in his translation of the Bible into the German vernacular accomplished more than he was conscious of at the time.

It was among the Anabaptists that the missionary and evangelistic obligation of every Christian was emphasized. Their concern for a recovery of the New Testament Church with its clear concept of a regenerate membership led them to oppose infant baptism, the state Church system, and other accretions that had brought distortion. As a result they were not only persecuted by the Roman Church but also were opposed by Protestants such as Luther and Calvin. The ensuing sufferings and martyrdoms, much like the early post-apostolic Church, served to scatter these throughout Europe and to contribute to their growth.

The Anabaptists had numerous preachers and evangelists during the sixteenth century. Best know representatives are Menno Simons (1496-1561), a former Roman priest, and the outstanding theologian, Balthaser Hubmaier (1481-1528), university professor at Frieburg and Ingolstadt. Hubmaier began his career as a Reformer in the manner of Ulrich Zwingli, but soon moved to more radical New Testament positions. His arguments for believers' baptism were widely disseminated. His view of Baptism and the Lord's Supper made them expressions of covenant relationships with Christ and with fellow believers. His eloquence as a preacher and his ability in theological debate led to persecution and martyrdom.

Menno Simons began his career as a Roman Catholic priest, but his continued study of Scripture and his observation of the seriousness of the Anabaptistic Mechiorites in Frisia where he lived caused him to renounce the Roman Church. He was reordained in 1537 and for some 25 years he traveled throughout the Lowlands, preaching, writing, establishing congregations of believers. During most of this time he had a price on his head, but this did not dissuade him from preaching openly and privately and developing a kind of underground Church throughout northeastern Europe. At one time in certain parts of Holland no less than one-fourth of the population belonged to the Mennonite movement.

The Anabaptists of continental Europe sparked similar movements in England. Here, in both the Independents, later known as the Congregationalists, and in the English Baptists, Anabaptists who not only believed in believer's baptism but saw this baptism as immersion, the Continental influence was seen. Most significant in this latter movement was John Bunyan (1628-1688). He was a tinker by trade but a preacher by choice and spent many years in the Bedford, England, jail because of his preaching. While imprisoned he wrote those enduring allegories, *Pilgrim's Progress* and *The Holy War*, which have been evangelistic tools through the years.

When some of these "Independents" moved to the New World, they found themselves

cheek-by-jowl with a non-Christian population... their reaction was unhesitating. They made the evangelization of the Indians a real part of their new life...Roger Williams, for example, the founder of Rhode Island Colony, learned their language in order to be able to preach to them in person. John Eliot, however, is the out-standing figure. He gave half a century of devoted service on their behalf and is rightly regarded as 'The Apostle of the Indians' (Chirgwin, p. 37).

Linked closely with John Eliot was David Brainerd, who also gave his life in the service of the American Indians. He left an autobiographical account of his service that became the inspiration of countless others and is today a missionary classic.

But the initial enthusiasm and evangelistic thrust of the Reformation began to wane. On the Continent, Protestant State Churches settled back into a formalism and this-worldliness that had afflicted State Churches through the centuries. The energies of Church leaders were directed toward theological definition and the development of a blighting creedalism. The Protestant Scholastic period had begun. Both on the Continent and in Great Britain, "another spiritual decline had laid hold on the Church, and...it seemed that religion had almost died out of the hearts of men. This was true not alone of the people in general but the religious knowledge and morals of the church herself including the clergy had sunk to the lowest ebb" (W.E. Biederwolf, *Evangelism*, New York: Fleming H. Revell Co., 1921, p. 27f).

On the Continent, Pietism attempted to bring about revival. This movement had no formal organization, "it was a movement of the Spirit and was marked by a deep devotion to the Bible and a firm belief in its evangelistic power" (Chirgwin, p. 39). It began in the Reformed Church of the Netherlands and soon spread to the German Lutheran Church. In this latter context it found congenial soil and grew. It found its focus in Halle where a burning passion for Bible Study and overseas evangelism developed. The leaders of the Pietist Movement were Philipp Jakob Spener and his disciple, A.H. Franke, professor of Oriental Language at the University of Halle. Here at Halle, Franke taught, began Bible Study groups among the populace, presided over a youth hostel, and supervised a publishing venture know as Canstein House. From this printing press flowed thousands of Bibles that were economical in price. In one sense this was the forerunner of later Bible Societies. Before the British and Foreign Bible Society was formed in the early nineteenth century, Canstein House had already printed more than three million Bibles and Testaments in various languages and had distributed them throughout Europe, in America and even in parts of Asia.

Through his influence among the young people that resided in the youth hostel he had established, many were led to dedicate themselves to missionary service. Halle, in fact, says C.P.S. Clarke, became "the first nursery of missionaries outside the Roman communion since the Reformation" (*A Short History of the Christian Church*, p. 403). One of these young men whom Frank influenced was Count Zinzendorf who would in later years become the leader of the Moravian Brethren and lead them into worldwide evangelistic labors.

It was through the Moravian Brethren and their influence in England and America that renewal came to the British Isles. That small group of men that formed the Holy Club at Oxford University to further piety among their members would all be influenced by Pietism as reflected in the Moravians. George Whitefield was the first of this group to break out of the legalism that dominated the Club in its earliest days and to preach salvation by Faith. Son of a Gloucester innkeeper, he left this family enterprise to study at Oxford. At Oxford he became associated with the Wesleys and joined the "Holy Club." As early as 1735, Whitefield was moving away from the ideas of the Holy Club which emphasized a "kind of monastic discipline based on good works" to proclaim the need for "rebirth and justification by faith" (Scharpff, p. 75). Ordained a deacon in 1736, he began to preach, gaining fame as a pulpiteer and an evangelist from the beginning. For the next 35 years he was to divide his evangelistic efforts between Great Britain and America, crossing the ocean thirteen times. He died in 1770 in New England in the midst of his labor.

Scharpff pens this assessment of this great Evangelist:

> Whitefield had an unusual gift for preaching, as well as an unusual spirit of joy in doing so. Preaching was his life, his love, even his balm of healing when he was ill. His entire life and strength were given to evangelism. He was fired by only one passion, that for souls. These facts explain his unusual power and penetration, the mighty earnestness of his testimony and his disarming love. He preached always as if he had a direct message from God Himself. Everything about him seemed alive and aglow. In addition, he possessed a marvelous command of language, and a fresh, dramatic style of delivery, and the ability to adapt his speech to each particular audience. His voice was strong and melodious, his bearing gracious. This 'Prince of English Evangelists,' it was said, preached like a lion (Scharpff, p. 75).

John Wesley, another member of the Holy Club, was

steeped in religious legalism even as a preacher in the colonies and as a missionary to Georgia. It was only after his association with some Moravians during a trip to America, and a continued association with one of their pastors, Peter Bohler, after his return to England that he finally came to a personal knowledge of assurance in Christ. All this came to focus on the 24th of May, 1738. Wesley describes the events of that day in his private journal.

> In the evening I went, very unwillingly, to a Society in Aldersgate Street where one was reading Luther's preface to the epistle of the Romans. About a quarter before nine, while he was describing the change that God works in the heart through faith in Christ, I felt my heart strangely warmed. I felt that I did trust in Christ, Christ alone, for salvation. And an assurance was given me that He had taken away my sins, even mine, and saved me from the law of sin and death.

This was the turning point in Wesley's life. Like his friend, George Whitefield, he began to preach this understanding of justification and assurance through Christ's death. Wherever he went there was renewal and, in spite of the opposition of the traditional church, he formed these converts into Societies who would continue to study the Bible, share with each other in mutual Christian support, and share this new-found faith with others. He trained "lay preachers" to carry this message throughout Great Britain and into the Colonies. By 1790 his religious societies (organized in the newly formed United States as the Methodist Episcopal Church) were located in 117 areas, numbered more than 77,000 members and 313 preachers. In addition, Wesley had organized several

schools to educate youth in Christian maturity.
Scharpff tells us that:

> The power of the Methodist revival movement lay in
> Wesley's and his workers' keen purpose to spread the
> glorious news of salvation throughout the land. Their own
> salvation showed itself in three ways especially. First, they
> expressed joyful thanksgiving for the gift of justification,
> forgiveness of sins, and assurance through the Holy Spirit
> of being children of God. This experience motivated their
> lively witness; the precious total golden lump of justifica-
> tion that Luther mined from the Bible, these Methodists
> broke into small nuggets of personal testimony. Second,
> they strove 'to pursue holiness,' that is, to separate them-
> selves from all known sins. This purpose was strength-
> ened by a sense of responsibility to the 'general rules,'
> according to which every society member was consciously
> to avoid all evil. To encourage this pursuit of holiness,
> they watched over one another in love; in meetings they
> confessed their sins, or witnessed of victory over sin. Such
> procedure was a practice session, as it were, for personal
> witnessing in the outside world. Third, the high ideal of
> each Methodist was to be so imbued with God's love
> through the Holy Ghost (Rom. 5:5) that their full heart of
> love to God and neighbor would bring a unique con-
> sciousness of being God's very messengers. As Charles
> Wesley described it, there would be a choosing, a calling,
> and a command by God to save the dearly bought world
> from eternal death.
>
> This striving for holiness made Methodism one of the
> most potent evangelistic movements of all time. It loosed
> extraordinary missionary, social, and cultural powers in
> ever new waves. Like few others, Wesley had grasped
> Zinzendorf's concept of 'warriorship'; and the members
> of his organization learned that the church of Jesus Christ
> is a living organism in which every member is a spiritual
> co-worker (Scharpff, pp. 78-79).

If the Wesleys, Whitefield and others were leading forces in the First Evangelical Awakening, the Second Evangelical Awaking, beginning in the early years of the Nineteenth Century and continuing on through the century, cannot be seen as the result of such specific leadership. Leaders there were; but these leaders did not have the overall influence as seen in the earlier Awakening. Much of this is due to the nature of religion in America where this Second Awakening begins.

First, American religious life was voluntary. There were no state churches to which citizens automatically belonged. Those who became members of American denominations did so voluntarily. Then, too, American religions were more individualistic. Each person, as a member, was conceived of as having certain inalienable, religious rights as well as the political rights that were his as a citizen of this new democracy. Some churches like the Baptists, saw themselves as a "spiritual democracy." American denominations also were less creedal and traditional than European religious groups. As a result, renewal and revival often led to division, with new doctrinal expressions of faith. Above all, American denominations, by and large, were more lay-centered than clerically-controlled. The freedom of the Christian man enunciated by Luther became more of a reality in America than anywhere else in the world.

The story of the Great Awakening, or the Second Evangelical Awakening, begins with the Frontier Revivals of 1796-1815. These reached their peak just shortly after the century (see the account of the Cane Ridge Revival in Kentucky in chapter 5). These Revivals were often interdenominational, with New Light Presbyterians, Methodists, and Baptists all involved. There were many excesses seen in these Revivals, but the overall good and the number of genuine converts far outweigh what is objectionable. These early Revivals led to the creation of two new religious groups — the Christians under Barton W. Stone and the Cumberland Presbyterians, both groups revivalistic and forced into independency by traditional, creed-bound Presbyterians.

After the first wave of revivalism was over, many religious groups developed other means of evangelistic thrust. Among Baptists, Christians and Disciples (those who followed the lead of Alexander Campbell) the "protracted meeting" became a most useful tool. "By 1805, the open-air revival had become mainly a Methodist institution" (Charles A. Johnson, *The Frontier Camp Meeting*, Southern Methodist University Press, 1955, p. 70), and throughout the century, Methodism used this institution effectively. The Methodist Camp Meeting became the means of Methodist ingathering and growth.

But the Frontier Revivals not only affected the frontier as it moved west, it also had an influence on the more settled, stable areas of this new country. To some degree this followed a general liberalizing of extreme Calvinism, and can be reflected in the life and work of Charles G. Finney. He began as a Presbyterian preacher in central western New York in 1824. Almost immediately under the vivid preaching of this ex-lawyer preacher a wave of revivalism began to spread throughout the region. Finney, though Presbyterian, had rejected the Calvinistic doctrine of predestination and insisted that salvation was for all. His revivalistic methods — often called "new measures" by his enemies — brought results but eventually precipitated trouble from his more strict Presbyterian colleagues. Such new measures included the "anxious bench," praying for people by name in public, cottage prayer meetings, and advertising his meetings in public media.

As Finney came more and more to approximate Methodist or Arminian theology, criticism by his own church became more severe. Moving to Oberlin College in 1836 as professor of theology, he continued to hold tent meetings wherever he could. However, students of Oberlin, imbued with Finney's spirit and theology, were finding difficulty in locating places to preach due to growing opposition. "But in spite of this hostility Oberlin carried on under Finney's leadership and by the eighteen-fifties had achieved a national and international reputation" (W.W. Sweet, *Revivalism in America*, Scribners, 1944, p. 138).

Timothy Smith says that: "The revival fervor which had earlier seemed typical of the rural West became in the years between 1840 and 1857 a dominant mood in urban religious life. Under the sponsorship of city pastors, the 'new measures' which had from their beginnings characterized Methodist and New School Presbyterian churches managed at last to conquer Calvinistic scruples against them in Baptist, Congregational, and Reformed communions, and to make deep inroads in Old School Presbyterian circles as well. Lutheranism's strongest party, though not by any means entirely urban, was as thoroughly evangelistic in work and worship as many of the German Methodist sects. The most provincial rural sections of the Lutheran, Baptist, and Presbyterian churches were now the strongholds of antirevival feeling, though the Cumberland Presbyterians, Disciples of Christ, and Freewill Baptists kept the fire burning on several frontiers. The common notion that, except for occasional sporadic out-bursts led by Finney, Moody, and the Y.M.C.A., revival-ism declined steadily after the great Western awakening burned out around 1840, seems in direct contradiction to the facts" (*Revivalism and Social Reform*, Abingdon, 1957, p. 62).

During the Civil War, evangelism continued. Organiza-tions such as the Y.M.C.A. supplied men (e.g. D.L. Moody) who encouraged the soldiers, leading many to Christ. Every regiment of the Union Army was assigned a field chaplain. Some of these field chaplains used an extended military encampment to carry on evangelistic campaigns. "In a New York regiment, for example, a pastor conducted thirty consecutive nights of evangelistic services in a tent supplied by a commanding general" (Scharpff, p. 173).

In the Confederate Army, pastoral care and evangelism seemed to play a greater part than among the armies of the Union. Both General Robert E. Lee and General Stonewall Jackson actively supported their chaplains. "In 1863-64 a great revival came to the troops of northern Virginia in which thousands were converted. One chaplain reported about 150,000 conversions among Southern troops in four years of battle" (Scharpff, p. 173).

Such interdenominational efforts of the Y.M.C.A., the chaplaincies of both the Union and Confederate armies and, later, the Sunday School Movement were to launch a new spirit of evangelism in American Protestantism. In fact, the vocational or professional evangelist came into existence out of this background. There were other forces that contributed to this rise, among which the rise of the city must be noted. In the city, notes W.W. Sweet, "religion had to meet a type of competition which it had never before experienced, in the cafes, beer gardens, shooting galleries, amusement parks, saloons, theaters...and a host of other types of entertainment" (Sweet, p. 168). To meet such competition a new type of spectacular city revivalism arose.

The greatest of all these professional evangelists was Dwight L. Moody. Moody was born in Northfield, Massachusetts on February 5, 1837. Following his conversion, he moved to Chicago, earning his living as a shoe clerk but giving himself to Sunday School work and personal evangelism. He became one of the famous "Chicago Evangelicals" who promoted evangelism through Bible study. It was from the platform of the Sunday School Convention that Moody would be catapulted into mass evangelism. Beginning in England in 1872, he began evangelistic campaigns in the largest cities of Great Britain and the United States. Accompanied by Ira Sankey as soloist and choir leader, Moody had phenomenal success wherever he went. "Conservative in theology, a literalist in his interpretation of the Scripture though never a bigot, with a flat voice, often ungrammatical in speech, with sermons preached over and over again, Moody's success in pointing men to the Christian way of life was truly astonishing" (Sweet, p. 169).

Like Wesley and Finney, Moody was a great organizer. Every campaign followed a definite plan. He would unite the leaders of various churches in the city for a single-minded cooperative effort. These co-workers would be encouraged to carry out months of intensive prayer and advertisement before the actual campaign began. Many times special tabernacles were erected in large cities to accommodate crowds and provide a neutral site for the meeting. Personal workers were trained, follow-up was encouraged so that those responding would become integral members of local churches.

The main factor in Moody's success was his preaching. He preached Christ in simple, everyday speech. Basic Biblical truths were presented as lucidly as possible; since Moody believed firmly that the Spirit of God worked through the word of truth. Thousands on both Continents came to hear and remained to pray. Many of these became faithful leaders of evangelical churches in years to come.

The professional evangelists who followed Moody (Moody died in 1899) were all more or less in the Moody tradition. His pattern of mass evangelism — careful attention to details, good organization, use of music — was followed by all his successors. Reuben Torrey, J. Wilbur Chapman, B. Fay Mills, Sam P. Jones, W.E. Biederwolf and Billy Sunday in those earlier years and Billy Graham and his colleagues in this day are all heirs of Moody's evangelism. Even the public evangelism going on in individual churches and among various religious groups have picked up on these methods that Moody utilized so well.

In the late twentieth century several factors have created the illusion that evangelistic preaching, whether in a mass or local church setting, is no longer effective. Theological liberalism has affected certain religious groups who formerly were very evangelistic. Such liberalism undermined the conviction that men and women were lost and doomed for hell. When this conviction has given up its corollary, the call to salvation and safety, also went by the board. Among several groups so affected, evangelistic efforts at various levels are seldom seen. In fact, evangelism is often equated with social action.

Another factor is the widespread emphasis upon Christian Education. Beginning in the nineteenth century with Bushnell's Christian Nurture, the idea of so environing and teaching the child in the home so that he will "grow" into Christianity became an option to extreme revivalism. As a result many children from Christian homes come to decisions for Christ without any perceptible crisis in their lives. Some would suggest that this is the only way to evangelize and have so emphasized "educational evangelism" as to eliminate, for all practical purposes, any notion of the older type of "crisis-evangelism."

Perhaps the most significant factor that creates the illusion that evangelistic preaching is no longer necessary is the strong emphasis upon personal evangelism as a week to week responsibility of the Church. In many evangelical churches today, visitation evangelism programs, such as Kennedy's "Evangelism Explosion," or evangelism through weekly Bible studies, etc., are used to reach people and there is often a corresponding elimination of week-long or protracted evangelistic meetings.

But, in spite of all these factors, evangelistic preaching still continues. When one sits with another in his home and shares the Gospel of Jesus Christ and brings that person to a decision, evangelistic preaching, as understood in the New Testament sense, has taken place. So, in all these newer expressions or methods of evangelism there is a continuation of preaching though it may not be in the form of a previous age. Then, too, in most of these churches in which such methods are reaching people for Christ, the pulpit is still a significant factor. Whenever there is excellent Biblical exposition followed by an invitation for decision, evangelistic preaching continues.

In conclusion it can be said that though the methods of evangelistic preaching may change, due to a change of circumstances, the heart of evangelistic preaching is there. Whenever and wherever one Christian "preaches Christ" to another (as Philip did to the Ethiopian officer of Acts 8) who stands in need of salvation, evangelistic preaching takes place.

3

Evangelistic Preaching
In the Restoration Movement

CHARLES R. GRESHAM

One of the most significant developments within that nineteenth century movement to recover essential Christianity was the recovery of the Ancient Gospel or the restoration of evangelistic preaching as reflected in the New Testament Scriptures. This important development needs to be seen in historical perspective.

But, first, what do we mean by the Restoration Movement? This terminology is used to refer to that movement in Christendom which began in early nineteenth century America[1] with a desire to achieve Christian unity upon the basis of the restoration of essential Christianity so that the task of world evangelism which Christ gave to His church might be accomplished.

From the leaders of this movement came a plea — the

Restoration Plea. Directed toward unbelievers it was a plea that Christ may be enthroned in their hearts as they respond to the Gospel and are incorporated into the body of Christ, the Church. Directed toward those who claim allegiance to Christ but who are related to human organizations and devoted to human theology it is a plea to recover essential apostolic Christianity as the only basis of fellowship and renewal in Christ. Directed toward themselves it was a plea to repentance and renewal so that they might constantly and consistently mirror the will of Christ in faith and action and continue to propagate this plea winsomely and persuasively.

This movement must be seen in historical perspective. In the early stages there are certain emphases that are stressed that later study will show are not essential to Christian faith. During these earlier stages certain Biblical ideas had not come to fruition in actual practice, so it is difficult to pinpoint definitely when all the factors that make up the movement came together. To express this, historians such as Dean E. Walker see the various earlier groups of concerned Christian people as tributaries contributing to the Restoration "river".

Certainly the concern for Christian unity, the primacy of Biblical authority, the understanding of restoring the "ancient order," etc., are seen by 1825. However, that which put the "move" into the Movement had not yet been recovered. Frederick Kershner may well be right in his contention that we do not really see the full-orbed movement until Walter Scott's recovery of the Ancient Gospel in his evangelistic campaigns as the evangelist of the Mahoning Association. Dr. Kershner says: "The Campbells, Stone, and their contemporaries were the pioneers who set in motion the great tide of Restoration. It was left to Walter Scott, however, to complete and adequately formulate the principles of the movement. In his introductory sermon, on the Ohio Western Reserve, which marked the beginning of the first great evangelistic campaign of our brotherhood, he definitely outlined the Restoration plea for the first time in all of its practical details. This outline...has never been surpassed or improved upon. It states the whole case for New Testament Christianity, and states it so clearly that there is nothing more to be said. For this reason it is fair to regard Walter Scott as the man who finally launched the Restoration plea upon its successful career" (*The Restoration Handbook*, Series 1, p. 26).

Yet there was evangelism of a sort going on prior to the significant recovery of New Testament evangelism by Walter Scott on the Western Reserve. This type of evangelism needs to be explored to get the total perspective of evangelistic preaching in the Restoration Movement.

I. Before Walter Scott

Twenty-five years before Walter Scott began his great work on the Ohio Western Reserve, Barton W. Stone and those associated with him were involved in a kind of revivalistic evangelism. The pattern had been set by that great New Light Presbyterian revivalist, James McGready. Barton Stone had heard McGready while he was studying in Guilford Academy in North Carolina. Later, when reports of McGready's revivalistic work in Logan County, Kentucky, came to Stone's ears, he determined to visit that area to examine carefully what was being done. Both McGready and Stone were Presbyterians, but the Orthodox Presbyterian interpretation of election had little meaning for either. In his preaching, McGready would maintain that "it is the will of God that the sinner should try to forsake his sins, and as a guilty, condemned criminal, fall at the footstool of sovereign mercy, crying for pardon" (James M. McGready, *Posthumous Works*, vol. I, p. 73). McGready believed that when the sinner so acted in humble supplication God made possible the saving faith. He never felt that individual salvation was really a matter of inevitability as some of his more strict Calvinistic brethren believed. In fact, McGready believed that the preacher had an essential role to perform in leading his listeners to consider earnestly their spiritual condition. He wrote:

> The preacher must use every possible means to alarm and awaken Christless sinners from their security, and bring them to a sense of their danger and guilt. He must use every argument to convince them of the horrors of an unconverted state; he must tell them the worst of their case — roar the thunders of Sinai in their ears, and flash the lightening of Jehovah's vengeance in their faces...Let them hear or not, though the world scorn and revile us, call us low preachers and madmen, Methodists — do this we must, or we will be the worst murderers; the blood of sinners will be required at our hands — their damnation will lie at our door" (Ibid., I, 316-317).

In the spring of 1801, Stone traveled to Logan County. What he witnessed there, he later wrote in his autobiography, was "passing strange. It baffled description" (see chapter two of Barton W. Stone's *Autobiography*, pp.

119-125). After witnessing these strange happenings for a number of days, he returned to Bourbon County, where he was ministering to both the Concord and Cane Ridge Presbyterian Churches, convinced that such revivalism was the "work of God."

That summer Stone reported the good results of the Logan County revival to his congregations and this report triggered a mini-revival which became widely known in central Kentucky. Stone immediately made preparations for a protracted meeting (centering around a sacramental service) to be held at Cane Ridge in early August, publicizing the scheduled meeting for over a month.

The crowds began gathering on Friday, August 8, 1801. Revival rumors all across the Cumberlands had created an unusual interest and curiosity here in the much more populous central portion of the state. By Saturday, the crowds were estimated to number between twelve and twenty-five thousand. These numbers were entirely possible for Kentucky's population had grown to 220,995 by 1800 and a large portion of this was located within a 100 mile radius of Lexington.

John B. Boles, in his work *The Great Revival, 1787 — 1805*, (Lexington: The University Press of Kentucky, 1972), gives an excellent extended description of this great revival.

> Thousands of worshipers were scattered across the hillside. A cacophonous clamor of shouted sermons, chanted hymns, ecstatic hosannas, and mournful wailing filled the air already thick with the smell of smoke, sweat, and excitement. 'The noise was like the roar of Niagara. The vast sea of human beings seemed to be agitated as if by a storm.' Perched atop stumps, standing among the limbs

of half-fallen trees, or astride wagons, ministers were warning of the judgment day to come with an emotional pitch proportional to the size of the assemblage. As many as eighteen preachers were present.

Curious listeners huddled around the ministers. In the resulting pandemonium the overwhelming majority of ministers neglected theological subtleties and tried with all their might to get these exhausted and exhilarated masses to accept Jesus Christ. Almost all the revivalists at first seem to have felt that the mere existence of the current revival season proved that God's spirit was moving among the people. In fact, many ministers assumed that the miraculous size of the throngs meant that those present were earnestly aware of their failings and desired to effect reconciliation with God.

In essence, the camp meeting circumstances, in which God was felt to be working in many ways, seemingly meant that all the conditions for salvation had been met. God had created a desire, a curiosity, which attracted multitudes; simultaneously his spirit was making possible the realization of personal repentance (with the orthodox alternative of a sizzling hell made clear) and return to God, through Jesus Christ. The unprecedented size of the services simply relegated Calvinistic talk of particular election to the background; the immediate, convincing effectiveness of the revival spectacle pushed an emphasis on personal volition to the forefront.

Using every technique known to their profession, the ministers urged their listeners to consider the terrors of hell and then imagine the glories of heaven. The willing crowd, their emotions buoyed by the scene around them, was easily swayed. In the swell of the sounds, sights, and numbers assaulting their imagination, God seemed quite evidently to be at hand. This then was to them an unprecedented opportunity to find security, avoid eternal torment, and gain everlasting glory. Even those who had never been devout were aware of the claims of religion, which, in such a situation, seemed difficult to doubt. Whenever a listener would fall, overcome by his emotions, large numbers of worshipers would crowd around him praising God and singing hymns. All this added to the clamor and confusion.

Everything acting together — the size of the crowd, the noise of simultaneous sermons and hymns, assorted shouts, cries, groans, and praises, the exhaustion brought on by continual services, the summer heat — simply overwhelmed the participants with their beliefs in providential omnipotence. The event itself generated further acceptance of its authenticity as heaven-sent, and this attitude further contributed to the frenzied commotion. In a very real sense, given the outlook of most of those in attendance, the camp meeting revival typified by Cane Ridge became a self-authenticating work of God.

These procedures, seen in the Cane Ridge revival (and earlier revivals), became the pattern for evangelistic preaching in the subsequent Christian Church or the "New Lights" as they were being called. Following the break with traditional Presbyterianism, the creation of the Springfield Presbytery and its dissolution in 1804, this New Light group led by Barton W. Stone and others adopted the name Christian to designate both individuals and congregations. This move was undoubtedly prompted by suggestions made by Rice Haggard who, ten years earlier, had urged James O'Kelly's Republican Methodists to accept the name "Christian." Richard McNemar, one of the original group of New Lights, was particularly impressed by Haggard's reasoning and, as Marshall and Thompson, (two other of the original leaders), would later write, began urging that "our bond of union with the Springfield Presbytery was a carnal bond — that we ought to be united by no bond but Christian love — and that this delegated body stood full in the way of Christ, and the progress of revival; which revival would run like fire in dry stubble, if our Presbytery was out of the way" (R. Marshall and J. Thompson, *A Brief Historical Account of the Christian or as it is Commonly Called, the Newlight Church*, p. 256).

Extremists such as McNemar and Dunlavy soon left the Christian Church to become a part of the Shaker movement, the United Society of Believers of Christ's Sure Return. Others, such as Richard Marshall and John Thompson, perhaps in reaction to some of the excesses seen in McNemar, returned to the traditional Presbyterian fold. Only Barton Stone and David Purviance of the original group of leaders remained within the Christian Church. Both of these — Stone in Kentucky and Purviance near Dayton, Ohio — continued to prosecute a revival of religion based upon the Bible.

The kind of preaching done by these who were leaders in the Christian Church in the West (as B.W. Stone would refer to the Movement in the *Christian Messenger* which he began to edit in 1826), was typical of revivalistic preaching of the day. There was, indeed, an emphasis upon emotion to gain the potential convert's attention and emotive consent. But, more often than not, these emotional harangues were not a part of the body of the sermon but were appended to the sermon or were separate talks given by another preacher to enforce the previous message. Often, certain preachers would become "specialists in exhortation" who would supplement and fervently apply the truth set forth in the sermon proper. Boles points out that this "division of labor made it possible for congregations to hear first an orderly and well-structured sermon, buttressed by biblical quotation and even historical and literary allusions, then to be urged passionately to accept Jesus Christ or imitate his life. The preachers hoped this would produce a combination of warmed hearts and filled heads" (Op. Cit., p. 111). An example of this is seen in Samuel Rogers' Autobiography where he tells of participating in a large meeting near New Paris, Ohio. He reports:

> On our arrival (he and Father Dooley), we found a great concourse of people assembled in the woods. A rough stand had been erected for the accommodation of the preachers, and the people were arranged on convenient seats around it. Being unwilling to enter the stand among the more aged preachers that already occupied it, I took a seat in the congregation, and was much edified and enthused by a discourse from Father Purviance (David). At length, having been called to speak, my diffidence left me, and I began to exhort sinners to contemplate Jesus, bleeding and dying for them on the cross. I do not remember of ever having been more completely transported in thought and feeling than on this occasion. Calling upon sinners to behold the Savior in his suffering I felt the warming influence of the cross in my own heart. I now have no recollection of what I said, or how I said it; I only remember my theme, and the transport of my soul in beholding the bleeding, dying One. No doubt, the effort was a humble one, but my soul was in it; the power of God attended it for scores came to the mourners' bench, crying and praying — crying for mercy" (*Autobiography of Elder Samuel Rogers*, pp. 29-30).

In retrospect, (and perhaps, nostalgically), Rogers continued:

We had mourners' benches in those days, and they were things unauthorized by the Word of God. We have long since abolished them, and we did right in so doing; but I almost fear that we did in such a way as to abolish the mourners too.

But within such emotionalism the sense of pardon often eluded those who gathered at the altar as "seekers." Samuel Rogers, John Rogers, and other preachers during those earlier days refer to this. Samuel Rogers wrote that he knew only "a part of the gospel" in those days. He knew "how to make sinners feel by presenting the facts of the gospel," but he did not know "what to tell them to do." "As it was," he confessed, "many professed faith in Jesus and were baptized, while as many more went on mourning" (p. 30).

There were times, of course, when the proper Biblical approach was taken but since it was so new nothing substantial resulted. Samuel Rogers tells of attending a meeting at Millersburg, KY, conducted by Barton W. Stone sometime in 1821. The interest was high, audiences large. Many had professed religion, but many more were at the mourners' bench, refusing to be comforted. After laboring with these mourners until a late hour of the night without being able to bring peace to them, Brother Stone arose and addressed the audience in this manner:

Brethren, something must be wrong; we have been laboring with these mourners earnestly, and they are deeply penitent; why have they not found relief? We all know that God is willing to pardon them, and certainly they are anxious to receive it. The cause must be that we do not preach as the Apostles did. On the day of Pentecost, those who were pierced to the heart were promptly told what to do for remission of sins. And 'they gladly received the word and were baptized; and the same day about three thousand were added unto them.'

He then quoted the commission: "He that believeth and is baptized shall be saved."

Rogers adds:

When Brother Stone sat down, we were all completely confounded; and, for my part, though I said nothing, I thought our dear old brother was beside himself. The speech was a perfect damper upon the meeting: the people knew not what to make of it. On a few other occasions, Brother Stone repeated about the same language, with the same effect. At length, he concluded that the people were by no means prepared for this doctrine, and gave it up (Ibid., p. 56).

Rogers also gives an extensive testimony of B.F. Hall, a Christian preacher who was ordained by B.W. Stone at the Old Union Church in Fayette County, Kentucky, May 15, 1825. Hall reports:

Early in the summer of that same year, I returned and preached through Middle Tennessee and Northern Alabama. We held many camp-meetings that fall. It was a season of much religious interest. It was no uncommon thing, at a camp-meeting, to see from ten to fifty weeping sinners at the anxious seat, crying out for mercy. Being naturally sympathetic, I thought they were the most affecting, touching scenes I had ever witnessed. At many of those meetings I spent nearly the whole night singing, praying for, and trying to instruct weeping mourners how to obtain pardon. I would weep with those that wept, and rejoice with those that rejoiced.

At one of those meetings, in the fall of 1825, an

unusually large number were constantly at the anxious seat, weeping, and praying, and begging us to pray that God would have mercy upon them. Some found relief during the meeting; but the greater number remained uncomforted. At the close of the meeting, when about to leave for another meeting, a brother proposed that we sing a parting hymn, and that the Christians first, and then the mourners, who had not found peace, should come forward and give the minister the parting hand. When the broken-hearted mourners came in a long line, weeping as if their hearts would break, I could sing no longer, but burst forth in a wail of anguish of soul. My pent-up grief found vent in a gush of tears. On the way to the next meeting, I said to a brother preacher:

"There is a wrong somewhere. Surely, we do not preach as the Apostles and first evangelists preached."

"Why do you think so?" he asked.

"Because our preaching does not produce the effect which theirs did. We nowhere read of persons who were convicted under their preaching, going away uncomforted."

"Wherein," said the brother, "does our preaching differ from theirs?"

I answered that I could not tell; but I was satisfied there must be a wrong somewhere. This idea haunted me through the whole series of meetings which I attended that fall.

Early next spring — 1826 — I set out for Kentucky to see my friends, especially my aged mother, whom I greatly desired to see before she passed to her reward. Late one afternoon, having traveled hard all day, I reached old Brother Guess's, whose house stood on the south side of Line Creek, a small stream which, at that point, divided Tennessee from Kentucky. As I rode up, Brother Guess came out to meet me. He told me, as I was tired, to go into the house and rest, and he would take my horse. He informed me that Sister Guess had gone to see a sick neighbor, but that she would be home directly and get me something to eat. As I entered the house, I looked for a book that I could read, while sitting resting myself. In a small book-case in one corner of the house, I saw some books. As I drew near I saw one with 'Debate on Baptism' printed on the back. It struck me at once that it was the debate between Campbell and M'Calla, which took place in Mason county, Ky., October, 1823. I had heard it had been published, but had never seen it. It turned out as I expected. I knew I should have but a short time to examine it, and began to turn over leaf after leaf to find something of special interest to read. Turning the leaves slowly over, my eye caught Mr. Campbell's speech on the design of baptism. I read it carefully from beginning to end; and I had scarcely concluded his masterly argument on that subject when I sprang to my feet, dropped the book on the floor, clapped my hands repeatedly together, and exclaimed: "Eureka! Eureka!! I have found it! I have found it!!" And, thanks be to God, I had found it! I had found the keystone of the arch. It had been lost a long time. I had never seen it before — strange that I had not. But I had seen the vacant space in the arch a hundred times, and had some idea of the size and shape of it; and when I saw baptism as Mr. Campbell had presented it, I knew it would exactly fit and fill the vacant space. I was converted over; and was one of the happiest young converts you ever saw; happier than when I was converted the first time, and a great deal more certain that I was right. Hitherto, I had been walking in the mud, or on the sand, and withal, groping in the dark. Now, all was light around me, and I felt that I was standing on a rock; and I have felt the same way ever since. From that day to this, I have never doubted that baptism is for the remission of sins. Not even a stray doubt has ever flitted across my mind. Every brother I met on my way from Line Creek home I told of the grand discovery. On the south fork of Green River, I met Brother

Sandy E. Jones — he was not a preacher then — and told him of it. He affected not to receive it — perhaps did not; but the next time I heard of him, he was a preacher, and was preaching baptism for the remission of sins.

In the summer of 1826, I met Elder B.W. Stone, and spoke of the idea to him. He told me that he had preached it early in the present century, and that it was like ice-water thrown on the audience; it chilled them, and came very near driving vital religion out of the church; and that, in consequence of its chilling effect, he had abandoned it altogether. I insisted that it was God's truth, nevertheless, and that I felt compelled to preach it at a meeting at Sulphur Well, to which we were then going. He begged that I should not preach it while he was present, but said he would leave after meeting Lord's-day morning; then I could do as I saw proper. I complied with his request, but preached it that night rather privately to persons who appeared to be concerned about their souls. Five, I think, was the number who were persuaded to take the Lord at his word. I immersed them the next morning for the remission of sins. Our venerable brother, Samuel Rogers, who is still living, was at that meeting, and was the only preacher who did not oppose the idea.

The next year, in September, I think, I preached baptism for the remission of sins on Cyprus Creek, in Lauderdale county, Ala., on Lord's day night. Tolbert Fanning was present and heard the discourse, was convinced of the truth, and, when the invitation was given, came forward and made the good confession, and was immersed the next morning for the remission of sins by Brother James E. Matthews. I witnessed the immersion. Brother James E. Matthews embraced the sentiment at or soon after that time, and at my instance wrote several articles on the subject, addressed to Brother B.W. Stone, which were afterwards published in his Christian Messenger (Rogers, pp. 57-60).

Samuel Rogers indicates that these cases are mentioned to show how slowly, but surely, the Christian Churches in the West were advancing "toward the full day of gospel light" and "preparing the way for this Reformation" (p. 60). But this also points up how significant Walter Scott's work on the Western Reserve was for the full recovery of the Gospel.

II. Walter Scott and
the Recovery of the Ancient Gospel

In the October issue of the 1831 *Millennial Harbinger*, Alexander Campbell, in advertising a new book written by Walter Scott says: "Brother SCOTT, who, in the Fall of 1827, arranged the several items of Faith, Repentance, Baptism, Remission of Sins, the Holy Spirit, and Eternal Life, restored them in this order to the Church under the title of Ancient Gospel, and successfully preached it for the conversion of the world...." Here, Mr. Campbell was pointing up the significance of Walter Scott's discovery for the evangelistic thrust — "the conversion of the world" — of the Church.

Walter Scott was a younger contemporary of Alexander Campbell. He had emigrated from Scotland in 1818 after completing his degree at the University of Edinburgh. Arriving in this new country he eventually came to Pittsburg where he became associated with George Forrester in his academy. George Forrester was also the minister of a Haldanian Scottish Baptist church and soon led young Walter to accept immersion and other positions that the Haldanes had found in the New Testament Scriptures. It was during this time that Scott became acquainted with the Campbells who were friends of the Richardson family, whose son, Robert, was enrolled in the academy. When Forrester drowned while bathing in the Allegheny River, Scott took over all his duties in both school and church.

It was while Scott was thus involved that a growing concern for religious reform according to the New Testament began to dominate his thinking. A pamphlet, *On Baptism*, written by a Mr. Errett and published by a Haldane congregation in New York City, fell into his hands. In this pamphlet the design or purpose of baptism was discussed. Errett asserted that baptism was for the remission of sins. A new understanding of Scriptural truth was thus revealed. Apparently Scott and his good friend Alexander Campbell, who had also perused a copy of the pamphlet, discussed the implications of this truth, for in the McCalla debate in 1823 (as indicated above), Campbell sets forth this Biblical truth about baptism's design. For the next few years these two men were constantly in contact by visit or letter. "They were thinking along the same lines, both seeking the reform of a desolate church, both intent upon the primitive Christian order, the destruction of creeds, the elevation of the New Testament, and the investiture of religious experience with reason" (Dwight Stevenson, *The Voice of the Golden Oracle*, p. 38).

In 1826, Scott (now married and with a growing family) moved to Steubenville, Ohio where he formed an academy and gathered a congregation. His contacts with Alexander Campbell were continuing and he was a frequent contributor to Campbell's journal, *The Christian Baptist.*

Late in August of that year, Campbell and his father, Thomas, stopped at the Scott home to invite him to attend a meeting of the Mahoning Baptist Association which was to meet at Canfield, Ohio, August 25-27. The congregation at Wellsburg, where Alexander held membership, had been a member of the Mahoning Association since 1824 and Campbell's influence, both personally and through the pages of *The Christian Baptist*, had been quite strong. Scott consented and accompanied the Campbells to the meeting.

Mr. Scott was asked to deliver one of the sermons at the meeting at Canfield (probably due to Alexander Campbell's influence since he was not a member of the Association, not even a Baptist), and he made a lasting impression on those gathered. When the statistical reports were given, sixteen churches reported a total of eighteen baptisms and six additions by letter, while during that same period thirteen had been dismissed by letter, twelve had been "excluded" and eleven had died. Here, indeed, was a field ripe for evangelistic harvest.

Returning to Steubenville, Scott continued to preach, teach and write. He submitted two articles on "Experimental Religion" which were published in the *Christian Baptist*, February 5 and June 4. In the latter article he affirmed that the Holy Spirit is given not before but after belief. He wrote:

> In reference to this good gift of God, I heard it observed a few nights ago that we had turned the gospel wrong end foremost — the modern gospel reading thus: 'Unless you receive the Spirit you cannot believe!' the ancient gospel reading thus: Unless you believe you cannot receive the Holy Spirit; or to give it in the terms of Peter, Believe and

be baptized, and ye shall receive the gift of the Holy
Spirit, for the promise (i.e. of the Holy Spirit) is to you,'
&c.&c.

One can see that he is beginning to put the pieces of the
puzzle (the Ancient Gospel) together.

Again, Alexander Campbell prevailed upon Scott to
attend the Mahoning Association meeting at New Lisbon,
Ohio, Aug. 23-25, 1827. Some have suggested that Mr.
Campbell was already anticipating Walter Scott's being
installed as the first full-time evangelist of the Mahoning
Association. Whatever may have been Campbell's inten-
tion, the Churches of the Association voted to secure "an
evangelical preacher to be employed to travel and teach
among the churches" (Stevenson, p. 55), and Walter Scott
was suggested by Mr. Campbell as this preacher. Finding
no reason to object, Scott agreed. He immediately began
to prepare for the work. Speaking of this, he would later
write:

> I immediately cut all other connections, abandoned my
> projected Editorship of a proposed paper entitled *The
> Millennium Herald*, dissolved my academy; left my
> church, left my family, dropt the bitterest tear over my
> infant household that ever escaped from my eyes, and set
> out under the simple conduct of Jesus Christ to make an
> experiment of what is now styled the Ancient Gospel
> (*The Evangelist* Vol. I, 1832, p. 94).

And it was an experiment at first. Although he had
come to see the New Testament pattern, he had not yet
preached it. All the elements were there: the presentation
of Jesus as Messiah, followed by faith or the belief in the
evidences of Jesus' Messiahship; then followed, in logical

order, by repentance, baptism, the remission of sins, the gift of the Holy Spirit and life eternal. "Just as one needs all the right letters to make a word and then must arrange them in the proper order to spell that word correctly, even so one needs for the restoration of the gospel both the right elements and the right arrangement of these elements" (Stevenson, p. 63). Scott now saw the whole scope of the Reformation. He would later write:

> The present century, then, is characterized by these three successive steps, which the lovers of our Lord Jesus have been enabled to make, in their return to the original institution. First the Bible was adopted as sole authority in our assemblies, to the exclusion of all other books. Next, the Apostolic order was proposed. Finally, the true Gospel was restored (*The Gospel Restored*, preface, pp. v-vi).

During that Fall of 1827, Scott arranged to move his family to a plot of land near Canfield whereon a house was being built for him. This allowed him to "try out" the Ancient Gospel on a church near Steubenville which was not a part of the Mahoning Association. He failed (as had those among the "Christians" of the West at an earlier time); his audience was taken by surprise by such a new program. Scott was crushed; but surely he had not been mistaken. He prayed fervently and decided that he must continue to preach as the Word directed.

His first preaching appointment within the bounds of the Mahoning Association was at New Lisbon, Ohio, November 18, 1827. He took as his text, Mt. 16:16, "Thou art the Christ, the Son of the Living God." After a masterful presentation of Jesus' Messiahship, Scott moved to speak of the conditions by which the benefits of Jesus' work could be secured. Quoting Peter's words at Pentecost, Scott pointed out that faith, repentance, and baptism are the necessary responses to receive God's pardon and God's presence.

Sometime toward the close of Scott's sermon William Amend, a devout Presbyterian, came into meetinghouse. Amend had been studying his Bible and had come to some of the same convictions as Walter Scott. Once upon reading the second chapter of Acts, he had said to his wife: "Oh this is the gospel; this is the thing we wish, the remission of our sins! Oh, that I could hear the gospel in those same words as Peter preached it! I hope I shall some day hear, and the first man I meet who will preach the gospel thus, with him I will go" (Stevenson, p. 67). As Amend listened to Scott, he knew he had found that man and promptly proceeded forward to comply with the invitation and was immediately baptized. Within the week, fifteen others had sought baptism on this Scriptural basis.

This pattern of evangelism and evangelistic preaching swept like wildfire throughout the Western Reserve. Other preachers — both those in the Mahoning Association, (as Adamson Bentley) and those among the "Christians" (as Joseph Gaston and John Secrest) — adopted the New Testament pattern. Gaston even traveled with Scott for a time and "the two did much, not only to advance the Reformation, but to cement the bond between the Baptists and the 'Christians'" (Stevenson, p. 72). In fact, this pattern became so generally practiced that one "Christian" preacher wrote Barton W. Stone about it. Stone replied in his journal, *The Christian Messenger*, (July 26, 1828): "I have no doubt that it will become the universal practice, though vehemently opposed."

Within weeks, what had been begun with much prayer and, perhaps, almost tentatively, became an assumed spiritual offensive. Scott was urgently preaching wherever he could gain a hearing. Opposed, he did not fight back, but continued to preach the Ancient Gospel. Hundreds came, scores were baptized, even a number of ministers from various denominations were won over to the simplicity of the New Testament practice. Whole congregations came over to the Movement. The evangelistic force begun by one man began to multiply itself.

By the Spring of 1828, the Western Reserve was in turmoil due to this growing evangelistic thrust. So much so that Alexander Campbell was concerned that his friend Scott's impulsiveness had run away with him. He sent Father Campbell to visit and report on what was happening among the Mahoning churches. Thomas Campbell arrived in April and after some days of investigation he wrote his son Alexander:

> I perceive that theory and practice in religion, as well as in other things, are matters of distinct consideration. It is one thing to know concerning the art of fishing — for instance, the rod, the line, the hook, and the bait, too; and quite another thing to handle them dexterously when thrown into the water, so as to make it take. We have long known the former (the theory), and have spoken and published many things correctly concerning the ancient gospel, its simplicity and perfect adaptation to the present state of mankind, for the benign and gracious purposes of his immediate relief and complete salvation; but I must confess that, in respect to the direct exhibition and application of it for that blessed purpose, I am at present for the first time upon the ground where the thing has appeared to be practically exhibited to the proper pur-

pose. "Compel them to come in," saith our Lord, "that my house may be filled."

Mr. Scott has made a bold push to accomplish this object, by simply and boldly stating the ancient gospel, and insisting upon it; and then by putting the question generally and particularly to males and females, old and young. Will you come to Christ and be baptized for the remission of your sins and the gift of the Holy Spirit? Don't you believe this blessed gospel? Then come away. This elicits a personal conversation; some confess faith in the testimony, beg time to think; others consent, give their hands to be baptized as soon as convenient; others debate the matter friendly; some go straight to the water, be it day or night, and upon the whole none appear offended (quoted by Stevenson, pp. 92-93).

When the 1828 meeting of the Mahoning Association convened at Warren, August 29, five new churches were received. There had been 307 baptisms in the older churches of the Association, and the new ones created wholly by such baptisms, numbered 284 more for a total of 691. The moderator that year, Stephen Boyd, wrote to sister Associations that these 691 were "but half of the actual number which have been by our means, immersed into the Lord Jesus during the last year" (Stevenson, p. 99).

Other Baptist Associations, such as the North District Association in Kentucky were following Scott's lead and were also seeing fabulous results. Jeremiah Vardeman and "Racoon" John Smith, both in Kentucky, were reporting hundreds obeying the gospel and immersed into Christ. The leaven implanted by Walter Scott was growing!

One must not suppose that with the recovery of the Ancient Gospel that a complete revolution in the style of preaching resulted. The message was changed, particularly, the appeal at the conclusion of the message. No longer was there a mourner's bench or anxious seat. Men and women were called upon to accept the Gospel as those did in New Testament times. But, there was still that older pattern evidenced, where one preacher would present the Gospel message and another would "exhort" or encourage auditors to respond. While Scott was in the field, James Mitchell and William Hayden served him in this manner. In Kentucky, John Allen Gano gained a wide reputation as an exhorter, leading people to note that whenever he appeared at a meeting there would always be responses. This pattern would continue through most of the nineteenth century. J.J. Haley refers to J.W. McGarvey and R.M. Gano participating together in a meeting sometime in the late sixties or seventies: "The Lexington Professor 'lightened' in those sermons, and General R.M. Gano came along soon after and 'thundered' and a great harvest of souls was gathered into the Kingdom" (*Makers and Molders of the Reformation*, p. 145).

III. Evangelistic Preaching in Post-Civil War America

The New Testament pattern recovered by Walter Scott and applied by the Restoration Movement generally produced tremendous fruitage. Thousands came to Christ as the Gospel was preached and responses were made. From 1827 to 1860 the Movement grew from some 15,000 (12,000 in the Stone movement and, possibly,

3,000 within the orbit of the Campbells) to an estimated 192,000 (see W.E. Garrison and A.T. DeGroot *The Disciples of Christ: A History*, p. 115, 329). In the forty years from 1860 to 1900 the growth rate was 500 percent, reaching 1,120,000. This growth was largely due to the simple presentation of the Gospel to people in need with their resultant obedience and organization into New Testament congregations.

Not long after Scott's recovery of New Testament evangelism the Christians in the West (under B.W. Stone's leadership) and the "Reforming Baptists" or "Disciples," influenced by A. Campbell, began to unite. Beginning in those meetings at Georgetown and Lexington, Kentucky, in December 1831 and January 1832, congregations from both groups merged into one and a vigorous program of evangelism resulted. These brethren were not only concerned about their own immediate area, they began to develop regional and state "cooperatives," supporting men in the field as the Mahoning Association had supported Scott. Many of these "cooperatives" developed into state "missionary societies" whose original concern was with evangelism — first at home, then at home and abroad.

Soon national missionary agencies developed. As early as 1849 concerned brethren met in Cincinnati and formed the American Christian Missionary Society. Originally this Society was interested in foreign missions or evangelism abroad, but after two or three ill-fated and poorly supported efforts on foreign shores, the ACMS became, for all practical purposes, a home mission organization. By the turn of the century, the Society was supporting some 300 people working in thirty-seven states and territories.

In one year there were 121 churches organized with almost 15,000 additions. Paralleling the work of the ACMS was the Board of Church Extension which provided loan funds for these new churches so that adequate facilities could be provided.

During these closing years of the nineteenth century and the first decade or two of the twentieth there were a number of outstanding men giving full-time to evangelistic preaching. In John T. Brown's work, *Churches of Christ*, he devotes a section to "some national evangelists" (p. 475ff). Here biographical sketches are given of T.B. Larimore, William F. Cowden, J.V. Coombs, Simpson Ely, John A. Stevens, Allen Wilson, J.H.O. Smith, Jacob Van Updike, James Small, Henry Clay Patterson, S.M. Martin, and Charles R. Scoville. In addition to these there were numerous "located ministers" who frequently held "protracted meetings" with great success.

Such an emphasis upon a rational approach to New Testament evangelism was having its effect upon American Protestantism. Extreme Calvinism with its anti-evangelistic thrust was breaking down; the hyper-emotionalism of revivalism was waning. Through most of the Protestant denominations a new spirit was at work and gave rise to "professional evangelists" such as Dwight L. Moody. Moody's evangelistic career began immediately following the Civil War, and ended with his death in the very midst of a great meeting in Kansas City in 1899. All his great meetings were union meetings (in which churches of different denominations participated), city campaigns conducted in such places as Brooklyn, Philadelphia, Chicago, Boston, San Francisco and even Great Britain. "Conservative in theology, a literalist in his interpretation of Scripture though never a bigot, with a flat voice, often ungrammatical in speech, with sermons preached over and over again, Moody's success in pointing men to the Christian way of life was truly astonishing" (W.W. Sweet, Revivalism in America, p. 169).

Among those who followed Moody in this era we find such greats as R.A. Torrey, William Chapman, Sam Jones, W.E. Biederwolf and, of course, the incomparable Billy Sunday. None of these, with the exception of the flamboyant Sunday, ever reached the heights of Moody in effectiveness, but they all made their impact upon the day and age in which they lived. In fact, the success of such "union evangelism" was so tempting that a few of the full-time evangelists and evangelistic parties within the Restoration Movement became involved, even though it meant playing down the significance of baptism in Gospel obedience.

But there were several factors that united to bring about the wane of such evangelism within Protestantism (and, to some degree, these same forces affected certain orbits within the Restoration Movement). First, theological liberalism tended to undermine the Biblical basis of evangelism. If evangelism is based upon man's sinfulness and the reality of salvation through Jesus Christ, theological liberalism's deemphasis, if not outright denial, of these Biblical truths caused this basic foundation to crumble. Accompanying theological liberalism was the promulgation of the Social Gospel. This emphasis tended to highlight the impersonal rather than the personal; to see salvation in terms of education reform, political action and amelioration of social condition. The new scientific psychology tended to play down any kind of emotionalism and to explain all religious experience in terms of biological or social causes. Such agnosticism in regard to religious reality, taught in college and universities and played up by the various media, became another undermining factor.

The influence of these factors on the evangelistic thrust of Restoration heirs can be seen as well. Within the agencies that had begun in the nineteenth century to bring the Gospel to the world at home and abroad, a gradual drift away from this original purpose was seen in the twentieth century. The major missionary organizations had merged in 1919/20 to form the United Christian Missionary Society, presumably to be more efficient and to accomplish more; but, in reality, less was accomplished and fewer personnel were involved in direct evangelistic activity. Not only that, but there was a move away from the New Testament emphasis upon immersion into Christ as the culminating act of initial obedience to the Gospel as more and more within the "cooperative" orbit (as it was known in the thirties and forties) were accepting "open membership." This segment of the Restoration Movement, in spite of its control of most of the older agencies and other institutions, has continued to decline largely due to its failure to maintain a strong evangelistic thrust.

Within that more conservative wing of the movement, evangelism continued to play a major role, although only in post World War II years have these churches become intensely interested in world-wide evangelism. Whatever charges may be leveled at some of these preachers because of their legalism, lovelessness, and lack of interest in genuine Christian unity, they must be commended for their evangelistic fervor. Wherever members of these congregations go, they plant new "churches of Christ" and share the ancient Gospel. From approximately 125,000 (in the 1906 Census where they are for the first time listed as a separate group) they have grown to number somewhere in the neighborhood of two million. Both through various kinds of personal evangelism, and through Gospel meetings conducted by congregations at set times in the year, evangelistic preaching is carried on.

As the "cooperative orbit" tended to move away from clear Biblical ground and began to emphasize denominational federation and ecumenicity, a large segment of those who were still reported as "Disciples of Christ" became dissatisfied. Developing their own colleges (basically institutions for educating and training Gospel preachers) and their own "direct support" missionary approach, they tried to remain true to the basic principles and practices of the Restoration Movement. As a result programs of evangelism were developed, full-time evangelists continued to share with concerned congregations, and missionaries were sent out to evangelize and disciple needy fields. Within this group, now known as "Christian Churches and Churches of Christ" (numbering one million two hundred thousand), there continues to be those who are concerned about Church Growth. They know that churches in this latter part of the twentieth century must be aware of new methods and means of reaching the needy people of the world. They also know that it is still the Ancient Gospel that must be presented; therefore, there will always be a need for some kind of evangelistic preaching.

NOTES

1. There were, of course, Old World backgrounds seen in the Haldanean and the Scottish Baptists.

4

Evangelistic Preaching at the End of the Twentieth Century

KEITH KEERAN

Let the church get back to apostolic methods of carrying out the divine commission. The saints then were witnessing and they were all witnessing. It was the private witnessing of all the disciples, reaching its climax and culmination in the public witnessing of one disciple, that brought the results of Pentecost. Let each Christian go with the gospel to his own sphere, and a spiritual revolution will soon take place. The church stands in need of such. Imagine a church full of soul-winners. My Lord! What a Millennium!

Such was the sentiment of Joseph W. Kemp in 1930. His urgent appeal to return to "apostolic methods" of evangelism penetrates even the closing chapters of the second millennium, Anno Domini. Evidences of any functional restoration of such an apostolic model is slow to emerge. The penetration has been quite gradual, and in many quarters unknown.

Evangelistic preaching at the end of the twentieth century must be carefully integrated with other forms of outreach if it is to contribute to the successful incorporation and result in the active participation of an ever burgeoning non-member community. The simple truth is that the New Testament never teaches, models, or sanctions the pulpit activity we call "evangelistic preaching" as the divine plan for carrying out local church evangelism. Yet, for many congregations this is the channel through which much, if not all, of their evangelistic energy is directed. Typically, once or twice a year a firebrand evangelist is summoned to "do the work of an evangelist," i.e. to evangelize by the means of pulpit eloquence. He, with clear and resonant tones sounds forth a clarion call for sinners to repent and make their peace with God. The fervent and well intentioned pulpit effort to reach the masses is not infrequently characterized by tasteless style, empty arguments, intimidating illustrations, false emotion, and canned cliches. At the end of the 20th Century the non-member demands something that will satisfy his intelligence; a challenge that will spur his devotion; a reasoned declaration that will enlist his life in service.

Evangelistic efforts accompanied by shallow sensationalism, high expense accounts and few genuine converts have contributed to an attitude of despair in the churches. Leadership no longer has a zeal to evangelize. Some have erroneously concluded that modern man is no longer interested in the gospel. Even many preachers are giving less attention to their sermon preparation, being persuaded that time would be better spent in other ministerial duties.

Is preaching as a communication event at fault? Is it no longer in vogue? Is it, in our time, an increasingly ineffective and hence inappropriate method for convincing men of their sins? NO! NO! A THOUSAND TIMES — NO!!! Preaching is still a vital event; and when done well, it is extremely effective. But to be effective, great evangelistic preaching as a pulpit activity must be orchestrated in harmony with other communication (witnessing) efforts, both private and public. "It was the private witnessing of all the disciples, reaching its climax and culmination in the public witnessing of one disciple, that brought the results of Pentecost."

PROLOGUE TO THE TWENTY-FIRST CENTURY

The church at the end of the twentieth century is experiencing a refreshing and exciting shift in its emphasis. A shift that will awaken flexible congregations from their evangelistic lethargy and restore the vitality of the pulpit.

For many years it seemed as though there was great emphasis laid on the ministry to the masses. There are always exceptions to any emphasis, but by-and-large ministerial training schools developed their courses around how one person could minister to many. Graduate seminaries did the same. The mindset of both seminary and church was such that the sermonic monologue was the method that God would bless. Evangelistic campaigns seemed to emphasize this. The small churches copied the larger churches who set the pace in evangelistic technique.

Then, during the early 1960's we as a nation began to hurt. We became conscious of our hurts in various ways.

We were suddenly aware that our population was not only predicted to explode — it had exploded! And then came the reality of pollution. We learned the word "ecology". It became a science. We all became increasingly more aware of the burgeoning problem of our growing nation.

Soon America's youth began screaming for attention. Professionals also told us they were losing their identity. The ghettos began to scream to the city for help and relief. Through sometimes foolish extremes they got our attention. Riots began to explode on college campuses all across America. We learned such words as "communal living" and "drop out". We began to notice previously unknown places such as Haight Ashbury and Greenwich Village.

All through the turbulent 60's and into the 70's the church seemed to be asleep as though she were paralyzed. She saw the culture and society around her convulsing, but because she was not trained to minister to the individual, she continued to try her approach. She was then branded by society as the "established church" and the "institutionalized church" which had no message. She was not touched by the infirmities of the individual nor acquainted with his grief. She could not weep with those that weep or mourn with those who mourn. She made noise but no longer communicated.

With the 1970's came evidences of change. Colleges and seminaries began to shift their emphasis from mass evangelism to ministering to the individual. This refocusing which began in the academic community is just now penetrating the churches. Churches are becoming increasingly aware of the individual, as demonstrated by specialized ministries to youth, senior citizens, singles, divorced, and the physically and mentally handicapped. More and more churches are offering counselling services staffed by well-trained, professionally credentialed Christian men and women. The needs of lonely, troubled and often desperate individuals are being met.

Of course much that happened during the restless 60's and early 70's was not good. The world was trying to get our attention. We have learned some hard lessons as a church. We have learned that we cannot ignore the individual. We have learned that ministering one on one or one with a few is not settling for less than the best but in fact is going right to the root of New Testament Christianity.

In Mark 3:13,14 we may observe the principle in concentrated form. Jesus had come to earth with an impossible mission before Him (humanly speaking). He carried out that mission effectively, not by preaching to the masses, but by ministering to a small group of individuals who continued to carry out the task of evangelism after He left the earth.

Mark reported: "Jesus went up into the hills and called to Him those he wanted, and they came to Him. He appointed twelve *that they might be with Him* and *that He might send them out to preach*." Let your eyes graze upon those two italicized clauses for a moment.

1) "That they might be with Him." That's discipleship; skills developmental, leadership effectiveness training, personal goals assessment, spiritual enrichment.

2) "That He might send them out to preach." That's reproduction, personal and corporate growth, missionary vision, evangelism.

Jesus appointed twelve men. He virtually ignored the

idea of discipling the masses. He chose twelve men; hand picked them one by one. One was from the ranks of the tax gatherers. A few were from the fishing fleets. Some were unknown Galileans. Labeled as "ignorant men," they were untrained and uneducated. Yet, with those men He poured out Himself in such a way that they became effective torch bearers after He left. They altered for all time the direction of history by the end of their generation.

Some will say that approach was all right for Jesus, but will continue to insist that their ministry is basically to the masses. Continued advocacy of the techniques of mass evangelism, i.e. the evangelistic meeting or crusade as the primary means of evangelism, will be evidenced in some quarters for years to come. Such changes in thinking do not come quickly. Whatever the conceptualization of evangelism, it must be sourced in biblical truth. To this, most will agree with their lips if not in practice. A cursory examination of Matthew 28:18-20 reveals that the same method Jesus used He commanded us to use. The ones He trained were to use it. Through them He modeled His method and commands us to "disciple the nations."

Do not think that I am opposed to evangelistic preaching. To the contrary! Its growing disappearance from the pulpit is alarming. Its decline is a signal to re-evaluate our preaching agenda, if not our homiletic priorities. Further, the absence of a significant treatise on this subject may suggest the place given to evangelistic preaching as an academic discipline among our Christian Colleges and Seminaries. Academic curriculums need to be reviewed, not to determine the positions of evangelistic preaching above, but to assess the position and emphasis being given to evangelism in general.

Without question, evangelistic preaching as it finds expression in the evangelistic meeting or crusade is a phenomenon of a period of history which is now fading from the American scene in general and the American restoration movement in particular. The disappearance of the crusade is not symptomatic of a dying movement as some may suggest. It is rather a signal to redirect our efforts; to realign ourselves with the method of Jesus; to restore a biblical approach to evangelism to orchestrate our pulpit activity in harmony with efforts to disciple personally another or a few others who in turn will become teachers of others also. Remember, "It was the private witnessing of all the disciples, reaching its culmination in the public witnessing of one disciple, that brought the results of Pentecost."

Our movement was born in the midst of revival fervor, but perhaps that is not so much a static characteristic of the movement as it is a dynamic of its birth and of the times which incubated its infancy. The ostentatious oratory that accompanied the frontier rebellion against the established religious order is well chronicled in the history of religious movements in American culture. The consequential impact of this pioneer faith upon the church has been a residual longing for "old fashioned" revival. In recent years however, the evangelistic meeting/revival/ crusade appears to be going the way of many cultural and sociological institutions. It is fading away to be replaced by other evangelistic expressions more suited to the unique requisites demanded by contemporary urban culture. We will grieve at its going, as we would at the parting of a dear friend; and similarly there will be those who will refuse to believe that it is gone. Old, cherished and established institutions do not die easily, and those of us who have tasted of its fruits will long remember "the glory days of yesteryear." At times we will long to return.

AN OPERATIONAL PRESUPPOSITION FOR EVANGELISTIC PREACHING

To be effective, evangelistic preaching at the end of the twentieth century (or in any century) must be based on a biblically sourced operational presupposition — a biblical homiletic, the roots of which can be traced clearly to the method of Jesus. It is not inconsequential that Jesus said of Himself, "For I did not speak of my own accord, but the Father who sent me commanded me what to say and how to say it" (John 12:49 NIV). Both content ("what to say") and method ("how to say it") were from the Father. Equally important — both content and method were "commanded" by the Father! It is therefore presupposed that if one studied the method of Jesus, he would discover an operational model for evangelistic preaching; a biblical homiletic not restricted by time and space, a method of communication fitted to all the ages of man. Is the method of Jesus appropriate to others? Indeed it is! In fact, Jesus Himself instructed His disciples, "As the Father has sent me, I am sending you" (John 20:21 NIV).

In the preacher's quest to discover an operational pre-supposition he has often settled for less than a biblical model. Evangelistic preaching is intended to persuade as Paul suggested in II Corinthians 5:11, "Since, then, we know what it is to fear the Lord, we try to persuade men." But more specifically it is intended to influence a listener's

92

attitudes, beliefs, and behavior with respect to his relationship with God. It must be remembered however, that evangelistic preaching is only a part of the process of influencing non-members with a view to establishing Christ in their lives. It is not in itself the total process. This process must include not only what listeners hear in the preached word, but also what they see and experience in the lives of members. The fact that every member has a contributing influence in the evangelistic process is stated clearly by Paul in I Corinthians 14:24,25.

Our primary concern here, however, is the preacher's role and his approach to the preaching event in particular. It is likely that most preachers have developed an operational model of evangelistic preaching based on a particular presuppositional view. Three distinct views may be commonly observed. Functionally, these views presuppose that evangelistic preaching is either 1) an information monologue, 2) a manipulative event, or 3) a dialogical transaction.

Evangelistic preaching as an informational monologue requires nothing more of the preacher than to prepare and deliver a message centered on the historic realities of the death, burial, and resurrection of Christ. The comprehension and assimilation of these life altering truths is then in the hands of the listener. This view requires only that the preacher preach. Beyond that he is not obligated.

Evangelistic preaching as a manipulative event requires less biblical accuracy in the skillful preparation of sermons but more care is required in the delivery of the message. More staging of the total preaching event is necessary. The forward movement of trained counselors during the invitation; the prolonged invitation; the emotionally intimidating, life-threatening exhortive illustration and stories of the "almost saved" are but a few of the earmarks of this sensationalistic approach. This view requires little if any exegetical/expositional effort on the part of the preacher.

Evangelistic preaching as a dialogical transaction is the most demanding approach for a preacher and his audience. It requires that he know his people and his message thoroughly. It necessitates the active involvement of the saints in the preaching event. It demands the private witnessing of all the people and reaches its climax and culmination in the public witnessing of one person — the preacher. Evangelistic preaching as a dialogical transaction is based on a communication model sourced solely in the method of Jesus. It is the biblical homiletic.

THE SEARCH FOR A BIBLICAL HOMILETIC

The Bible is not, of course, a homiletics textbook — just as it is not a science textbook — but in the same way that its scientific observations have been found accurate, so its homiletic principles have been found to be true and in keeping with the most widely reasoned view in the discipline of communication.

What are the characteristics of a biblical homiletic which make evangelistic preaching, in this or any century, a dialogical transaction? To answer this question, it is necessary that we briefly review the "method" of Jesus.

Jesus spoke as one who had authority. His word was with power. This remarkable characteristic was what distinguished Him from other preachers of His day. He had tremendous insight. His eyes could penetrate the heart.

He knew men's hearts because He had become flesh and dwelt among them. He was touched by their constant struggle. He understood. He was one with them, because He was one of them — yet He was much more. He knew hardship, pain, grief, hunger and poverty. Power is born of weakness. He had earned the right to be heard and when He spoke there was the ring of compassion mingled with personal privation, and yet hope and salvation were in His eyes and on His lips. You can sense when a man is touched by your personal grief and shares your sorrows. You are moved by such men. There is power in their presence when they enable you to see light in the midst of darkness, hope in the midst of despair, victory in the midst of defeat, strength in the midst of weakness.

If it was His power that earned Him the right to be heard, it was His simplicity that attracted men to listen. The common people, uneducated and unsophisticated, heard Him gladly. They were moved by language they understood. Technical jargon may impress some but it will not move many. It is amazing that He who made the worlds and hence could have astounded His audiences with mathematical explanations of the laws of physics, did not. He could have — but He did not! Such was not His purpose, and had He done so they certainly would not have understood. His purpose was to be understood. Of course there is danger even in speaking so simply that you are understood. Jesus did, and you remember what they did to Him! The gospel is a simple announcement, yet profound. It requires that he who proclaims it, first experience it, understand it, continue to explore it, and live within it. Its simplicity is evidenced best in the lives of those who exhibit its timeless truths in their own spheres of life. Then a spiritual revolution will take place as others "see" the message. If the lives of the saints are the only Bible the world will read, we are in desperate need of a "revised version" — one that communicates truth through the simplicity of a godly life. When the simplicity of our speech unites with the simplicity of our lives then common men will gladly hear us, understand and believe.

Both the power and simplicity with which Christ spoke are evidences of a genuine uniqueness in the preaching style. How could men not be attracted to Him? They may challenge Him, argue with Him, defy Him, even crucify Him, but they cannot ignore Him! The words of Christ are alive and active; piercing words; words that penetrated men's hearts and challenged their lives. "The word of God is living and active. Sharper than any double-edged sword, it penetrates even to dividing soul and spirit, joints and marrow; it judges the thoughts and attitudes of the heart"(Hebrews 4:12 NIV). The words of Christ were anointed words. "The Spirit of the Lord is on me; therefore he has anointed me to preach good news to the poor" (Isaiah 61:1 and Luke 4:18). The same Holy Spirit that anointed Jesus and gave life and power to His words is available to those who preach in the twentieth century. So important was the role of the Holy Spirit in the preaching event that in Acts 1:4-8 Jesus actually forbade His disciples to preach until they received power by the Holy Spirit. A short time later Peter and John experienced a quenching of the Holy Spirit in their lives brought on by the intimidating threats of the Sanhedrin. Their power receded. Their boldness was restored only through prayer. "After they prayed, the place where they were meeting was shaken. And they were all filled with the Holy Spirit and spoke the word of God boldly" (Acts 4:31).

Evangelistic preaching at the end of the twentieth century will be dynamic when characterized by simplicity and spirituality — the kind of spirituality exhibited by a godly life anointed by the Holy Spirit. Mere human efforts at eloquence will never do. As E.M. Bounds has said, "Men are looking for better methods, but God is looking for better men!" Better men begin their sermons on their knees, petitioning God, not for persuasive words, but for a demonstration of the Spirit and of power. Paul confessed, "My speech and my preaching were not in persuasive words of wisdom, but in demonstration of the Spirit and of power: that your faith should not stand in the wisdom of men, but in the power of God" (I Corinthians 2:4,5). That was Paul's approach to evangelistic preaching in the first century. It is a timeless method — a New Testament model — a biblical homiletic.

5

The Evangelistic Messenger

The preacher is a herald of the everlasting evangel. It is said that in the past the messengers of a certain king wore three letters across their breasts — H.M.S., which stood for the words, "His Majesty's Service." Their messages were the king's messages. They carried them with dignity, promptness, and courage.

It is a high honor to be the herald of the King of kings and Lord of lords! To bear his message from his throne to his people is a privilege and a responsibility. He who bears the message of his King is on important business. He is never to think of himself as some little subcommitteeman fussing around with trivial matters. Nor is he to think of himself as a bellboy coming into a hotel lobby with inconsequential announcements. Rather, he is the

King's spokesman. The evangel he bears is not his, but that of his King who said, "You did not choose me, but I chose you and appointed you" (John 15:16).

There is a glory in this call to be the King's heralds. Isaiah, the prophetic preacher, saw the Lord in the year that King Uzziah died. The Lord's "train filled the temple. Above him stood the seraphim: each one had six wings: with two he covered his face, and with two he covered his feet, and with two he flew. And one called to another and said:

'Holy, holy, holy is the Lord of hosts;
the whole earth is full of his glory'" (Isaiah 6:1-3).

A vision of God came with Isaiah's call.

God goes to peculiar and unlikely places for his messengers. He went to the plains and called Elisha. To the sheepfold for Amos. He walked along the seashore and called four fishermen from their nets to become his heralds. He went to the School of Gamaliel in Jerusalem for Paul, to a farm for Barnabas, and to the seat of customs for Matthew. He calls his messengers from every station in life to be his voice. Today, as always, he is still surprising men by his ways of selecting his messengers. He goes to the shoestore for Moody; to the baseball diamond for Billy Sunday; to the cobbler's bench for William Carey; to a little community in Scotland for Robert Moffat; to a university for John R. Mott and Albert Schweitzer.

The heralds of the Christian message today are in a mighty succession of the great hearts of the calling from Jesus until now. Simon Peter, the Pentecost preacher; Paul, the tireless evangelist; St. Francis of Assisi who "married my lady poverty"; Chrysostom, the golden mouth; Luther, the preacher of God's judgments; John Wesley, savior of England and helper of the world; Alexander Campbell, scholarly interpreter of the scriptures and able preacher of the gospel; Dwight L. Moody, herald of the love of God; J.H. Jowett, peerless interpreter of the word; Charles E. Jefferson, unique expositor of the evangel; and George W. Truett, mighty preacher of God's amazing grace.

It is not easy to be the herald of Christ in any day. It has always been serious and exacting work. This present generation of preachers not only faces difficult days in which to preach, but they have some of the greatest opportunities for preaching that have ever been presented. This generation needs the gospel, which is the "power of God for salvation to every one who has faith" (Romans 1:16).

The question before preachers now in this kind of world is this — "What manner of men should we be who are called to voice the evangel of Christ to this generation? What are the basic qualifications we should have for this high calling? What equipment do we need?"

PREPARATION

Physical Preparation — The preacher's preparation should include his body, mind, and heart. The physical man has an important part to perform in the heralding of the message. God fashioned the body and without it the soul can do nothing on this earth. It is the soul's medium of expression. The herald of God cannot speak his message without his body, and other things being equal the more healthy his body, the more effective his message. In these exacting days physical strength is needed to "endure hardness as a good soldier of Jesus Christ." By our modern ways of living, nerves get on edge, vitality is sapped, and exhaustion is frequent. We live fast. We rush from one appointment to another. It is quite easy to work with mud, brick, and stone. They stay where they are put. It is easy, comparatively speaking, to work with flowers, for having no emotions they do not lose their tempers. But the preacher works with people who have appetites, dispositions, wills, and passions. These get out of order. He who seeks to deal with frustrations, inner tensions, and complexes must be without such things himself. He must not be a problem seeking to solve the problems of others.

Every herald owes it to his ministry to bring to God, the church, and his work, the best possible physical preparation. Habits that will impair his health and reduce his physical strength should be conquered. God's herald needs to give constant care to his body, for he preaches and works through his body. He is not a disembodied spirit.

Preparation of the Mind — No matter how fine the physique, something besides a healthy body is needed in preaching. He who speaks for God must give constant attention to the making of his mind. His memory must be disciplined. His imagination needs to be kept alive. There are two kinds of heralds of God's message — those of thoughts and those of thought. Continuous study and hard thinking must characterize the ministry today if any man would keep up to date, know God, know the Book of books, understand people and know his world. A preacher cannot give out that which he does not have first himself.

The heralds of God's message of redemption need the best mental equipment that this day affords. God has never put a premium on ignorance. The preacher, as well as others, needs to "love God with all his mind." The herald of today should seek to secure the best education and the finest training possible for his work.

The church at her best has always placed a strong emphasis on education and on an educated ministry. We need head culture. Now and then every herald needs to ask himself the question which Charles L. Goodell used to ask of preachers, "Is your culture a load or a lift? With some men the more they know, the less they do — the more culture, the less feeling." Preaching is the unfolding of truth. It is the evolution of an idea. A herald who can take a great idea and, by sheer force of brain power, unfold it until it glows and hangs glorious before the eyes of man and so burns that hard hearts melt and consciences are awakened is a preacher indeed.

The Spiritual Man — The messenger of God must have not only a strong body and a trained mind but a cultured heart. It is not only how a preacher thinks but also how he feels, which largely determines the success or failure of his ministry. There is a heresy of the heart as well as of the head. The time is here when the measuring tape needs to be put around the heart as well as the intellect of the one who would speak for God. The herald should speak with his heart and from his heart. He needs to work not only on his message but also on himself. Jonathan Edwards once said, "I make it my first business to look after the salvation of my own soul." This reminds us at once of Paul's concern about himself, saying "lest after preaching to others I myself should be disqualified" (I Corinthians 9:27). There is an orthodoxy of the head and there is an orthodoxy of the heart. It is possible for the herald of God to lay claim to an orthodoxy of the head, while at the same time he is heterodox in his heart. Sometimes in his heart he is irritable, unkind, unbrotherly, unco-operative, unappreciative, impatient, domineering, insincere, unsympathetic, and dishonest.

The herald's heart must be set afire. The Word of God confronts the preacher again and again with the fact that the divine fires on the altar of his heart will burn low unless he replenishes the flame at the altar of God. Paul, in writing to the Christians in Rome, stated this, "Never flag in zeal, be aglow with the Spirit" (Romans 12:11).

PERILS

There are perils for preachers just as there are for the laity within the churches. Only three will be considered here.

Lost in his Machinery — In these days of a multiplicity of organizations within the churches, the herald needs to be on his guard lest he become a mere tinkerer of machinery. It is quite easy for a preacher to get lost among the belts, pulleys, and wheels of church machinery, unless he is on constant guard. Organization is important and necessary. It is not the end but only the means to an end. Preachers are sometimes so interested in creating the machinery of the church that they let the fire go out in the boiler.

In many congregations, organizations multiply until the minister and those associated with him often feel that it takes almost all his time and strength to build, repair, and run the machine. A preacher one time tried to install an electric light in his study. There was a dry-cell battery in one corner of this study by means of which a series of bells over the church were rung for the church school classes. He decided that he would attach an electric light to the dry-cell battery. He bought the necessary electrical equipment, completed the wiring and when all was finished he pressed a button — but there was no light. He sent for an electrician who was a member of his church. The man came and looked the situation over and laughingly said, "Well, pastor, you have preached many sermons to me. Let me preach one to you which will be a sermon in one sentence, 'It takes more power to make a light than a noise.'"

Outside Interests — A second peril of the herald of God is to be found in the many calls that come to him from outside interests. There are many civic organizations, lodges, luncheon clubs, and other community groups that call on him frequently for his services. Unless he is very careful concerning these many requests for his services, he will discover that he does not have much time left to give to his study and his congregation. It is right for a preacher to take some responsibility for civic matters in his community but the best of his time and strength should be given to his church. By his ministry to and through his church he can accomplish more in the long run for the betterment of his community than apart from his church.

Sometimes a minister allows himself to be a server of

tables. The herald today, of all days, should not forget the word that comes out of the New Testament church:

> It is not right that we should give up preaching the word of God to serve tables. Therefore, brethren, pick out from among you seven men of good repute, full of the Spirit and of wisdom, whom we may appoint to this duty. But we will devote ourselves to prayer and to the ministry of the word (Acts 6:2-4).

Misplaced Emphasis — A third peril of the preacher today is a misplaced emphasis. He needs continually to check up on himself to see if he has primary things in primary places. Any ministry can become a tragedy if and when secondary things are put in primary places.

A preacher's emphasis determines the character and quality of his work. A misplaced emphasis by the artist changes portraiture into caricature; a misplaced emphasis by the bugler changes attack into a retreat; a misplaced emphasis by the preacher changes the Christian evangel into man's evasion and it is more fatal than many heresies. A preacher can have anything he wants if he will emphasize it long and prayerfully enough, hard enough and tactfully. If he needs and wants a new church building, he can get it if he will keep on emphasizing it. If he wants a missionary church, he can have that, too, if he will emphasize missions strongly enough. If he really wants an evangelistic church with many baptisms annually, he can have this, too, with a proper, sustained emphasis.

PULPIT

The Pulpit an Altar — The herald's pulpit is not his

throne. It is his altar. Here he gives himself sacrificially for Christ and the people. This makes for the romance of preaching. No other attitude will get results which really matter.

The spiritual temperature in the pulpit is determined by the temperature in the mind and heart of the preacher. In a certain Missouri church there is a pulpit. On one Sunday morning the writer was in this particular church, preaching from this pulpit. He looked at the side of the pulpit during the service and saw a thermometer hanging there. There is no more appropriate place in a church for a thermometer than on the pulpit, for when there are sincerity, concern, and enthusiasm (of the right kind) in the pulpit, there is a warm atmosphere pervading the pews. A good question for every preacher is, "What is the temperature registered by my pulpit thermometer?"

A Movable Pulpit — Every pulpit should be a movable piece of furniture. The herald (speaking figuratively of course) should take his pulpit out of the church on Monday morning. He should keep it out all week, speaking from behind it to men and women, one by one or in groups. In other words, from behind his movable pulpit all through the week he gives his personal witness in the community, in the homes, offices, shops, factories, and on the farms. Like his Lord he seeks men out one at a time and in groups. The preacher should have his own prospect list containing names of those who should be members of his church. He should interview men, one by one, seeking to win them to Christ and church membership. For many preachers it is easier to preach a sermon from behind the pulpit on Sunday than it is to interview persons one at a time throughout the week and try to secure decisions for Christ. The path from a preacher's study to his Sunday pulpit should never be a straight one, but a circuitous path, leading from the study over rural roads and city streets to give his redemptive witness in behalf of the One who called him "to seek and to save the lost."

The Pulpit Message — Paul said, "We preach Christ." (I Corinthians 1:23.) He is the message for today. Preachers are a group of men called of God to keep the soul of the world alive through the preaching of the timely, deathless message — the evangel of Christ. They bring the glory of the timeless into time. It is the good news of God the Father to man the sinner. This message is not of man's devising. It is from God. It was said of Dante that he was the voice of ten centuries. Sylvester Horne, speaking of the preachers of history, says, "They and not kings and warriors have been the moulders of history. The sermons of Isaiah, Micah, Paul, and Peter will outlast the pyramids."

The gospel needs dedicated voices that speak out of trained minds and cultured hearts. The prophet Isaiah (58:1) says, "Lift up your voice like a trumpet." A trumpet sends out a clear musical tone. It never screeches or thunders. The prophet here is thinking of the tone that is characteristic of a trumpet. Its tone is positive. The world judges the preacher today not by what he is against, but by what he is for. The need is for affirmative heralds of the evangel. The tone of a trumpet is penetrating; it sets the nerves vibrating; it awakens the mind and stirs the heart. One cannot sleep when trumpets are blowing. It is a moving tone. It moves to action. It is aggressive. This is the tone needed in preaching today — a trumpet tone. On the first Christian Pentecost, Peter "lifted up his voice." Following his penetrating sermon men cried out, "Brethren, what shall we do?" Peter said to them, "Repent, and be baptized every one of you in the name of Jesus Christ for the forgiveness of your sins; and you shall receive the gift of the Holy Spirit" (Acts 2:38). The apostle on this occasion preached for a verdict and as a result, "those who received his word were baptized, and there were added that day about three thousand souls" (Acts 2:41). Preachers need to preach on big themes. Preachers cannot drop the big themes of the gospel and create great saints. They must always preach upon the great texts of the scriptures; the tremendous passages whose vastnesses almost terrify us as we approach them. Yes, preachers must grapple with the big things of the Christian faith, the things about which their people will hear nowhere else. The message of salvation must be presented to men with a view to securing a decision for Christ. Paul said, "We persuade men" and in all his preaching of the evangel, this is what he did in season and out of season.

Bishop Ralph Cushman of the Methodist Church comments about the preacher like this —

> I do not ask
> That crowds may throng the temple
> That standing room may be priced;
> I only ask that as I voice the message
> They may see Christ!

> I do not ask
> That men may sound my praises
> Or headlines spread my name abroad;
> I only pray that as I voice the message
> Hearts may find God![2]

The seeking note is often absent in the pulpit message. When this seeking note is present in preaching, it is then that the herald becomes an evangelist. Jesus came saying, "The Son of man came to seek and to save the lost" (Luke 19:10). His entire ministry was a seeking and a saving ministry. He never allowed himself to forget why he came for he was always seeking and he was always saving.

Said a minister, "I simply do not have the evangelistic gift." One wonders how much prayer, thought, and energy he put into it. Francis Peabody once said, "Capacity grows out of desire much more often than desire grows out of capacity." Jesus said, "This gospel of the kingdom will be preached throughout the whole world." (Matthew 24:14.) That was his word for a troubled world. The civilization of his day had a death rattle in its throat. This message of redeeming love was his hope for a lost world. The Christians took the message out. They matched the power of Christ against the powers of the Caesars. They set something living in a decadent age.

POWER

Power Through Prayer — Luther one time said, "Prayer and provender hinder no man on his journey." Men who would preach with power must pray. The diary of the Son of God states, "He went up into the hills by himself to pray" (Matthew 14:23).

At Lake Wales, Florida, is a building called the Singing Tower. It was built by Edward Bok, the publisher, and dedicated by Calvin Coolidge. John Burroughs suggested a sentence for one of the rooms, which reads, "It is so easy to get lost in the world, I came here to find myself." Prayer does much for the herald of the Good News, that he may find and keep his directions. He needs to pray often in order to meet all his responsibilities with poise and to preach the word with power.

Walter Rauschenbusch was a great scholar. His books have done much to change the course of American Christianity. He emphasized the need of applying the gospel to social needs. For ten years he served a little church on the edge of Hell's Kitchen in New York City. There he labored untiringly to meet the needs of his people — most of them the victims of misfortune. To explain both his personality and power, one must study his prayer life. Once, during a time of great trial and pain, he wrote:

> In the castle of my soul
> Is a little postern gate,
> Whereat, when I enter,
> I am in the presence of God.
> In a moment, in the turning of a thought,
> I am where God is,
> This is a fact.[3]

Power Through the Herald's Passion — One of America's great preachers used to say, "We are the heralds of a passion but we cannot be the herald of a passion we do not feel." Truth never amounts to much unless it is felt truth. Jesus says of John the Baptist, "he was a burning and a shining lamp" (John 5:35). He burned to shine. Robert McCheyne of Scotland died at the age of 29, but after only a few years of preaching he had shaken all Scotland with his message. In 1938 the Archbishop of

Canterbury, William Temple, addressed a letter to his clergy requesting them to meet with him for a "quiet day" in London. One of the clergy replied, "Your Grace, in my village we do not need a quiet day but an earthquake."

A few years ago in an address at the Harvard tercentenary celebration President Conant quoted as a warning the words of Edward Gibbon in the *Decline and Fall of the Roman Empire*, written about the Greek scholars of tenth-century Constantinople,

> They held in their lifeless hands the riches of their fathers, without inheriting the spirit which had created and improved that sacred patrimony; they read, they praised, they compiled, but their languid souls seemed alike incapable of thought and action....A succession of patient disciples became in their turn the dogmatic teachers of the next servile generation.[4]

These are solemn words. Such degeneration has happened over and over again in history. It can happen to a religious communion. It can happen in a local church. It can happen in a family. Heralds of God may well read these words on their knees, "They held in their lifeless hands the riches of their fathers without inheriting their spirit."

Power Through the Holy Spirit — Christ said to the first disciples, "You shall receive power when the Holy Spirit has come upon you." Halford Luccock says, "The Holy Spirit is the present tense of God." He states that this definition is inadequate, but it does picture the truth enshrined in the words, "the Holy Spirit." It affirms that God is here now, active. To believe in the Holy Spirit is to believe in a God not located back in the past or off in the future, but God in the present. On Pentecost they "were filled with the Holy Spirit." This was the secret of their evangelistic success on this day when the church was born and 3,000 were baptized.

It is quite easy to tell if the herald of God has the Holy Spirit. If he is daily and continually seeking to win men to Christ and the church, he possesses the Holy Spirit, for the Holy Spirit is an evangelistic spirit. Theodore Adams, minister of the First Baptist Church of Richmond, Virginia, was ordained by his preacher father who said in giving the charge to his son, "Ted, my son, keep close to Christ. Ted, my son, keep close to men. Ted, my son, bring Christ and men together." This is the herald's supreme task — to keep close to Christ and to bring men to Christ for salvation.

Paul said to Timothy, "Do the work of an evangelist" (II Timothy 4:5). This is a timely word from a seasoned veteran to a raw recruit. This word needs to be displayed in every Bible college and in every seminary; carved into every pulpit; placed in every preacher's study and stamped indelibly on the heart of every herald of the Good News.

NOTES

1. Jesse M. Bader, *Evangelism in a Changing America*, (St Louis: Bethany Press, 1957). Used with permission from publisher.

2. From *Practicing the Presence*, copyright 1936 by Ralph S. Cushman. By permission of Abingdon Press.

3. From "The Postern Gate," from *Walter Rauschenbusch*, by Doris Robinson Sharpe, 1942. Used by permission of the Macmillan Company.

4. From Chapter LIII.

6

Preparing Evangelistic Sermons

ROBERT C. SHANNON

The evangelistic sermon requires greater care and preparation than any other type of sermon. There are several reasons for this. One is because so much rests upon it. "It pleased God through the foolishness of preaching to save them that believe." Much is at stake when an evangelistic sermon is preached. Souls may be won or lost for all eternity.

Of course, there are those who say people are not won to Christ by sermons anymore. They say that it is only the personal, one-on-one encounter that wins people to Christ. If this is the case, then the fault may lie with the kind of sermons they hear rather than with the preaching itself. Historically, preaching has been the vehicle for winning the lost. It was so in New Testament times. It has been so down through the years. If we are not winning people with our sermons, then it is time to take a look at the kind of sermons we are preaching.

Listen to this quotation: "The greatest avalanches in human history have all been launched by the force of a single power, the power of the spoken word." Those words are from Adolf Hitler. His life and early success demonstrate the fact that he knew what he was talking about — the power of the spoken word. That is the power that resides in us and in our pulpits. The power of that spoken word is not going to be eclipsed by any of the other ministries of the church. They are all good and they are all important and we need them all; but they are not going to eclipse the power of the spoken word. Sangster said, "Preaching is essential because Christianity is essentially revelation; and revelation must be told."

When George W. Truett came to the end of his career, the church decided to install a microphone so that he could preach from his sick bed at home to the congregation in the church. He did this for six Sundays to overflowing congregations. At the end of each sermon an invitation was given and people came forward to join the church, even though the preacher was not there in person to receive them. All they heard was the voice. So when Isaiah said, "God has given me a tongue," he speaks about a tremendous and potent force.

Why did they come forward in that great service at the preaching of George W. Truett in absentia? Because beneath his voice they heard another voice. As John Sutherland Bonnell says, "This is the only valid test of great preaching, that beneath my voice there is heard the voice of God."

116

Albert Speer was the man in charge of wartime production for Adolf Hitler. He spent twenty-five years in prison and then was released. In his memoirs, he told about the first time he went to hear Adolf Hitler speak. He said,

> Till then I tended to view him as a vulgar, rabble-rousing fanatic in a comic opera brown shirt uniform. But that meeting in a dirty, ill-lit beer hall drastically altered my image of him. He spoke earnestly, persuasively, almost shyly. His manner was completely sincere. Within a few minutes, he had his audience in his grip and, by no means, was everyone there his supporter. Soon his low-key manner disappeared, his voice rose to an hypnotic pitch, and there was a palpable aura of tension and excitement in the hall. A crackling, emotional voltage. That kind of supercharged atmosphere I'd encountered before, only at a dramatic sporting event.

Do you see how the personality of Adolf Hitler began to emerge as he spoke and captured this brilliant man, Albert Speer? And Speer became a devoted follower of Adolf Hitler. He said, "I believe there may be a tendency of man, perhaps rooted in Jung's concept of the collective unconscious, to surrender himself to the yoke of a stronger personality. This was certainly true of Hitler's mass meetings. He did not convince his audiences — he conquered them."

H.H. Farmer said, "The necessity of preaching resides in the fact that when God saves a man through Christ, he insists on a living, personal encounter with Him here and now." Preaching is the earlier encounter. Before they have that personal encounter with Christ, they have that personal encounter with us. Somebody has written an article on the "Energizing of Truth." That's what we are talking about.

It can be demonstrated over and over again that a man who takes the trouble to prepare and the pains to excel can move people. It has been well said that "the halcyon days of Christianity have always been the days of the right kind of preaching. All the decadent days of Christianity have been the days of the wrong kind of preaching." People cry out to us as they did to prophets of old, "Is there any word from the Lord?" They cry not out of curiosity but out of deep need. He who answers with words of purely human wisdom will fail them. He who seeks the real questions of life and offers the Bible's answers will not find his pews empty very long. The value of preaching is seen in the fact that both the forerunner and the Saviour chose it as their method.

A single sermon, a poor one at that, converted Charles Spurgeon. Sangster was blessed, he said, for twenty years by a sermon he had heard. One of Moody's sermons changed the life of Wilfred Grenfell. One sermon by Charles G. Finney brought the Chief Justice of the Court of Appeals of the State of New York to the front seat. The sermons of Niemoller and Bonhoeffer and Ludwig Steil so threatened Hitler that their mouths had to be stopped. They were lighting fires like those that Savonarola had — from his pulpit — kindled in Florence so long ago. Our sermons are not straws in the wind. The sound of our voices is not lost in the night. Cowper was right when he said that "while the world shall stand" the pulpit must stand as "the most important and effectual guard of truth."

Sangster is right when he says:

On his way to preach the gospel the most modest man

may whisper to himself, 'Nothing more important will happen in this town this week than the work I am doing now.'

Spurgeon's influence has reached farther and lasted longer than Queen Victoria's. Luther made a deeper impression on Germany than Charles V. Mary, Queen of Scots, said to John Knox, "I perceive that my subjects shall obey you and not me." England would have lost but little if George III had died in infancy; but the whole nation would have been impoverished if the infant John Wesley had not been rescued from the flames of the burning rectory at Epworth. Two centuries later, we may still say with George Whitefield, "The Christian world is in a dead sleep. Nothing but a loud voice can wake the people out of it."

Another reason that the evangelistic sermon needs the most careful preparation is that we do not know how many opportunities we will have. The person who needs to be won to Christ may not be as regular a church goer as the Christian who needs comfort or instruction or encouragement. We may have many opportunities in a year to meet the other goals of preaching. The object of the evangelistic sermon may attend very rarely.

Furthermore, we must prepare carefully for the evangelistic sermon because of the delicate balance that must be maintained in such sermons. We must have instruction but not so much instruction that we cause the listener to be discouraged. We must have logical reasoning but not such involved reasoning that the listener gets lost. We must have an emotional appeal to motivate but not a sermon that is so emotional that it has no lasting foundation.

Stewart reminds us that,

Nothing could be more narrowless and stultified and futile than the preaching which is forever exhorting 'Thus and thus you must act' and neglecting the one thing which essentially makes Christianity: 'Thus has God acted, once and for all.'

Dr. L.P. Jacks said, "Every truth that religion announces passes insensibly into a command. Its indicatives are veiled imperatives!" He urges us to avoid "academic speculation" and "cold, insipid moralizing."

Speaking of the doctrine of God's redemptive work in Christ, Dorothy Sayers wrote:

We may call that doctrine exhilarating or we may call it devastating; we may call it revelation or we may call it rubbish; but if we call it dull, then words have no meaning at all. If this is dull, when what, in Heaven's name, is worthy to be called exciting?

Scolding and haranguing from week to week will kill interest more quickly than anything else. In "Go Tell the People," Theodore Parker Ferris reminds us that preaching should be indicative, not imperative. Occasionally, one must deal with imperatives, but remember that Jacks says "every indicative is a veiled imperative."

Affirmations are better than arguments. While evangelistic sermons cut, they must also heal. There must be both diagnosis and prescription if the message is to be complete. The Bible says, "The goodness of God leadeth thee to repentance." The best way to get people to repent is to keep emphasizing how good God is. When they see themselves by comparison, they will turn to Him.

A woman of the slums worshipped in George Matheson's congregation. She came to know, under his preaching, the power of the gospel. For a long time, she lived in a cellar, taking for granted that she could do no better. One day she astonished her neighbors by moving to a new place. She said, "You canna hear George Matheson preach and live in a cellar."

How does a man manage to preach like that? He does not do it simply by condemning. We must do that, of course. John the Baptist did and so did Jesus. We miss our calling if we do not sometimes pronounce the woes of God's judgment. It is a poor sermon that is all diagnosis and no prescription. Hope and forgiveness are themes the world hears too little — and needs desperately to know. Have we, perhaps, traded the role of the shepherd for that of the sheep dog — nipping at the heels of the flock rather than leading them on to higher ground? The ecclesia consists of those called out, not those driven out! We are called to joyfully announce good news, not mournfully relate bad news.

It is not that we ought to be like the speaker at the Women's Club who was introduced in this fashion: "This is Professor Smith, who is going to address us on Europe today; and she promises to leave out all the nasty things." There is no way we can declare the whole counsel of God and leave out all the nasty things. It is, however, no gospel, no good news, that does not hold out a blessed hope, a forgiving love, an amazing grace.

Care must be exercised in the selection of a theme for an evangelistic sermon. It may well present the dark side of sin; but it certainly must present the bright side of hope. Many people do not come to Christ, not because they do not realize they are sinners but rather because they believe there is no hope for them. While it is necessary in such a sermon to induce a genuine and recognized repentance, it is essential in such preaching to give people hope.

H. Grady Davis, in his book *Design for Preaching*, says that a topic should be narrow enough to be sharp; that it should have a force that is expanding or exploding or fermenting. It must be loaded with realities, dealing with the universal questions of life: life, death, love, hate, fear, trust, doubt, guilt, forgiveness, shame, remorse, compassion, hope. They are the realities of life and the things with which we must deal.

There is a line from Tristram Shandy, "The excellency of this text is that it will fit any sermon and of this sermon that it will fit any text." That kind of thing ought to be avoided.

Generally speaking, an effective evangelistic sermon is not overly concerned with the means of grace but has as its thrust the reality of grace. Naturally, an evangelistic sermon must end with an invitation to respond to the grace of God. It puts a further demand on preparing an evangelistic sermon in that it must conclude with a moving appeal and a clear invitation or summons to follow God.

An evangelistic sermon must not have convoluted reasoning. It must be clear as crystal. There must be no detours. The way you are going ought to be plain. You may or may not announce your flight plan in advance, but as you move along it ought to be clear now how one gets from A to B to C.

Sometimes you may want to show the ribs and sometimes you may want the flesh to hide the ribs. Which is more beautiful, a skeleton or a fully-fleshed body? The body, of course. But the skeleton may be more instructive! Sometimes the ribs may show and sometimes not; but the arrangement must be logical.

Throughout the process of preparing the evangelistic sermon the preacher must mentally sit in the pew. He must imagine himself to be the listener rather than the speaker. He must not think of the way he will feel when he says these words. He must imagine how he would feel if he were a lost sinner hearing these words.

There is a distorted kind of evangelistic preaching in which the preacher greatly enjoys getting something off his chest. However, no one is won by such preaching. It is not a matter of getting something off the preacher's chest. It is a matter of getting something into the hearer's heart.

The preacher must perform the very difficult task of supposing he is hearing the gospel for the first time when he hears his own sermon. He must imagine what it would be like not to have any of the great stock of information that he has previously gathered. Will the sermon make sense under these conditions? Will it be convincing under these conditions? Of course, many who hear evangelistic sermons do have some previous knowledge. Sometimes they have considerable previous knowledge. However, the preacher cannot take that into consideration since he does not know how much knowledge they have nor how accurate it may be.

Rising to meet this challenge, he faces a danger from the opposite quarter. He must not fall into the trap of explaining the obvious. He must not insult the intelligence of his audience. That means he must make things clear at the very primary level without appearing to speak on a primary level at all. Nothing calls for greater skill in the choice of words or figures of speech.

We must define without appearing to give a definition. Can we explain without appearing to give an explanation? Yes, we can. We can employ qualifying phrases such as, "As you well know," or "As you are no doubt aware," or "As you may have heard," or "Perhaps you are way ahead of me on this, but let me be very basic." We can employ illustrations, figures of speech, similes, and metaphors that will make the meaning clear to the first-time hearer without making the sermon dull for the person with an extensive background.

Here is where fresh, new illustrations will help us. Every man who undertakes to prepare evangelistic sermons ought to have a very extensive file of illustrations he has clipped from newspapers, magazines, or noted from his own observation of life.

Evangelistic preaching challenges us to be transparently clear without being dull or juvenile. The text that is chosen ought to be relatively short. It ought to be a text that has a thrust to it, a sharp point. In selecting our text we must exercise care. We must not select texts that require labored explanation. The texts we select ought to be colorful, clear, and almost self-explanatory.

Here are examples of evangelistic texts. "Repent ye, for the kingdom of heaven is at hand" (Matthew 3:2). "Repent, and be baptized every one of you in the name of Jesus Christ for the remission of sins, and ye shall receive the gift of the Holy Ghost" (Acts 2:38). "What must I do to be saved?" (Acts 16:30). "How shall we escape, if we neglect so great salvation" (Hebrews 2:3). "It is appointed unto men once to die, but after this the judgement"

(Hebrews 9:27). "Behold, I stand at the door, and knock: If any man hear my voice, and open the door, I will come in to him, and will sup with him and he with me" (Revelation 3:20). "And the Spirit and the bride say, Come...And let him that is athirst come. And whosoever will, let him take the water of life freely" (Revelation 22:17). "Come unto me, all ye that labour and are heavy laden, and I will give you rest" (Matthew 11:28). "God so loved the world, that he gave his only begotten Son, that whosoever believeth in him should not perish, but have everlasting life" (John 3:16). "Repent ye therefore,and be converted, that your sins may be blotted out, when the times of refreshing shall come from the presence of the Lord" (Acts 3:19). "As the hart panteth after the water brooks, so panteth my soul after thee, O God" (Psalm 42:1). "The blood of Jesus Christ his Son cleanseth us from all sin" (I John 1:7).

The topics we use must be sharp. They must be topics that meet some felt need on the part of the hearers. Here are some topics for evangelistic sermons. "There's a New World Coming," "Can Man be Righteous Before God?" "What Is so Amazing about Grace?" "Grace That Is Greater than All our Sin," "There Is Power in the Blood." "Beginning Again," "How to Please God," "Hope for the Hopeless, Help for the Helpless."

As with all sermons, the evangelistic sermon needs an arresting introduction, a convincing argument, and a motivating conclusion.

Having settled on text and topic, the evangelistic preacher must now develop an outline. It needs to be relatively simple, though it may be expressed in vivid, colorful words. It ought not to have too many parts. It ought to

125

have no more than four divisions and, of course, there can be no fewer than two.

Once the subject has been divided into two, three, or four parts, it is ready for further development. There is a need for analysis or explanation. These must be brief. Let the words be carefully chosen. Let there be no fuzzy words or hazy ideas that are not sharp and clear. Do not put all of the explanations together in one big, indigestible lump. Intersperse explanation, application, and illustration. Interweave teaching, reinforcing, encouraging, and inspiring. Put any humorous material in the first half of the sermon, touching or dramatic material toward the end. Be sure that you have only one climax. Move gradually but certainly to it.

Choose your words carefully. Try not to be flowery or too poetic. Choose vivid words, concrete words, picturesque words, warm words, words that are easily understood but perhaps not commonly used. When you speak of colors, be specific. Scarlet is better than red. Ebony is better than black. Keep the adjectives to a minimum, just one or two. Something may be white as snow; it may sparkle like silver.

An evangelistic sermon cannot be dull. Committed church members may listen to a sermon out of a sense of duty. People that need to be won to Christ must be drawn to the sermon. There must be a warmth to it and a friendliness to it. Yet, there must be something quite definite and uncompromising about it. The call to accept Christ must be clear and emphatic and delivered without hesitation.

Imagination is necessary if we are to be interesting. Can you, like Stephen, see Heaven opened? Can you, like

Stephen, describe what you see? Chalmers was described like this: "His imagination was endless, his diction and imagery were colorful."

The value of word pictures is seen here. Jesus used them. He spoke of a sower who went forth to sow, of birds and sheep and seeds. Paul used them. He spoke of sounding brass and tinkling cymbals and runners in a race.

Jesus spoke more in pictures than in precepts. They asked Him, "Who is my neighbor?" He didn't launch out on a definition of Hebrew word for neighbor and its Chaldean cognate. He told a story, a story filled with vivid picture words. "A certain man went down from Jerusalem to Jericho and fell among thieves."

"The Bible is full of ideas," says Paul Rees, "But they are not primarily ideational. They have skin on their faces and a glint — good or bad — in their eyes...imagination is a kind of coagulant by which ideas held in intellectual and theological suspension are precipitated in the form of images." He quoted Gustave Frenssen:

> First of all I take the text out of its ancient setting and plant it in our own life and in our own time. My text so to speak, saunters up and down the village street once or twice with thoughtful eyes and meditative mind. It becomes accustomed to the village, learns to feel at home in it.

Said John Ruskin, "The greatest thing a human soul ever does in this world is to see something and tell what he saw in a plain way...To see clearly is poetry, prophecy and religion — all in one."

The best preaching then, says Rees, is pictorial; and he quotes an old Arab saying: "He is the best speaker who can turn the ear into an eye." Perhaps after we have spoken someone can say with the disciples of old, "And we beheld His glory."

We must, of course, know the meaning of words, both the denotative and the connotative meaning. The word "scheme" means something quite different in England than it does in America. The words pride, dignity, arrogance, self-respect, vanity all may have the same denotative meaning but the connotative meanings are quite different. We must know the meaning of words and use them precisely. We need to avoid words that are too strong or too weak. It would be too strong to accuse your congregation of being rotten and too weak to say that there is room for improvement. Charles Jefferson reminds us that "Words have moods as people do."

Poems may add sparkle on occasion, if properly used; but they should be used sparingly. Personal illustrations are great, but not every Sunday. Vary them with illustrations from literature, nature, history, and current events.

Humor can be used every Sunday, if it fits the subject and truly illustrates a point. It may pick up lagging attention midway in the sermon.

There is a very old book of anecdotes entitled Pearls from Many Seas. Our sermons ought to have pearls from many seas — not all from the same sea. The illustrations in a single sermon ought to come from many sources. Perhaps one is from sports. Then, let there be only one from sports. Perhaps one is drawn from history; but let there be only one from history. Perhaps there is one personal experience; but let there be only one.

We must avoid all that clouds or obscures the message. Big words obscure the light. Why should anything be immutable when it can be changeless, efficacious when it can be helpful, promulgated when it can be spread, auspicious when it can be great, multitudinous when it can be vast.

John Bunyan said that he could have stepped into a much higher style and adorned his preaching more than he did. He saw it as a temptation to be severely resisted. Jesus is, of course, the best example of simplicity of speech in preaching. It was said of a certain congressman that he never used one word if two would do as well. It may be said of some of us that we never used a plain word if a fancier one would do. We must prune away needless adjectives and adverbs. We must strive to be lean, not wordy. Lincoln's Gettysburg Address has only 266 words. The Ten Commandments have 321 words. Moses told the story of Creation in 761 words; and Luke related the story of the birth of Christ in 284 words. The Declaration of Independence has only 1,321 words.

Do we have Biblical models for evangelistic preaching? Certainly, we do. The sermons in the book of Acts are our best examples. You will discover that each has a single subject, has a sense of unity, that it is tightly focused, that it builds to a climax. Above all, every sermon in Acts lifts up Christ!

An evangelistic sermon ought not to have too many scripture references. This is not to minimize the importance or the impact of the word of God. It is rather to maximize it. If we read or quote thirty passages of scripture in a single sermon we diffuse the impact of scripture in that sermon. If, on the other hand, we concentrate on one passage with four or five others to support it, we increase the impact the scripture will have on the hearer.

Too many scripture references in a sermon will confuse the unlearned. A few carefully chosen scriptures, properly presented, will move his heart and will.

Jowett once called on a cobbler in a little seaside town in England. The man worked alone in a very tiny room. Jowett asked him if he did not sometimes feel oppressed by the smallness of the chamber. "Oh, no," he said. Then he opened a door that gave him a glorious view of the sea.

For some, life has shrunken into an incredibly small room. They are confined in by the narrowness of life. It is our privilege to open the door and let in the light. It is our joy to help them see the larger view — to help them see the image in which they were created and the destiny for which they were made.

"Light," cried the dying Goethe, "more light!" That is the cry of all humanity. Until the Light of the world comes into their lives in the person of Jesus, that cry will echo still. Only when men know Him can we say, "The people that walked in darkness have seen a great light; they that dwell in the shadow of death, upon them hath the light shined."

A popular magazine carried a review of plays of the two Russian writers, Chekov and Gorki. The review described the two as being quite different in these words: "Chekov was a cardiologist of a wounded heart and Gorki was a cartographer of a scarred, social landscape." The effective evangelistic preacher does not find his model in the cartographer of a scarred social landscape. He finds it in the cardiologist of a wounded heart.

7

Delivering Evangelistic Sermons

RAYMOND L. ALBER

PREFACE

Who is there among us that can teach another how he should deliver his sermons? What is right for one will be all wrong for another. Learning to preach is like learning to swim. One can read book after book after book on "How to Swim" only to discover that the most effective way to learn to swim is to get in the water and go to it. This does not suggest that an instructor may not be of some help, but it does show that reading books is not enough.

Preaching and churches make preachers. Why did we include "churches?" Because the congregation to whom one preaches can be of inestimable value in helping its preacher learn the fine art of preaching.

The writer was asked to preach a trial sermon in a town of about 300 people in western Kansas. He was still in college, in fact he had just finished the freshman year. He delivered the sermon as requested. After the service was over Bob Schnelle, an elder in the church and one of those spiritual giants, came to the writer and said, "Ray, there is one thing sure, you sure can't preach." I replied: "Well, I guess I blew it." "Oh no," said Mr. Schnelle, "we are going to hire you and make a preacher out of you."

We could only wish that every young preacher's first church had that attitude toward their preacher. So many churches are critical, fault finding, and a tremendous discouragement to their preacher. Most of us have our faults, but learning to preach, (and we can never say we have arrived) is a cooperative venture. May the suggestions in this chapter be of help to those who plan to preach and may the chapter be a genuine aid to those who see their ministry as an evangelistic enterprise.

DELIVERING EVANGELISTIC SERMONS

The delivery of the evangelistic message is an extremely personal responsibility. Every man has his own way of doing his work and delivering his message. Every man is different from every other man. Paramount in sermon delivery is to BE YOURSELF! There is no one else in this world just like you. That is no accident. Each one is a personal creation of God Himself, hence different from every other person.

In Phillips Brook's lectures on preaching he writes:

"Preaching is the communication of truth by man to man. It has in it two essential elements, Truth and Personality. Neither of these can it spare and still be preaching. The truest truth, the most authoritative statement of God's will, communicated in any other way than through the personality of brother man to men is not preached truth."

The way each man will deliver his message is different from that method of delivery of every other man. It is God's Truth that must motivate the evangelist. As he becomes more and more knowledgeable of that Word of truth his personality will be stimulated and thus his effectiveness will be enhanced.

The force with which the evangelist will deliver his message will be determined by the volume of truth and knowledge of his subject, which is in the recesses of the evangelist's mind, even though it never gets expressed in any particular sermon. It is like the force with which the waters go over the mighty Niagara Falls that is determined by the volume of water miles upstream from the falls themselves. This principle holds true, especially for the preacher. When one's knowledge of a subject becomes exhausted then the message will just dribble from his lips. No one speaks powerfully who has only a slight knowledge of his theme.

Yes, the best of sermons must be preached. Effective delivery will demand hours in the study, reading, noting, searching the scriptures, seeking inspiration from the Lord. When that preparatory work is completed the sermon can now be put on paper. Write it out in full. Read it again and again. Correct any errors in grammar. Do not underestimate the importance of this last observation. Errors in grammar are a reflection on the speaker.

Each error is noted by someone in the audience. It will weaken every message and in some cases will turn the hearers off completely.

The radio and television have brought into the home of our land all manner of subjects and speakers who articulate to perfection. For the evangelist to mumble or stumble in grammar and in other ways "murder the King's English" — no matter what he says — he will demean himself and greatly reduce his effectiveness.

The writer is aware that Dwight L. Moody often "murdered the King's English"; he called Gideon "Gidjin" and Daniel "Dannel"; he often used such constructions as "seen and went," etc., but remember, you are not Dwight L. Moody.

Let us give further thought to the above observation on writing one's sermons out in full. Remember — as important as delivery is — it is second to content. This cannot be emphasized too much. If one does not have something meaningful to say, no matter how splendidly he delivers the sermon, his objective will elude him. If one wants clarity of thought, if he wants his sermon to be free of ambiguities, he needs to learn this discipline early. We are not suggesting that one read his sermon. The writer has never been comfortable with reading his sermons, though some do it very effectively. But, by writing it out in full, he will achieve a clarity and confidence not obtainable otherwise.

As one develops his technique of delivery he will at times launch out into some great moments of inspiration. Sometimes when one is preaching it seems the Spirit lifts him and he can depart from his manuscript or notes into a magnificent moment as his audience is swept along with him. Time and again we see this in the New Testament writers. They start in one direction then move off into another. Those are great moments, and lapses in grammar and content are forgiven.

However one may deliver a sermon, the continuity of message and the assurance of clarity will come, if he has made this message a part of himself. We cannot stress this matter of personal saturation with the message too much. Freedom of delivery will come, often depending upon the carefulness of preparation and construction in the study. If you would soar among the clouds, you must first baptize your entire being with the content of your message.

The pace one sets in preaching is a very personal matter, yet clarity of pronunciation is essential no matter what pace one may use in delivery. There are those who seem so leisurely in presentation that some listeners will tend to doze. That is the time to pick up the pace and possibly increase the volume.

FREEDOM OF DELIVERY

Whether one reads his sermon or speaks it from memory or notes, we must emphasize that whatever style one may choose depends on carefulness of construction in the study. Whatever approach one may take it must be emphasized that the evangelist must be free for those flights of inspiration that all of us have at times. Avoid stiltedness, which is the danger that comes from mechanized memorizing.

Clarity of logic is essential. Avoid long unbroken stretches. Short paragraphs are always encouraged. When one is reading a written article he may find the author is straying from his subject. The reader can stop, go back, and re-read the paragraph. Such a course is not an available alternative for the one listening from the pew.

Always begin quietly so that you will have some latitude as the sermon develops. Learn to modulate your voice and avoid like the plague what some call "the conventional pulpit monotone." It is important, as you preach, to bring yourself back again and again to the conversational level.

Above all, be yourself — and forget yourself. You may give free reign to your personality in so far as it does not take from the message. One man's mannerisms may fit perfectly into his message, another's may take attention away from the message. The evangelist's life may come into play here. Remember the adage, "What you are speaks so loudly that I cannot hear what you are saying."

INTEGRITY AND DELIVERY

There are many factors that enter into the delivery of an evangelistic sermon, whether it be delivered from a formal pulpit or in someone's living room. Basic to all of this is the personal integrity of the evangelist. You cannot listen to a man preach very long, or even converse in the living room, without sooner or later making a judgment about his integrity. If one is found to be an honest upright person, his message will come across far more forcefully than if he is found to be of questionable integrity.

Many of us are disturbed with any evangelist who is more concerned with "up front" results than with the total commitment of the one he is seeking to evangelize. Then there are those self-styled evangelists who rely upon "people manipulation." It is bad enough to see this in the secular world, but when we see it pawned off by those who claim to be men of God it turns us off completely. When an individual finds that he has been manipulated a sense of wrath rises up within him. Unfortunately many are never aware that they have been manipulated.

Probably the best illustration of people being manipulated is the television commercial. Integrity has nothing to do with many of those involved in their production or the commercial itself. Their motivation is not for the good of mankind but for the advertiser's lucrative benefit. The writer confesses that many of these commercials so infuriate him to the point that he turns the set off completely. That unsuspecting viewer is apparently not aware that many super-sales people know the methods of psychology and salesmanship so well that they can make people believe that black is white and white is black.

There is a relationship between a man's integrity and the methods he uses in evangelism. The T.V. evangelist is another illustration. Many of us turn them off simply because we question their integrity.

Real evangelism is tough. Real evangelism is strenuous. Real evangelism is demanding. "Evangelism is dangerous," as George Sweazey says, "but not as dangerous as the lack of evangelism."

FAITH AND DELIVERY

If one believes something with all of his heart he will express it far more forcefully than if one's faith is just a casual matter. Effective preaching and one's faith cannot be separated. "Give a man a message and he will find a way to deliver it," says Dr. Dean E. Walker. The real problem is to give a man a message. How often have you heard a man preaching who had nothing to say?

Faith is not something that one inherits or casually picks up. Jesus said to the father of the afflicted boy, "Everything is possible to one who has faith" (Mark 9:23). The kind of faith Jesus is speaking of is very difficult to obtain. Let the evangelist beware; if his faith is not in line with his message few will believe.

What a man believes has everything to do with the urgency of his message. Read the eleventh chapter of Hebrews. In doing so you will marvel at the capacity of man to believe and to endure. Faith is stronger than knowledge. Men will die for the things they believe when they will not turn a hand for the things they know.

If the evangelist is to deliver an effective message he better be sure of his faith. The Bible says the waters of the Nile were turned to blood. Do you believe that? The Bible says: "And the sun stood still" (Joshua 10:13). Do you believe that? The Bible says that Jesus was born of a virgin. Do you believe that? The Bible says that Jesus is the incarnation of God. Do you believe that? The Bible says that Jesus was raised from the dead. Do you believe that?

Do you believe that men are lost without Christ? One cannot be very effective in telling his fellowman what to do to be saved if he does not believe that he is lost. This is where theology comes into evangelism. What one believes is his theology (more on theology later). There is no room in the pulpit for the doubter. Give people your faith.

It is said that a certain young man was having difficulty with the doctrine of the virgin birth. One Sunday he preached a sermon on his doubts about the virgin birth. After the sermon one of the fine elders of the congregation took the young minister off to the side and said, "Give us your faith, we have enough doubts of our own."

Nothing will do more for one's evangelizing than a deep and abiding faith. Phillips Brooks tells of two young men who preached the same sermon word for word. With one the audience was electrified while with the other the message fell flat at his feet. It's a matter of believing what you are preaching.

ATTITUDE AND DELIVERY

If the evangelist is to be successful he must have a positive attitude. People are not won to the Christ of love by negative, accusative, belligerent, "holier than thou" attitudes on the part of the evangelist. These attitudes will show through his delivery and message and will turn people off. It's one thing to be "right" and "confident"; it's another to attack everyone with whom one disagrees from behind the pulpit. Teaching Bible truths is one thing, but to be arrogant and abusive toward those who may not have been taught those truths is unexcusable. The evangelist is not a judge. He is a teacher as well as a preacher and his attitudes will come through his delivery.

Early in the writer's ministry of evangelism, his Evangelistic Party was holding a meeting in Western Kansas. The meeting was going very well. On this particular evening, there was a full house and included in the congregation were a number of visitors from various churches in the community. The young evangelist thought this was the opportunity of his life. He roared out his sermon on baptism. He was really "telling them off." No one came forward that night. After the benediction the pastor of the church approached the young evangelist. "Raymond," he said, "Your father and I are the best of friends. I do not want to offend you, but let me ask you one question, why did you preach that sermon tonight?" He continued, "Did you really want to baptize people or were you just telling them that you were right and they were wrong?" Fortunate is any young preacher (or older one for that matter) who has a friend who will be so frank. From that day on the writer checked his motivation, his attitude in his preaching, especially if the sermon dwelt on a controversial theme.

Another incident comes to mind. The writer was holding meetings in the far west. In one of his meetings in Portland, Oregon, an elderly gentleman attended nightly. He was not a member of the church where the meeting was in progress. One evening the minister of the church said to the writer, "Fred H. was not present tonight." He was not there the next night, and he was absent for several nights. We visited the elderly gentleman. He was cool to both of us. Finally the writer asked if he had offended him in some way. Fred responded, "I won't listen to a man preach who says my mother is in Hell." Immediately I responded that I did not recall saying his mother was in Hell, and if I did I owed him an apology. I tried to point out that it was not my prerogative to pass judgement on anyone. I had been called to preach not to become judge. To make a long story short, as the minister and I were leaving, Fred asked if he could be baptized that night. It is one thing to be right. It is another to be arrogant and "self righteous" about it. It is very important that the evangelist not assume the role of judge in teaching the great Bible Truths. He is a messenger. Let him keep his place.

ENTHUSIASM AND DELIVERY

Enthusiasm must be a part of the evangelist's delivery. It really makes a difference. Enthusiasm is a good word. It comes from two Greek words, *en* and *theos*, meaning "God in us." Surely a man should have God in him if his evangelism is to be effective.

Enthusiasm is contagious. As he prepares his message the heart of the evangelist will burn because he is close to Christ. When he steps into the pulpit that burning will come through and his audience will share his enthusiasm. If the evangelist is not enthusiastic he need not be surprised if those who hear him are cool and unmoved. Another word for enthusiasm is that word zeal. Be zealous in your delivery. The evangelists in the New Testament were filled with zeal.

A reporter, having attended worship in an American church, gave the following report: "One felt as if the preacher had gathered a little loose talk around a subject which itself had no greatness in it. He spoke faultlessly, harmlessly, aimlessly. All that he said might be so, but it did not grip or fasten the attention, made no form of spiritual appeal, awoke no deep or answering emotion, and left the hearers as untouched as it found them."

The Quakers got their name because they trembled and

shook. At least their religion shook them. All too few of us are shaken by our faith, many preachers included. Some may be "shaky" ABOUT their faith but all too few are shaken BY their faith. Is it any wonder that one deacon said, "The clock struck twelve on Sunday noon and the church gave up the dead."

Come to life, preacher man! The world is dying to hear your message. Don't fail them with a few casual phrases and little personal feeling in the delivery. Unfortunately we have reached that tragic hour when the situation is desperate but the saints (evangelists) are not.

URGENCY AND DELIVERY

Webster defines "urgent" as follows: "pressing; plying with importunity; calling for immediate attention; instantly important."

Urgency must come through if the evangelist is to be effective. No two men will be alike in their presentation, but urgency must come through the message.

Every sermon must be a testimony of the evangelist's deep convictions. It is a personal witness. John writes, "That which we have seen and heard we proclaim unto you" (John 1:3). It is not a matter of hearsay — it is his own personal experience. He must know and feel the love of God if he is to get it across to his hearers. His life blood must be a part of the message if it is to come across with power.

No matter how loud one may shout or how one may "stomp" his feet or how one may pound the pulpit, if he doesn't have an urgent feeling about his message his hearers will be left cold and unconvinced. Lung power and urgency are not necessarily related. Some men will shout with emphasis, others will whisper with equal emphasis. A sense of urgency must illumine his message. Light is the need of the hour.

"Behold, NOW is the accepted time; behold, NOW is the day of salvation" (II Cor. 6:2). There is urgency there.

Some evangelists just make a big noise, no light comes through. A man once wired power to a light bulb and nothing happened. He learned that it takes more power to light a bulb than it does to ring a buzzer. The need of the hour is light, not noise. Nor do we seek to defame the evangelist who shouts at times. Some of us find there are times when we cannot help it. Fine! Sometimes the best way to get the hearers attention and assure him of the urgency of the matter, is to turn up the volume.

However one does it, be sure the sense of urgency comes across. "Except you repent you will perish!" There is urgency! Time is short for you and me. God can take his time for the eternities are His — but you and I must hurry before it is too late.

The evangelist must be patient, he must be humble, — and he must speak with a sense of urgency. This is a strange mix. Patience and humility are two characteristics of God — "God never hurries — but he is never late," says a card under the glass of the writer's desk. What we are saying is, don't let your desire for the patience of God (who has the eternities) keep you from reminding your hearers that time is of the essence.

Every sermon delivered must be the evangelist's own. He delivers it because he believes in the urgency of this matter. If, in every sermon, you give some of your life blood you will not preach in vain.

THEOLOGY AND DELIVERY

What one believes theologically has everything to do with effective sermon delivery. As stated earlier, you cannot be very effective in telling one what to do to be saved if you don't believe he is lost. Some people "pooh-pooh" theology but it is because they do not know what theology is. What one believes about God, man, atonement, sin, incarnation, the church, heaven, hell, etc., is his theology. Do not let this truth escape you. Belief and action (even in the pulpit), are inseparably united. Deep convictions spur one to action. Shallow convictions leave one passive and unconcerned.

If a passer-by sees one's house on fire, does he casually saunter into the dwelling and suggest that the occupants really ought to leave because their house is on fire? On the contrary, the alarmist will come running and, in as forceful way as he can, urge the people to leave immediately for their lives are in danger.

The story is told of a man in the Tower of London. He had been given the death sentence. On the day of his execution a minister was permitted to speak with the man about his soul. The minister's efforts were fruitless. As the minister was leaving the condemned man said to him, "Sir, if I believed as you claim to believe that every person must either accept this Christ you were speaking of or spend eternity in hell, I would crawl across England on my hands and knees to save just one soul."

Get your theological priorities in place. They will affect

your delivery more than you imagine.

QUOTATIONS IN DELIVERY

Use quotations sparingly, except, of course, quotations from scripture. But even long laborious passages from Scripture may distract from the presentation. No one wants to hear endless paragraphs and pages read during the sermon.

Be cautious about using quotations that are threadbare with use. Take, for example, Sir Oliver Lodge's remark, "The modern man is not worrying about his sins." In how many thousands of sermons has that remark made its appearance? On the other hand, quotations can illumine one's message. However, if the quotation is too dramatic the rest of your sermon may suffer. A passage the writer finds particularly exciting is from T. DeWitt Talmage of Brooklyn. The impenitent thief on one of the crosses with Jesus has just shouted in his agony, "If thou be Christ, save thyself and us" (Luke 23:39). "If..." writes Mr. Talmage. "Was there any doubt about it? Tell me, thou star, that in robe of life didst run to point out his birthplace. Tell me, thou sea, that didst put thy hand over thy lips when he bid thee be still. Tell me ye dead, who got up to see him die. Tell me, thou sun, in mid-heaven, who for him didst pull down over thy face the veil of darkness. Tell me, ye lepers, who were cleansed, ye dead, who were raised. Is He the Son of God? 'Aye, aye' responds the universe. The flowers breathe it — the stars chime it — the redeemed celebrate it — the angels rise upon their thrones to announce it. And yet on the miserable malefactor's 'if'

145

millions shall be wrecked for eternity."

That is preaching at its best! The quotation is not too long and it electrifies those who hear it. May each one who reads these words have, again and again, the elation of such inspiration. Those are the moments when you realize that someone is speaking through you — and you pray that it might be Him.

Quotes should not be used profusely; but, in their proper place, they will cause your theme to shine like the stars above. Many times, probably more than you will ever know, someone in your audience may hear only your text or possibly some high moment of inspiration. May we seek such moments and give thanks to Him above, for God indeed may be speaking through you more often than you know.

Charles Spurgeon says that he was converted by a lay preacher. This man chose as his text: "Look at me and be ye saved, all the ends of the earth." Spurgeon noted later that the lay preacher had little to say, but the text that he chose and read kept running through Spurgeon's mind again and again. This led to his conversion.

ILLUSTRATIONS IN DELIVERY

In spite of its many pitfalls the art of illustration is a matter no evangelist can afford to neglect. Truth made concrete will find its way past many a door where abstractions knock in vain. Word pictures will captivate an audience when mere abstractions will leave them empty.

It is an art, but of course, like any art, the matter of illustrations can be carried too far. Any illustration that is only partially meaningful in the context may even distract the mind of the listener.

Illustrations dragged in at random weaken the message and will leave the hearer with the thought, that you were more interested in the illustration as such, than you were in getting your point across. James S. Stewart offers this advise: "No matter how vivid it may be in itself if it does not immediately light up the particular subject under discussion, exclude it ruthlessly. Otherwise it will simply detract attention and defeat your purpose. On the other hand, illustrations sparingly and appropriately used can be a vital source of power and illumination."

Continuing under this same theme Mr. Stewart writes:

> How is the preacher to obtain an adequate store of illustrative material? I would warn you against being content to allow others to do this garnering for you. Ready-made collections of illustrations are those which come to you as the harvest of your reading and observation. In this realm as in others, there is far more zest and thrill in personal discovery than in second-hand borrowing. Be your own anthologist. Little incidents of daily life, significant happenings in the world around you, moving pages in the books you read — all can serve to illuminate the truth committed to your charge. Better one illustration that is strong and apt and gripping than ten that are shoddy and irrelevant and sentimental.

GESTURES IN DELIVERY

Here again we do not want to encroach upon the evangelist's freedom. You are not a graven image, nor are you a windmill. You are not immobile nor are you to act like a school boy who has the fidgets. In general, avoid mean-ingless mannerisms which may distract the listener. James Stewart once put it this way: "You are not to cramp or stifle your individuality; but you are to offer it so com-pletely to God upon the altar that, when the service closes, the dominating thought in the worshippers' mind will be, not of any obtrusive human proficiency, but only this — 'The Lord was in His holy temple today!'"

We want our hearers to see the Christ and not the mes-senger. To illustrate: A man and his wife were listening to an evangelist. They were enthralled. As they left the meet-ing the husband was overheard to say to his wife, "My, isn't he a wonderful preacher." On the following night they listened to another preacher in a neighboring church. As they left the service the husband was overheard to say to his wife, "My, isn't He a wonderful Saviour."

It is no easy task, this matter of obscuring your own personality in such a way that the audience leaves with a devotion to Jesus rather than an excitement over the "wonderful preacher-evangelist's" personality and manner-isms.

THE INVITATION IN DELIVERY

If you are preaching for a verdict, give the hearer an opportunity to respond. What could be more frustrating than to hear a moving sermon with no opportunity to answer the call. The invitation is critical. It calls for far more space than we have in this discourse.

The importance of the Good Confession demands that the evangelist give ample time for those under conviction to confess their faith. The Good Confession is to our Christian faith what the sun is to the Copernican system of astronomy. According to the Copernican theory, all planets revolve around the sun and from it gather all light and luster. In the same manner, Christ is the center of the spiritual universe. From Him the spiritual world gathers all its life, light and luster. Christ is at the "storm center" and the "power center" of the Christian religion.

It was the custom in the Roman government to demand of its citizens a simple loyalty oath of allegiance. The form of that oath was simply "Kyrios Kaisar" which meant "Caesar is Lord." Over against this Roman pledge of loyalty the Christian Confession was often simply, "Kyrios Christos" which means "Christ is Lord."

The importance of this Confession must not be minimized. It is the simplest Creed ever written. It opens the door of the Kingdom to all who care to enter. The importance of this confession is seen in who made it:

God made it at the baptism of Jesus (Matt. 3:17) and again at the Transfiguration (Matt. 17:5). Christ himself made it. While He was on trial the high priest cried: "I adjure you by the living God, tell us if you are the Christ, the Son of God." Jesus said unto him, "you have said so," or "yes I am" (Matt 26:63ff). Simon Peter made it (Matt. 16:16). Stephen made it, and died for his testimony (Acts 7:56). Timothy made it (I Tim. 6:12). The Secretary of the Ethiopian treasury, (the eunuch of Ethiopia) made it (Acts 8:37).

Must we name more? It is of such importance that its delivery honors His preeminence. How often have we heard a splendid sermon only to have it ruined by a poorly prepared invitation.

We are not suggesting that the Invitation Hymn be long. It must carry an invitation in such a manner that those singing it will feel it is directed right at them.

Let your style be positive in nature. Have an air of confidence and assurance. Be expectant. Encourage the folk to "pray as you sing." Ask the congregation to be in prayer while the organist plays a verse of a hymn. If possible choose a hymn that carries the message of the sermon just delivered. Caution is suggested here. The writer heard of an evangelist that had just delivered a very moving sermon on Hell. The announced invitation hymn was, "I Want To Go There, Don't You." The invitation hymn is of major importance.

Generally it is best not to have a long drawn out invitation. Let the evangelist express compassion and deep concern during the singing. Avoid death-bed stories like a plague. While the congregation is singing let the evangelist take a prayerful attitude and posture, perhaps with bowed head. Occasionally, the evangelist may make a plea while the singing is in progress, however, do not push it to the point that folk become uncomfortable. Be sure the potential convert(s) leave convinced of the evangelist's deep concern for them.

Offer to talk with anyone after the benediction. Discourage folk from trying to persuade a potential convert by conversing with them during the singing of the Invitation Hymn. There are exceptions to this, of course — such as a husband to his wife or a friend to someone that is very special to him.

The length of the Invitation will be in direct relation to the responses. If one announced that there will be just one more verse, keep your word. On the other hand one may announce that this will be the final verse unless someone else comes forward.

This is a time for patience. Do not overly push the potential convert or make him feel conspicuous. Don't offend him. Let the potential convert know that he alone can make this decision. No one is going to embarrass him during the invitation. Let him leave with a warm and wanted feeling so that he may return another time.

During the singing of the Invitation Hymn the evangelist may glance at the potential converts from time to time to let them know that he is praying for them. Any remarks during the invitation should be short and to the point.

Finally, the Invitation Hymn should be a hymn with which the congregation is familiar. Well know hymns such as, "Just As I Am," "Give Me Thy Heart," "I Surrender All," etc.

THE PUBLIC ADDRESS SYSTEM

Finally, let me offer a purely personal suggestion. Get rid of the public address system. Such systems have limited the effectiveness of many a preacher and evangelist. Often it is only a matter of self-importance; when they put in the public address system the preacher really feels he has arrived. Well, if one can do without it, do so. Of course, there are exceptions. In a large auditorium or sanctuary it may be necessary, but in the average auditorium it is a hindrance.

Preachers need to learn to develop their voice to its most impressive tone. They need to learn to project, then their message will come across far more meaningfully and they can get along without the P.A. System. Voice projection is an art — but it can be learned. Search out a speech teacher or effective homiletics professor. Learn the art of projection without increasing the volume. It is hard to put into words but as one preaches, he needs to practice speaking to the people on the back row without raising the volume in his presentation. Also note that a voice that is projected will come across with far more urgency than one that is frail and weak.

8

The Evangelistic Invitation

O. GEORGE STANSBERRY

At the conversion of Singing Evangelist Knowles Shaw, his biographer, William Baxter says,

> What a treasure now would be a full report of the doings of that bright autumn day; the discourse of Uncle Gabriel, as the preacher was affectionately called; the exhortation of George Campbell, a Boanerges in zeal, and rising, as many still remember, when calling sinners to repentance, to the highest degree of tender and pathetic entreaty....

In one of the last sermons he ever preached, Knowles Shaw gave the invitation by saying,

> All our days are fast passing away; and oh, the thought of meeting God in the judgement, without reconciliation — an enemy! To be banished forever! Hear the word of

reconciliation now: Turn ye, O turn ye, for why will you die? The Savior calls, Mercy pleads, the Spirit woos, and the Father smiles, while all glory beams, and angels are ready to rejoice. Come while you may.

Shaw baptized more than 11,000 persons before his tragic death in a train accident that took his life at age 44. His last words were, "Oh, it is a grand thing to rally the people to the Cross of Christ." The evangelistic invitation is designed to rally people to the cross.

The end result of an evangelistic sermon should be the evangelistic invitation for people to accept Christ for salvation. This is the natural climax. This is the moment that heaven has been waiting for. It is the most important moment of the service for the sinner.

It is disheartening to watch your favorite football team march down the field with precision until they reach the five yard line and then not be able to score. Some lose their intense drive and others call the wrong plays. Many a minister has marched his message with intellectual precision down to the final moment and then failed to use the right appeal or else lost his compassionate concern.

There are biblical precedents for asking people to make a decision to follow the will of God. Though there is no precedent for the exact form for conducting a public invitation at the close of a service, neither is there a precedent for the opening of a service or the form that the service should follow.

In the Great Invitation of Matthew 11:28, Jesus says, "Come unto me, all ye that labour and are heavy laden, and I will give you rest." The evangelistic preacher stands before his congregation and issues this invitation in Jesus' name.

When Moses came down from the mount and found the people worshipping the golden calf, he cried, "Who is on the Lord's side? Let him come unto me." The sons of Levi accepted that invitation and the other tribes refused the same invitation. The evangelistic invitation is designed to call men to the side of the Lord and to turn from the world.

Joshua was issuing an invitation when he said, "Choose you this day whom ye will serve; whether the gods which your fathers served that were on the other side of the flood, or the gods of the Amorites, in whose land ye dwell: but as for me and my house, we will serve the Lord" (Joshua 24:15).

In the parable of the Great Supper the lord said to his servants, "Go out into the highways and hedges and compel them to come in, that my house may be filled." The word "compel" ("constrain," ASV) implies strong persuasion.

Paul wrote to the Corinthian church and said, "We are therefore Christ's ambassadors, as though God were making his appeal through us. We implore you on Christ's behalf: Be reconciled to God" (II Cor. 5:20 NIV).

Peter stood in Jerusalem before thousands and "with many other words he warned them; and he pleaded with them, 'Save yourselves from this corrupt generation'" (Acts 2:40 NIV). About 3000 accepted that invitation. How did the apostles know whom to baptize that day? By some means an invitation was offered so that those accepting Christ could publicly be separated from those who refused the invitation.

The invitation must be given PLAINLY. How frustrating it is for the sinner to be invited and to not have been told what he must do to be saved. I believe that most sermons end with the words, "And now we'll stand and sing the invitation hymn." No scripture verses are quoted. No recapping of the plan of salvation is mentioned. There is no explanation of how one transfers his life and membership.

An invitation to the lost must be specific. "He that believeth and is baptized shall be saved, but he that believeth not shall be damned" (Mk. 16:16). Peter said, "Repent and be baptized every one of you in the name of Jesus Christ for the remission of sins and ye shall receive the gift of the Holy Spirit" (Acts 2:38). I usually pause after the word "remission" and say that the word means "forgiveness" since more people understand that definition. Then one can say, "Put these two verses together and you have God saying, 'Faith, plus repentance, plus baptism equals the forgiveness of all your sins.'"

No invitation for salvation should ever be given without telling the prospects what one must do to be saved. If one is hesitant about repeating this then eliminate the invitation. One can vary this explanation from service to service so that it does not become monotonous. P.H. Welshimer was criticized by some of his members for continually emphasizing the plan of salvation, Sunday after Sunday, month after month. But the great Canton Christian Church would not have experienced the phenomenal growth that it had without this emphasis.

Explaining the minor details is often helpful especially for those who are not acquainted with the church and its practices. "There are three aisles in this building — the center aisle, the right aisle, and the left aisle (point to each). For those of you who are in the middle of a row, you can move to the aisle that is the nearest and come forward. Our people will graciously step back or move out of the pew to give you free access to any aisle. You won't have to say "Excuse me," as our people know exactly what to do at this time of invitation.

Other details can be spelled out. "Everything is ready for your baptism into Christ. We have private robing rooms. Clothing and towels are provided. The baptistery is filled with warm water. I (or someone) will meet you at the front in Jesus' name. There will be no embarrassment. There will be someone to show you each step of the way." Some people worry more about these details than they do about the actual decision to accept Christ.

For those who need to transfer membership it should be stated that they do not need a church letter. "Just come and be welcomed." I have met many who thought they could not respond until they had contacted their home congregation. It should also be made clear that the transfer of membership invitation is for those who, with faith and repentance in the heart, have been baptized (immersed) into Christ. Otherwise you may have some one to respond who has been sprinkled and thinks that he needs only to "transfer his membership."

A minister-friend related to me an incident in which the evangelist had obtained a decision of a man in his home to become a Christian. To reinforce the decision he asked him to sign a decision card stating that he would make this commitment publicly. He was told to bring the decision card with him and present it when he came forward at the invitation time. The man definitely committed himself to respond that evening at the service. That night the evangelist gave the invitation. The man didn't respond.

Verse after verse of the invitation hymn was sung with the evangelist pleading, "I know there is someone here who wants to come." No response. As the man was leaving the evangelist asked, "Why didn't you come tonight?" The man replied, "I forgot to bring my decision card with me." Make the invitation plain.

The invitation must be given PERSUASIVELY. The preacher who is not thoroughly convinced that men are lost without Christ will never be able to persuade others. You can only effectively persuade others of a truth that has persuaded you. We have lost the sense of urgency in inviting men to Christ. Paul knew how to persuade men both privately and publicly. "And he went into the synagogue, and spake boldly,...disputing and persuading the things concerning the kingdom of God" (Acts 19:8). "This Paul hath persuaded and turned away much people, saying that they be no gods, which are made with hands" (Acts 19:26). "Agrippa said unto Paul, 'Almost thou persuadest me to be a Christian'" (Acts 26:28). "...there came many unto him into his lodging; to whom he...persuaded them concerning Jesus..." (Acts 28:23).

Have you ever watched a defense attorney pleading for the life of his client in a murder trial? In his closing argument he stands before the jury. He uses every known means to persuade twelve people that his client is innocent. He appeals to their intellect, will, conscience, and emotions. If an attorney can do this to save the individual he represents, can we do less in pleading for the salvation of our hearers at invitation time?

An invitation must be given POSITIVELY. Eliminate the word "if" from your vocabulary. Do not say, "IF there are those here who are without Christ..." Instead say,

"For those of you who are here without Christ..." Eliminate, "IF you decide to become a Christian...." Say, "WHEN you decide to become a Christian then everything is ready. Christ is ready to receive you and we are ready to help you obey the Lord." Even invitation songs such as "Why Not Now?" leave a negative impression that there may be a logical answer to the question being answered. Expect people to respond. You have prayed for them. Your mental and spiritual attitude will be reflected in the way you offer the invitation.

Some approach the invitation merely from an intellectual point of view. The sermon is logical. It has appealed to the intellect. Then the preacher routinely asks the audience to stand and sing an invitation hymn. No exhortation is usually made. The impression is left that this is the way we close our services and if you want to come it is all right with us. The audience does not sense any compelling reason or desire to respond.

Others approach the invitation from a purely emotional point of view. The sermon may or may not have an intellectual appeal. An over-emphasis is made on tear-laden stories and appeals. The one directing this may be a master of crowd psychology. His main interest may be to merely get people down the aisle. This is a cheap and shoddy way to conduct an invitation.

In one church where I was conducting an evangelistic crusade there was a high school youth who came down the aisle crying at invitation time. Another youth followed him, and another, and another until more than twenty young people stood at the front weeping. I knew something was wrong. I quietly brought the invitation to a close before it got out of hand. I could have emotionally wrung that audience until there would not have been a dry eye. But I didn't. Later I found that the young man's girl friend had been killed in an automobile wreck the day before. The emotional trauma of that tragedy had spilled over into the invitation.

The ideal invitation is one that is a blend of both the intellectual and emotional approaches. The intellect must be appealed to in order that men may know that they are sinners in need of a Savior and what the Savior wants them to do to have their sins forgiven. Then the emotions are used to break the stubborn will of men. Tears may come. The emotion filled story may be told. But these logically follow after an intellectual foundation has been made for a response.

Interruptions should be discouraged when the invitation is given. Unconcerned members begin to reach for their coats and possessions. When the last stanza is being sung there are those who close their books and put them back in the racks. Some carry on a conversation with a friend. The worst scene is when some begin to leave early. Any movement towards the back is distracting to those who should be moving towards the front to answer the invitation.

I WAS LOST......YOU WERE IN A HURRY

I attended your church this morning. The choir sang hymns about a living Lord that made my heart beat faster. I felt a tight choking sensation in my throat as your minister described the condition of a lost person.

'He is talking about me,' I said to myself. 'Being saved must be very important.'

The minister finished his appeal and you began to sing another of the beautiful songs you know so well. I swallowed a lump in my throat and wished I knew the joy of which you sang. Your minister looked at me and started telling me how I could have this joy — but his words were drowned out...

When I glanced around you were putting on your little girl's coat and telling her to get her things. I looked on my other side and saw you touching up your lipstick and rearranging your hat.

Looking in front of me I saw you frown at your watch as if time were running out. Suddenly, I didn't want to look at any more of you. You didn't really care — you only wanted to get away.

I waited until the service was over and walked out among you — alone — lost.

-Condensed. Author unknown.

In Nowata, Oklahoma I had just finished an evangelistic message. All was ready for the invitation. Just as we stood to sing the hymn, everyone heard a loud, strange sound like a sucking noise. Both the custodian and minister quickly headed toward the baptistery. Unknown to me, they had been filling the baptistery during the service and the water had just reached the overflow pipe. Needless to say, it ruined the invitation. I had them sing one stanza of a song and we had the benediction.

At the invitation time in Johnston City, Illinois, a retired Seventh Day Adventist minister interrupted the hymn to tell us that we were worshipping on the wrong day. In a kindly, yet firm, way I had to stop him by saying that the audience did not come to hear him and that if he wanted to preach he would have to secure his own audience. Nevertheless, it ruined the invitation.

Music plays an important part in inviting men to Christ in a public service. The right kind of music can touch the emotions and sway the will. Some evangelists prefer a march type that will invite people to become soldiers of the cross. A song like, "I Am Resolved," fits this description.

> I am resolved no longer to linger
> Charmed by the world's delights
> Things that are higher, things that are nobler
> These have allured my sight."

My personal preference is the slow, meditative type. I work best with songs like, "Just As I Am," "Where He Leads Me," "Have Thine Own Way, Lord," and "Lord, I'm Coming Home." The organ and piano should play softly, and I do mean softly, during these songs. I like a song service that is enthusiastic and has an upbeat tempo. But when it comes to the invitation hymn I want it sung slowly and played softly. Always choose a familiar hymn. This is not the time to try out a new hymn. New hymns should be learned during a regular song service and repeated enough to make them familiar.

The purpose of the invitation is to give men the opportunity to decide for Christ and the church TODAY.

> We have sung one stanza and not even one person has come forward. If there were none here who should respond to this invitation then I would have suggested that we close the service without an invitation hymn. We do not sing the invitation hymn in the Christian churches and churches of Christ because it is a nice way to close a service. We do it for one reason — to give you this moment of present opportunity to do something for Christ today.
>
> If I were in your home I would urge you to accept Christ and be baptized right then. Why? Because it is the moment of present opportunity. And right now I urge you to do the same thing? Why? Because it is the moment of

the present — the only moment in which you can act. Yesterday is the cancelled check. Tomorrow is the promissory note. But today you can accept this wonderful Lord. Come, as we sing the next stanza.

Occasionally there may be those who step forward who have a background of kneeling at the altar and "praying through" for salvation. How do we handle these situations? We know that people are not saved in this fashion. The person is already kneeling at the front pew or communion table. There is a beautiful way to handle what otherwise might be an awkward situation. Kneel beside the person. If he is praying and pouring out his heart to God, then let him continue for a moment. Then ask him to let you pray. "Oh God, I thank you for this one who has come because he realizes he needs a Savior. Thank you that Jesus died to save him. And now, Lord, we know that Jesus said, 'He that believeth and is baptized shall be saved.' Bless him as he now goes to be baptized just like Jesus was baptized. In Jesus' name. Amen!"

Gently encourage him to stand and make his confession of faith. You need not be concerned about his desire to pray. Saul of Tarsus prayed for three days and nights before his baptism. Just be sure he understands that he is now to "arise and be baptized and wash away thy sins" (Acts 22:16).

The length of the invitation should be determined by the response. If after about three stanzas are sung and there is no response then this is probably long enough unless there is reason to believe someone is about ready to come. If people continue walking the aisles for Christ, then continue singing. I never stop to exhort between stanzas when someone has responded on the previous stanza. Keep singing. Exhortations can be made after a stanza on which no one comes forward. Even when you reach the last stanza one can say, "This will be the last stanza and the public invitation will come to a close unless there is someone (or others) who responds." Be honest with the audience. If you say you are going to close after a certain stanza, then close. If you anticipate a longer than usual invitation then one can shorten the sermon or song service to give more time for this climactic event. Remember that every part of an evangelistic service is to be geared toward the invitation.

Here comes the repentant sinner down the aisle. Visibly shaken by the momentous decision for Christ that he is making, his eyes are filled with tears. Then some well meaning person sticks a card in his hand and asks him to answer a trivial question such as his birth date. One must be more considerate at a time like this. First, assure him of your joy in seeing him come. Tell him that this will be a blessing to him for the rest of his life. Praise God for his decision for Christ. Then you can introduce any needed card that contains only essential information needed at this time. Additional information can be obtained after his baptism.

The confession of faith and baptism is the logical conclusion to an invitation. Don't let it become a mere ritual. Ask the convert what he believes about Jesus and let him answer in his own words. Let him repeat the "Good Confession" ("Thou art the Christ, the son of the living God") after you. Make it meaningful. Don't fall into the trap of saying, "This is the only question that I have a right to ask you...." The Bible never says anything like this. You have just as much a right to ask him if he repents, for both faith and repentance are prerequisites to baptism.

The late J. Halbert Brown of Charlottesville, Virginia would have those coming forward for baptism to go immediately to the robing rooms while the invitation hymn was still being sung. Those coming to transfer membership would remain at the front row. Trained workers would go to the robing rooms, give any needed instructions to, and have prayer with, the baptismal candidates. When the candidate was brought into the water he would make his confession of faith at that time.

Should the invitation be extended to those who are asked to rededicate their lives? Some have overworked the rededication appeal. Others have labeled it as unscriptural. Unscriptural it is, but not anti-scriptural. Personally, I very rarely issue an invitation for rededications. My main appeal is for the salvation decision and then the transfer of membership. However, I rejoice if there are those who do come to rededicate their lives. This is especially true if they are coming because of public sin in their lives. In private conversation with membership transfer prospects one can urge this to also be a time of rededication if the prospect is a backslider.

Jim Rutherford of the old Cincinnati Avenue Christian Church of Tulsa, Oklahoma was a master in giving an invitation for rededications. He would say to respondents, "We don't want this to be a cheap rededication. Does this mean that you will be faithful in your attendance? Will you be diligent in your Bible study and prayer life? Will you be a tither and give God what is due Him? Will you lead a clean, moral life?" He would wait for an answer after each of these questions. You can be certain that if one were going to come forward, knowing that these questions would be asked, he would more than likely have a greater sense of the meaning of rededication. Perhaps this was one reason why the Cincinnati Avenue church was the largest Christian church in the city for many years.

A song leader should not direct the invitation hymn with his hands. There is no need for this if you use a familiar hymn. He can stand to one side, facing the audience, and lead with his voice. All attention should focus on the evangelist giving the invitation.

There are a number of practical suggestions that will enable you to conduct an effective invitation and lend variation to this important segment of the service. Here are fifteen ways to offer the invitation.

1. At the close of the sermon and just prior to the invitation hymn, offer a prayer for the unsaved (Rom. 10:1) and those who need to identify with the local church. The congregation may either remain seated or stand for the prayer.

2. Let the choir sing a stanza and the audience hum. Have a soloist sing and everyone else hum. Invite everyone to hum "with bowed heads and praying hearts."

3. After standing in the middle of the platform, step to one side and say, "If Jesus Christ were to appear in bodily form and stand where I have been standing and invite you to "Come," — would you come? If He were to offer His nail scarred hands (spread your hands) and say, 'Come unto me, all ye who labor and are heavy laden and I will give you rest,' — would you come? I believe you would. So I'm going to invite the Lord Jesus to stand where I have been standing. You will not see him visibly, nevertheless He will be in our presence. What will your answer be now?"

4. Interrupt the singing in the middle of a stanza. "Let us stop singing...." At this point you may have a little difficulty getting the organist to stop playing and the congregation to stop singing but when they see you are serious about stopping the invitation hymn they will stop. Then you will say, "What if Jesus had come at this moment? Would you have been ready? Someday He will interrupt an invitation hymn like this in His second coming. Somewhere over the face of this earth services will undoubtedly be in progress when He rides down the slant of the skies to claim from the world His own. But He hasn't come during this moment when I interrupted the hymn. Why? Because He is 'not willing that any should perish but that all might come to repentance.' As we start this stanza over again, step out and make life's greatest decision — for Christ."

5. Use an illustration between stanzas. Personal illustrations are best. Tell about someone who became a Christian (or who refused to become one) or placed his membership and the result of that decision. One minister tells of two teen age girls who stopped by the church office to discuss becoming Christians. They agreed that they would be baptized the following Sunday. However, on Friday afternoon one of the girls was killed as she left a school bus and an approaching car did not stop. When the one girl came forward on Sunday the minister said that all he could think about was the girl who couldn't respond because of her death. He would then make the appeal, "It doesn't pay to wait even for one day, one hour, or one minute. Let's decide for Christ now while there is still time."

6. Use a soloist. Have the congregation stand for

prayer at the close of the sermon. As their heads are bowed the soloist will sing just the first line of "Have You Any Room For Jesus."

"Have you any room for Jesus, He who bore your load of sin...." Offer a prayer as the organist continues to play and chord into the invitation hymn of the night. Other songs that could be used in this manner are, "There's Room At The Cross For You," and "Precious Lord, Take My Hand."

7. Walk the center aisle and extend an invitation. I witnessed an effective use of this method in the National City Christian Church, Washington, D.C. The minister left the platform and paused briefly at each row on his right. He extended his hands and the expression on his face seemed to say, "Will you come?" He then walked backward down the aisle and did the same thing to the left section. There were those who responded as he came to their row and elders were at the front to receive them. He had timed his walk so that as the congregation finished the four stanzas that were sung he had arrived back at the front of the auditorium.

8. Demonstrate the intangible with a tangible object. Light a small birthday candle and let it burn during the invitation hymn. "Life is short." If the candle has not burned all the way down you can "snuff" it out and conclude that our lives can quickly be "snuffed out" with the heart attack or accident. Use a six foot rule the same way. Pull it out to 72" and let each inch represent a year of life. Push it half way in and say that life may be half over for many in the audience. Push it in until only one inch is left. "Some of you standing here may only have a year at the most...." If funeral flowers are in a vase nearby then take

one out, slowly pull the petals off and let them filter through your hand to the floor. "Just a few short hours ago these flowers were in the presence of death. If this were your last day on earth would the flowers placed on your casket be in the presence of a body that housed your spirit that went to be with the Lord in heaven?"

9. Change the invitation song. After singing two or three stanzas of the hymn and no one has responded, announce a new number to be sung that may be more appropriate for the occasion.

10. Direct your remarks to a specific problem that you know someone is facing. However, extreme caution must be used or else this may be offensive. Use this sparingly and with discretion. At the invitation hymn in one of my evangelistic crusades there stood an ex-Marine with his family. He was bitter because he had been an outstanding athlete and then had lost his leg in World War II. For his sake I said, "The greatest cripple in all the world is not the physical cripple — he is the spiritual cripple who has never come to the Great Physician for healing...." His wife leaned over and whispered in his ear. He came forward and became a Christian. Today he is an elder in that congregation.

11. Demonstrate that older Christians do not regret their decision for Christ. Ask those who have been Christians for fifty or more years to raise their hands. Then address your remarks to these people. "If you had it to do all over again, would you make the same decision for Christ? Or would you be willing to say, 'I'm disappointed in Jesus Christ. He has not kept His promises to me and I now regret that I ever became a Christian.' Now, will any of you who have been Christians for at least 50 years

raise your hands and say that? (Wait for a response). Not one hand is raised. You see, those who have tried Christ over a long period of time have never regretted accepting Him. Will you now come and join these aged saints and know the joy they have known?"

12. Demonstrate the urgency of deciding for Christ now by showing that fewer people become Christians as they grow older. "How many of you became Christians before the age of 20? (Count the hands and announce the number). How many became Christians between the ages of 21 and 30?" (Count). Continue with 40, 50, 60, 70. "Now do you see why I urge you to come now? It will never become easier in the future to accept Him...."

13. Describe an attorney before a jury. I have mentioned this earlier as an attitude for the one offering the invitation. Now you can use it at the invitation time. "Do you wonder why I stand here night after night (Sunday after Sunday) pleading with you to decide for Christ? Have you ever watched an attorney pleading for the life of his client before a jury? If he really believes his client is innocent he makes every possible appeal for an acquittal. Do you think that I could ever do less when I'm appealing for the souls of men? I appeal to your intellect, your conscience, your will, and your emotions to make Christ the Lord and Savior of your life."

14. The acapella invitation hymn. Do not use the organ or piano as is the usual custom. Start the invitation hymn in the right key (or have someone else do it). Be sure to use a very familiar hymn. Since this is different from the usual way we conduct the invitation it produces a beautiful atmosphere.

15. Encourage the officers and teachers to take a public

stand for Christ and the church. "I now address the elders of this congregation. If you are willing to say by your coming forward that you will be supportive of this evangelistic crusade with your prayers and effort then I would like for you to come forward to stand beside your minister." (Pause for the response). Then ask for the deacons to do the same. Then the teachers. As they face the platform offer the invitation to any who need Christ or who will place their life and membership with the local church to step forward. If there is a response at this point you can then join hands and have a prayer circle with one leading in prayer. If there is no response then a variation would be to have all officers and teachers kneel for prayer and ask two or three to offer a brief prayer. This is a good invitation for the opening night of a revival meeting.

There are certain phrases and thoughts that can be introduced as psychological jolts during an exhortation.

a. "One step from God is still a million miles from home."

b. "Tonight you can be brought from disgrace to amazing grace."

c. "You can be saved from the guttermost to the uttermost."

d. "God has already mentioned the very day that He wants you to become a Christian. That day is (mention the month, day & year). Do you know where that is found in the Bible? In Hebrews 3:15 God says, 'While it is called today, if ye will hear his voice, harden not your hearts.' What day is today?" (Mention the date again). "Then this is the actual day that God intends for you to decide for Christ."

e. "Today is mine. Tomorrow may not come. I may not

see the rising sun. But today is mine. Tomorrow may never come."

f. "Let me take the four words of the song we are singing, 'Just As I Am' and put them in a different order. 'I am as just' as other men are. Is this your excuse before God that you are as good as other people are? But your goodness cannot save you...etc."

g. "God is a gentleman of the first order. He will not force you or embarrass you into becoming a Christian. Neither will we. It's your choice."

h. "Did anyone ever die for you except Jesus? Since He died for everyone, including you, He intended for everyone to become a Christian."

i. "At Calvary He paid a debt He did not owe and you owe a debt you cannot pay. But out of gratitude you can give your life to Him who gave His life for you."

j. "This is not my invitation nor the invitation of this local church. It is the invitation of the One who said, 'Come unto me all ye that labor and are heavy laden and I will give you rest.'"

You will want to develop other phrases that are effective in causing men to THINK about their decision. Plan your invitation just as you plan your sermon. Don't leave it to chance or to the "Holy Spirit to put words in your mouth." But the Holy Spirit will use your prayerful words and His words in scripture to bring conviction to the hearts of sinners.

The last invitation in the Bible is found in Rev. 22:17. Someone has said that it seems as though the Holy Spirit was saying to John, "Don't lay the pen down yet. Dip it into the ink and write on the parchment one final invitation." And John wrote, "And the Spirit and the bride say,

'Come.' And let them that heareth say, 'Come.' And let him that is athirst come. And whosoever will, let him take the water of life freely."

EVANGELISTIC SERMONS
FROM THE PAST

Introduction to Part Two

In this section the editors have chosen five evangelistic sermons preached by five outstanding evangelists within the Restoration Movement. These five evangelists lived in different eras of the Movement. Benjamin Franklin is among those early pioneers and his sermon is quite representative of the rational, Biblical approach to conversion. One need only consult such works as Z.T. Sweeney's *New Testament Christianity*, and W.T. Moore's *The Living Pulpit of the Christian Church*, to see how typical the Franklin sermon is as seen in those first two generations of Christian leaders and preachers.

The next two sermons — one by Charles Reign Scoville and the other by J.V. Coombs — come from third generation men. Evangelistic preaching is changing. The rational,

Biblical approach has won the day, but there is need seen to appeal to the emotions and will as well as to the intellect. Profuse illustrations attempt to do this; and Scoville and Coombs were masters of the art.

The final sermons are from more recent days. A.B. McReynolds and James Earl Ladd are representative of the middle third of the twentieth century. The tendency is for evangelistic sermons to be more topical, profusely illustrated, emotionally appealing with a strong conclusion to move directly into an impassioned invitational appeal.

Other preachers and other sermons could have been chosen. The editors believe that these five preachers and sermons are representative of the development of evangelistic preaching within the Restoration Movement.

9

"Conversion, or Turning to God"

BENJAMIN FRANKLIN[1]

Text. — "Repent, therefore, and turn, that your sins may
be blotted out, in order that the times of refreshing may
come from the presence of the Lord." — Acts iii:19.

The introduction of the religion of Christ into the world,
is the grandest event connected with the entire history of
man. The founding of empires, kingdoms and republics,
their revolutions and downfalls, hold no comparison in
point of magnitude, with the one grand and transcen-
dently sublime event of founding this new institution of
religion, called the kingdom of Christ. The infidel that
denies Christ and the divine authority of the Bible, still has
this wonderful event, the most astounding one ever
recorded — the founding of Christianity — to reason on

179

and account for.

There stands the undeniable fact, confirmed by the testimony of Jews, infidels, pagans and Christians; the united testimony of all history; uncontradicted by any authority, at the time, in the place, and by the persons, as reported in the Bible. Admitting all this, as a man of reason, and one who claims to account for the position he takes, it devolves on him to tell us how it was that a poor carpenter, a Nazarene, who had never received even common schooling, the society of influential persons, any power from wealth or birth, at the head of a dozen fishermen of Galilee, fresh from their humble avocation, uncouth, unaccomplished and unlettered, stood up in Jerusalem, the center of the most violent religious bigotry, in opposition to the sanhedrin, the distinguished rabbis, scribes, and doctors of Jewish divinity, with their magnificent temple, imposing synagogues, altars, victims, and ancient ritual on the one hand; and outside of all this paganism, with the civil governments, the money and philosophy of the world at command, on the other; and in defiance of this combined opposition of the Jewish and pagan world swept away their religious rites, forms, ceremonies and institutions, declaring them null and void, and established a new religion on the ruins?

How was this done if God was not in the work? How did twelve unaccomplished, unlettered and moneyless fishermen, in defiance of the doctors, priests and scribes in a few days after their leader had been put to an ignominious death, and they had shown themselves to be cowards, stand up boldly in Jerusalem and induce three thousand of the people to believe that God had raised this same leader from the dead and turn away from their former religion, associations, and everything earthly that was dear to them, and commit themselves to this new faith? How did they persuade five thousand on another occasion, to fall in with them? How did they, in a short time, extend the doctrine to Samaria, and in ten years to the Gentiles, bringing thousands to the faith? By what means, natural or supernatural, human or divine, did they, in forty years, extend it the length of the great Mediterranean Sea, to all the cities, towns and villages of note throughout Asia Minor, in the mere strength of ignorant fishermen? This they did, if the skeptic is right. How credulous the man must be who believes all this!

Paine, in his book, falsely styled "The Age of Reason," delighted to array Moses, Jesus, and Mahomet, in the same class, as three great imposters, and skeptics still delight to speak of the similarity between the rise of Mohammedanism and Christianity; but certainly there was no similarity between the early progress of Christianity and Mohammedanism. Christianity proselyted three thousand persons the first day the death, resurrection and glorification of its founder in the heavens was fully unfolded, but Mohammedanism did not make one hundred converts in the first ten years. No imposter ever converted three thousand persons at the first speech, nor five thousand at the second; nor could the religion of Christ have done this, if nothing more than human power had been in it. Its success was not attained either by pandering to the pride of life, the lusts of the eye, the customs of the world, nor by enticing words of man's wisdom, or any effort to please man. The holy life, the pure morals, the austere manners it enjoined, forbid this. Nor was it done by sympathizing with other and false systems of religion in the world, nor the true one which the Lord had abolished; nor by aping the priesthood who taught these systems and bound them on the necks of the people. They remembered the command of their leader, "Be you not like them."

On the one hand, they openly declared the Jews' religion null, void, abolished, taken out of the way, and that by the deeds of its law no flesh could be justified. On the other hand, they declared all paganism an abomination in the sight of God; that pagan idols were not gods, but the workmanship of men's hands; that there was no salvation in them. They openly declared the whole world to be under sin, under the power of the wicked one — guilty before God; and that there was no other name given under heaven nor among men by which any person could be saved, but the name of Jesus. This was offensive to all, both Jew and Gentile alike, sweeping away every thing they held sacred under the name of religion. It was revolutionizing religiously, in all its bearings. He who can believe that twelve fishermen, without learning or any superior natural ability, money, or popularity, in their own mere human strength, stood up in the face of the priests and scribes of Israel, on one hand, and the statesmen, philosophers, and men of wealth, combined with the entire pagan priesthood, on the other, as described; and advocated this new doctrine, defended, propagated and perpetuated it, as the facts in the case, admitted by Jews, pagans and skeptics show they did, never ought to speak of the credulity of mankind. The man who can believe all this is too credulous to be a Christian. He can believe without evidence. The Christian system only requires a man to believe with credible evidence.

Shortly after the great Pentecost, Peter and John went up to the temple at three o'clock in the afternoon, as we count time, it being the hour the Jews were accustomed to assemble for prayers. There were two causes moving them, if no more, in going there at this time:

1. The natural desire of the human soul, when in possession of good news, to tell it — to publish it abroad. They had the best news ever published — the news of a free and gracious pardon for a guilty and condemned race.

2. They had a divine commission from the great head of the Church, to "Go into all the world and preach the good news to every creature" — to "Go, and disciple all nations."

Impelled, then, by the natural desire, burning in their breasts, to publish the good news of salvation to a perishing world, and a divine commission requiring them to do it, they went up to the temple. As they were passing the gate called Beautiful, their ears were greeted by the importunities of a beggar, a man lame from his birth, who was carried and laid there to implore the charities of the people as they passed into the temple. Looking on Peter and John, he asked them for money. These preachers were in a similar predicament with many others of whom we have heard; they were poor men and had no money, nor were they ashamed to acknowledge the fact. Peter with John looking intently on the man, as he lay before them, helpless, said, "Look on us." He anxiously gave heed to them, expecting to receive something. Peter said, "Silver and gold I have none; but what I have I give you; in the name of Jesus Christ of Nazareth, rise up and walk. And he took him by the right hand and raised him up.

And immediately his feet and ankle bones received strength; and leaping up, he stood, and walked, and entered with them into the temple, walking, and leaping, and praising God." This attracted the attention of the people, and thus served one of the principal designs of miracles. Miracles never converted anybody, nor was their design to convert. The design of this miracle was twofold:

1. To attract the attention of the people to get them to hear.

2. To prove to them that God was with these men, or, in other words, to confirm their divine mission.

Another matter worthy of note, in this grand transaction, is, that it occurred in broad daylight and openly, as if the Lord would challenge the world to investigate — to test the claims of the newly authorized ambassadors of Christ. Nor was this done in vain, for in the council held over the matter, by Annas the high priest, Caiaphas, John Alexander, and as many as were of the kindred of the high priest, alluding to the healing of the lame man, they admitted, not only that a miracle had been done, but a noted miracle; and not only a noted miracle, but that it was known to all who dwelt in Jerusalem, and that they could not deny it.

Peter, seeing the eyes of the people earnestly fixed on himself and John, proceeded to guard against another evil against which no imposter ever does. "Why," says he, "look so intent on us, as if by our own power of holiness this man has been made whole?" This is in a very different spirit from that of Pope Pius IX, who claims to be a successor of the apostle Peter. When they look intently on this modern Peter — the false Peter — the Man of Sin — or when they bow down before him, he never inquires,

"Why look you so earnestly on us, as if by our own power or holiness this man had been made whole?" He claims that it is by his own power and holiness that wondrous things are done, and requires them to address him by "His Holiness," "Vicar of Christ," "Visible Head of the Church on Earth," "Lord God the Pope," etc. But the Peter whom Jesus sent, unlike this venerable head and representative of the great apostasy, when Cornelius, in his unenlightened condition, desired to worship him, forbade it, saying, "I myself also am a man." He would not permit any person to fall before him, as to the Lord. In the same style in Solomon's porch, he inquired, "Why look you so earnestly on us, as if by our own power or holiness this man has been made whole?"

This was abundant caution that he might not fall into the sin of Moses, on account of which he was not permitted to lead the Israelites into the promised land. Some have supposed this sin was, that Moses became angry. Others think it consisted in his striking the rock. There is no evidence, however, that it consisted in either of these, but clear evidence that it consisted in an entirely different thing. He took glory to himself and Aaron, that was due to God alone. Said he to the Israelites, "You rebels; must we bring you water from this rock?" The Lord says to him, "Because you sanctified me not in the eye of this people, you shall not go before them into the land I have promised them." He did not set God apart before that people, or in their eyes, as the source of the water from the rock, but said, "Must we give you water from this rock?"

Peter avoids a similar sin, in inquiring, "Why look you so intently on us, as if by our own power or holiness this

185

man has been made whole? The name of Jesus Christ, through faith in His name, has given this man this perfect soundness in the presence of you all." How bold, manly, and self-denying this language, losing sight of himself, and carrying the minds of his hearers to his Lord and King. The name of Jesus Christ, through faith in His name, has made this man whole. This is done, too, in the presence of you all. As Paul said, before Agrippa, "This thing was not done in a corner," but openly and in broad daylight, before the gaze of a numerous multitude. This convinced them of the truth, and he proceeded as follows: "Repent, therefore, and turn, that your sins may be blotted out."

This opens the way for the main topic of this discourse, which is conversion. Many fears of unsoundness are entertained on this subject. On this account, it will be necessary to examine the subject with much care. The first thing, then, will be to consider the word convert, and examine its use, and ascertain its meaning in Scripture.

The original Greek word, *strepho*, occurs eighteen times in the New Testament, and is translated turn, in every instance, in the common version, except Matt. xviii:3: "Except ye be converted and become as a little child," etc. The Bible Union translate it turn, here, and read it as follows: "If ye do not turn and become as little children," etc., thus making the turning their own act, and at the same time making them accountable beings. If man can turn from sin to the Lord, he is an accountable being and may justly be condemned for not turning. But if a man can not turn from sin to the Lord, he is not accountable, and can not be justly condemned for not turning. We do not condemn the wheel, which can not turn itself, for not turning, when there is no power on it sufficient to turn it.

186

In every instance where the word *strepho* occurs in the New Testament, except the last one, Rev. xi:6, the person, or that which was turned, turned itself, as for example, Acts vii:42, "God turned"; Acts xiii:4, Paul says, "We turn to the Gentiles"; Luke vii:9, Jesus "turned him about"; Luke vii:44, "He turned to the woman."

The original Greek word, *epistrepho*, occurs thirty times, and is translated, in the common version, turn, or its equivalent, twenty-two times. It is eight times rendered converted, or convert. In a large majority of these cases, that which was turned, turned itself, as Matt. ix:22, "Jesus turned him about"; Matt. x:13, "Let your peace return to you"; Mark v:30, "Turned him about in the press," etc. There is nothing in the meaning of this word, showing which way the turning, or conversion is, whether from bad or good. This must be learned from the connection, as for example, II Pet. ii:22, "The dog turned to his vomit again;" Mark xiii:16, "Let him not turn back," etc. In one instance, where the turning is to the Lord, the turning is ascribed to the preacher; as, for example, Acts xxvi:18, Paul was to "turn them from darkness to light, and from the power of Satan to God." The turning is here ascribed to the preacher, in view of his agency, or instrumentality, in turning them. The turning is never ascribed to God, or Christ, or to the Holy Spirit. Still, it is true, when we are looking to God as the author of the entire scheme, by which we are turned and saved, we say that God turns us. When we are looking at the instrumentality of the preacher, we ascribe the turning to him. When we are looking at the act of turning, we ascribe the turning to man.

Converted to God, means turned to God, and nothing

else. It is the purpose of this discourse to elucidate this whole matter fully. In order to do this, it is necessary to make a few preliminary statements:

No person turns to God properly, or in the sense of the Gospel, without undergoing three distinct changes:

1. A distinct divine change in the heart.

2. A distinct divine change in the life, or character.

3. A distinct divine change in the state or relation. When a man is divinely changed in heart, life and relation, he is a new creature, a child of God.

In order to these three distinct divine changes, there are three distinct appointments in the Gospel.

1. The Lord has appointed faith to change the heart.

2. He has appointed repentance to change the life.

3. He has appointed immersion to change the relation.

The heart is never changed by repentance. The character is never changed by immersion. The state is never changed by faith. Faith and repentance together, never changed the state or relation. Immersion never changed the heart, or life.

These three grand items, in turning to God, can not be reversed in their order. The state or relation can not be changed first, then the life, and then the heart. The life can not be changed first and then the heart. The heart is the beginning place. The change in the heart must be produced first. There can be no repentance, or change in the life, produced by repentance, till the heart is changed. The change in the heart leads to repentance, and produces it. Repentance results in a change of life, or it is worthless. The order of heaven is, that faith must come first, producing a change in the heart. Repentance must follow next, producing, as its legitimate fruit, a change of life. When the heart and life are both changed, the person is ready for a new state or relation.

The way is now clear for the investigation of this work, as a whole, and each of these items separately, in particular:

1. What, then, is meant by a distinct divine change in the heart? Such a change as destroys the love of sin and establishes the love of God in the heart of the sinner. The love of sin must be completely destroyed in the heart, so that the subject hates it and no longer desires to practice it; and the love of God, of righteousness, and holiness, established in the heart, so as to create hunger and thirst after righteousness. In nine-tenths of the cases where preachers talk of "experimental religion," and require persons to tell experiences, the amount of the experience is no more than that the subject experienced a change — that what the subject once loved he now hates, and what he once hated he now loves. This is all right as far as it goes, but in many churches, it is taken for more than there is in it. It is taken not only for what it is — a change in the heart — but for the entire process of turning to God; a work of grace, evidence of pardon, the impartation of the Holy Spirit — a new creature. This is too much. All this is not in it. Where the statement is true, there is this much in it, a change in the heart — no more. The love of sin is destroyed in the heart and the love of God established there. That is all. There is no repentance, no change of relation, no pardon, no impartation of the Holy Spirit. The person is simply prepared in heart for all the balance of the work which should follow. Those who thus limit conversion do not comprehend the work. They stop with a single item.

2. What produces this distinct divine change in the heart? It has already been stated that faith produces it. This must now be elaborated and elucidated. Perhaps a description of a case and the manner in which the change in the heart was effected will, at least, illustrate the subject.

Let us suppose a man in your community forty-five years old. In his business operations, he has prospered greatly. Success attends all his plans and financial operations. He is a true gentleman in the worldly sense. He attends fairs, takes the premiums; has fine stock, bets on them when he can find a gentleman who will bet five hundred or a thousand dollars. When he drinks, he only drinks enough imported wines and brandies to make him feel a little richer and sharper in trading than he would otherwise be. He never swears, only when angry and "can't help it." He attends the races; goes to the theatre; never gambles, except where the first class, in some place of refinement and elegance, engage in games for large sums. He assists to build churches, especially if he thinks it will enhance the value of his property two or three times as much as he gives; he give a little to the poor, but does not see any use in being poor. He never goes to meeting, except on some extraordinary occasion; and has no use for preachers, Bibles, and churches. They are of service only to moralize and keep down ignorant and vicious people. Thus a rich and successful operator goes through the world to the eternal judgment, making money, seeking pleasure, thoughtless about his soul and his relation to God.

In the midst of this mad career, the Lord puts His hand on a little son of seven years, and after some fifteen days of terrible suffering the precious and innocent child breathes the last breath, struggles the last time, and closes its eyes in death. He stood over and ministered to the little sufferer till the last struggle was over, and saw it sink away in death. Many times already he had planned for the education of that child in some fine university and thought of the property he would give him, but alas! he is gone. His breast wells, he heaves a deep sigh, and groans inexpressibly. Secretly, he inquires, "What is the meaning of all this?" Down he sinks with his heart broken. The world appears now to be one vast gloom. A new theme has come up for his consideration, and one that can not be put off.

Arrangements for the funeral, the coffin, cemetery, and grave are the matters that now rush before him. In awful solemnity and inexpressible grief they are considered. But now what is to be done? A preacher must be had and a funeral sermon must be preached, but what preacher shall be had? He knows nothing of preachers or churches; but he had a grandfather or a grandmother that belonged to some popular Church, and if he leans at all, it is toward that Church and preacher. He remembers how said preacher entered the "sacred desk" with a black robe on, in a very solemn manner, with other evidences of wisdom, piety, and orthodoxy. It is decided that he is the man to preach the funeral sermon. He is sent for, comes, and preaches the sermon.

The heart of the afflicted man has become tender, and it is susceptible of good impressions. He is willing to hear something about the soul and the other world. He is satisfied that his little child has gone to rest. In the sermon the preacher repeats the words: "What shall it profit a man if he shall gain the whole world and lose his own soul?"

What an awful question! He meditates on it, and, in inexpressible grief, looks back at his effort to gain the world, or as large a share of it as possible. He looks at the other part of it, losing his own soul! Is it possible that a man may lose his own soul?

The funeral is over. He and his wife return to their fine mansion. But pride is stricken down. Their hearts are broken. All is gloom. The sweet voice of a dear little son is heard no more. His quick step is no more heard. His little toys are found and laid carefully away as mementoes. He inquires, "Wife, where is that scripture quoted by the preacher?" He can not repeat it, but gives her some idea of it. She knows not where it is, but after a long search, they find and read it many times over: "What shall it profit a man if he shall gain the whole world and lose his own soul?" They sit and weep over it. "Shall we," said he, "in our stretch to gain the world, lose our own souls?" This theme engages their attention much of the time till the next Lord's day.

By this time they are both anxious to attend meeting. In the discourse, the preacher repeats the words: "The wages of sin is death, but the gift of God is eternal life through Jesus Christ our Lord." In his mind he repeats the words, "the wages of sin is death." "Is it possible," says he, "that this is the wages for which I have been working all my life?" He ponders this in his mind during the week, and commences reading his Bible and talking of what he reads, in his family. He longs for the next Lord's day, that he may hear preaching again. You can see now that he is changing rapidly. He attends meeting again, and the preacher quotes the words: "These shall go away into everlasting punishment, but the righteous into life eternal."

This strikes down deep into his heart. "And," he exclaims, "is this the end to which I am coming?" Thus he continues on, week after week, struggling under the power of faith. He now is reading and talking about religion much of his time, and inviting religious people home with him. He begins to approach the preacher, and invites him to visit him, and to find his chief delight in religious conversation.

About this time, one of his former associates informs him of some great races to come off, and invites him to accompany them. He replies kindly, but very decidedly, "I shall not be there." Another invites him to attend a great ball, soon to come off. He replies, with decision, "I shall not be there." All such follies and vanities have lost their attraction to him. The change that he has undergone is so great that the amusements and pleasures, as he once called them, not only have no attraction for him, but would make him unhappy if he were where they are. He has no taste or relish for them. The love for them is utterly destroyed in his heart. The matters of the kingdom of God are opening up to him. His soul is now seeking rest, peace and joy in the things of God. His moral sensibilities are all alive and shocked at the thought of vanities and follies such as here alluded to. Truly can he now say, "The things I once loved I now hate, and the things I once hated I now love." This is what is meant in this discourse by "a change of heart" — such a change as destroys the love of sin in the heart and plants the love of God in its place. This would be received as a divine change of heart in any church in the land. The affections are changed from the love of the world to the love of God. As the popular style of expressing it is, "his feelings are changed."

One grand mistake, very current at the present time, is to regard this change in the heart and, as they say, "in the feelings," as an evidence of pardon! It is no evidence of pardon, nor of acceptance with God. Pardon is not a change in us, but an act of pardoning power in heaven for us. We do not feel pardon in us, as it is not in us, but done in heaven for us.

In time of the war, a man was condemned to be shot, and the day set for the execution. His friends sent a petition to the President to pardon him. No reply came, and the general expectation was that he would be executed. His wife took cars and went in person, to make her plea for pardon. She obtained admittance to the President's apartment, and as she entered his room, she shrieked out, "Oh, my husband!" The President took her by the arm, raised her up, and inquired, "Madam, what of your husband?" She exclaimed, "My husband is condemned to be shot, and I have come to seek and obtain pardon for him." The President wiped away his tears and invited her to be seated, adding, "Your husband shall be pardoned." She instantly sprang to her feet, thanked him from the depths of her heart, and praised God. But her husband did not rejoice yet because this work was not going on in him, but in Washington for him. The pardon was written out and handed to his wife. She hastened to the telegraph office and dispatched to a friend near the prison of her husband, in the words, "I have obtained a pardon for my husband." Still the husband felt no pardon, and did not rejoice. The dispatch was soon read to him, and he then wept tears of inexpressible joy, though yet bound in prison, and praised God for the pardon that had been obtained.

The change in the heart of the sinner, as described in this discourse, is not pardon, nor an evidence of pardon, but a change in his heart, preparing him in heart for pardon. This change, then, is here taken for just what it is, no more, no less. The heart is turned to the Lord. He is now right in heart. This is the first distinct divine change.

3. The next distinct divine change, is a divine change in the life. All the change a man can have in his heart amounts to nothing, unless there is a corresponding change in his life. The Lord's appointment to produce this, is repentance. Repentance is a change in the mind or purpose. When this repentance is what it ought to be, and what must be to be acceptable to the Lord, it is a change of mind or purpose sufficient to result in a change of life, or in a reformation of life. Repentance does not change the past life. This is beyond the reach of the sinner. Nothing short of the hand of God can change the past life. Pardon separates the sinner from the past life, all its guilt, and the consequences that would follow in the world to come without pardon. The penitent regrets the past life, sorrows for the sins with which it is filled up, and grieves over them, but this in no way changes his relation to the past life.

Nothing but an act of mercy from the Sovereign, in graciously granting pardon, can change the sinner's relation to his past sins. This is not repentance. Repentance looks to the future life. When it is genuine, such as it must be in order to be acceptable to God, it is a change of mind or purpose so great as to result in a change in life for the time to come. It looks forward and promises to cover the whole future life while pardon looks back and covers the whole of the past life, saving him from the past as repentance does from the future. This repentance prepares the sinner in life or in character for pardon, but is not pardon itself. When the sinner is changed in heart, so that the love of sin is destroyed in his soul and the love of God established in him, and so changed in his mind as to destroy the practice of sin, as to induce him to cease to do evil and learn to do well — to desire from his heart to do the will of God — to hunger and thirst after righteousness — he is a proper subject for pardon.

4. Though the sinner is now changed in his heart and life, the love and practice of sin both destroyed in him, there is yet no change in his relation. He is still in the same state. He is greatly changed, but the relation is not changed. The change, so far, is only in him, not in the relation, at all. Being now changed in heart and life, and thus fitted for the new relation, he is now a proper subject for a new state or relation. What is it, then, that transfers the person into the new state or relation; the person whose heart has been changed by faith and whose life has been changed by repentance? Immersion into the name of the Father and of the Son, and of the Holy Spirit, is the divine appointment to change the state or relation. Immersion does not change the heart nor the life, but the state or relation of the person whose heart and life have been changed by faith and repentance. This accounts for one trouble that many people find. They find many good people who have never been immersed, and many bad people who have been immersed. This is a plain matter. Immersion does not make them good. It changes neither their hearts nor lives. If persons are immersed who have not the faith to change them in heart, or the repentance

to change them in life, as, no doubt, is the case with many, they will be no better than they were before. But that does not prove that the person who is changed in heart by faith, and changed in life by repentance, is in the new state till immersed into Christ, or that he need not be immersed into Christ. He is the very person that ought to be immersed into Christ.

Some one may inquire, What do you mean by a change of state or relation? The very act itself of entering into the kingdom or Church, is what is meant. It is not the change in the heart that prepares a man in heart to enter, nor the change in life, that prepares a man in life to enter, that is here meant by a change in relation, but the act, on the part of one already changed in heart and life, of entering into the kingdom. Faith changes no relation, but changes or prepares a man in heart for a change of relation. Repentance changes no relation, but prepares a man in life for a change in relation. Immersion changes no man's heart or life, but changes the state or relation of the believing penitent, transferring him into the new state or relation.

But it is very desirable to have a distinct idea of what is meant by this new state. A change of state, is simply to change from one state to another. The change alluded to, in the state or relation is expressed in several clear passages of Scripture, as the following: "Immersed into one body" — "immersed into Christ" — "enter into the kingdom" — "immersing them into the name of the Father, and of the Son, and of the Holy Spirit." Each of these expressions has the idea of transition from one state to another. The transition is into the state of justification. Every man immersed into one body is in a justified state.

"Immersed into Christ" amounts to the same thing. To "enter into the kingdom of God," amounts to the same, for all who enter into the kingdom of God are justified, and none who do not enter into the kingdom of God is justified.

All believing penitents, immersed into the name of the Father, and of the Son, and of the Holy Spirit, are in the kingdom, in one body, in Christ, in a state of justification. When the Lords says, "He who believes and is immersed shall be saved," it is equivalent to he who believes and is immersed shall be pardoned or justified. When He says, "Except a man be born of water and the Spirit, he can not enter into the kingdom of God," the amount of it is the same as if He had said, Except a man be born of water and of the Spirit he can not enter into the body of Christ or be pardoned. A man can be changed in heart, be good in heart, and not be in the kingdom of God. He can be good in life and not be in the kingdom of God; but no matter how good he is in heart and life, he is not in the kingdom or body of Christ unless immersed into the body. Immersion into the name of the Father, and of the Son, and of the Holy Spirit, on the part of a believer penitent, is the visible act, in which he is transferred from one kingdom to another. Before this act, though he may be prepared in heart and life to enter, he is out of the body or kingdom; after this act, he is in the body or kingdom.

No two persons can properly enter the marriage relation without three similar changes:

a. A change in heart.

b. A change in the life.

c. A change in the relation or state.

In the acquaintance the parties form, the faith or confidence in each other becomes such as to change their hearts or affections. Here there is a change in their feelings, and the desire to enter the marriage relation is established. This is followed by a visible change in their lives. A series of preparations for an anticipated new relation commences. They are still single, notwithstanding the change in heart and life. The time is appointed and the marriage ceremony is performed. Before that ceremony they were each in a single state. Now they are married, the state is changed. When did they enter the marriage covenant? When did they enter the new state? When their hearts and feelings were changed and a change was seen in their actions? By no means. But when the marriage ceremony was pronounced. This is the time when they entered the new relation. The whole relationship throughout the entire train of connections, on both sides, was changed the moment that ceremony was pronounced. It did not change their hearts or lives, make them any better, or love any more ardently, but it changed the relation. The marriage is not dated from the time of the first change they experienced in their hearts, not from the time of the first change in their lives, but from the time when the marriage ceremony was performed.

If the gentleman is worth a million of money, and falls dead one minute before the ceremony would have been performed, the lady is not legally entitled to one dollar interest in his estate. If he falls dead one minute after the ceremony is pronounced she has an interest in it. There is something in an "external performance," an "outward act." The changes in the heart and life were necessary, and they were not prepared to enter the new relation without these changes, but the act of entering was a separate thing. So the changes in the heart and life of the sinner are necessary, and he would not be prepared to enter into the kingdom of God without these changes, or to enjoy the kingdom when in it, but they only prepare him to enter, and do not transfer him into the kingdom.

And in like manner, immersion into the name of the Father, and of the Son, and of the Holy Spirit, of a penitent believer, has no tendency to change the heart, and is not designed for that purpose, but is solely to change the relation. In it the proper subject is transferred "into the name of the Father, and of the Son, and of the Holy Spirit," "into Christ," "into one body," "into the kingdom," into a state of justification or pardon.

The person, then, being turned to the Lord in heart by faith, in life by repentance, and in his relation by immersion, is, in heart, and life, and relation a new creature.

It is of great advantage, in looking at all subjects, to keep the items all distinct. Men sometimes say, the Lord gives faith. This is true in a certain sense, but not the sense generally intended. In creating man, He gave him intelligence, or the ability to believe facts on credible testimony. He gave us the Gospel; sent men to preach it to us, that we might hear and believe it. When men ask whether they can believe in and of themselves, if they mean without the facts given to believe, or the Gospel that brings them to us, they should be answered that they can not. But if they mean to inquire, whether a man can believe the Gospel when preached to him, without some supernatural power performed directly on him, to enable him to believe, or on the Gospel, to make it believable, they should be answered, he can. If he can not, he can not be justly condemned for not believing. The part, then, the Lord performs in making a believer, is in giving a man the Gospel, which he can believe. He will, therefore, condemn him for not believing.

The part that believing performs, in preparing a man for the enjoyment of God, is in changing his heart, thus destroying the love of sin and establishing the love of God in him.

The part that repentance performs, is in changing his life; destroying the practice of sin for the future.

The part that immersion performs, is in changing the state or relation of the man previously prepared in heart by faith, and in life by repentance, for the kingdom of God. He is immersed into the name, the body or kingdom.

Pardon is not done in the sinner, in the water, nor on earth, but in heaven, for the sinner, separating him forever from all past sins, and receiving him as innocent, as if he had never sinned.

The impartation of the Holy Spirit, is in consummation in turning to God. Because you are sons, He has sent forth the Spirit of His Son into your hearts, saying, Father, Father.

Now, is Peter the same in Solomon's porch as Peter on Pentecost? Where did he begin on Pentecost? He began by preaching the Gospel. He did the same in Solomon's porch. On Pentecost, when they heard the Gospel preached, they were cut to the heart. They would not have been cut to the heart if they had not believed. When he made his appeal in Solomon's porch, upon the healing of the cripple, they heard and believed. On Pentecost, he commanded them to repent. He did the same in Solomon's porch. On Pentecost he commanded them to be immersed in the name of Jesus Christ for the remission of sins. Instead of this, he commanded them, in Solomon's porch, to "be converted," as it reads in the common version, or "turn," as it reads in both the New Translation, by Anderson and the Revised Version by the Bible Union, "that your sins may be blotted out."

There will be no difficulty in seeing that "the remission of sins," and "sins blotted out," amount to the same. But some will be troubled to see how "be immersed" and "be converted," or "turn," amount to the same. Yet this is the case. "Be immersed," is a literal command. There is nothing figurative about it. But the command, in Solomon's porch, to "turn," puts the result accomplished in immersion for immersion itself. These persons were already turned in heart by faith, and they are, in the connection, commanded to repent, which turns or changes the life. There was nothing remaining to turn or change but the relation. This was the turning commanded, and as this is effected in immersion, the command here amounted to the same as the command to be immersed on Pentecost. That on Pentecost was "in order to the remission of sins"; and that in Solomon's porch, "that your sins may be blotted out." On Pentecost he says "and you shall receive the gift of the Holy Spirit"; and in Solomon's porch, he has "the times of refreshing from the presence of the Lord"; the same, expressed in different words.

A man says, "That is all clear enough, but I am afraid I have not the right kind of change of heart." The following case will illustrate a proper change of heart, and the Lord's mercy and love in receiving the penitent sinner when he turns to Him:

A young man ran off from his father and mother, and

was absent a year before they knew where he had gone. Many prayers had fervently gone up to heaven for him, many tears had been shed over him, and many long and solemn conversations had been held, by an anxious father and mother about him. After about a year, a friend found him in California, and, knowing, the anxiety about him, immediately wrote his father a letter, informing him where he could write to him. The father received the letter, and lost no time in writing his son. The young man took the letter from the office and said, when he saw his father's handwriting, it moved him to his heart. But he determined to read it, as he expressed it, "like a man," and not shed any tears over it, as he thought "weak people" do. He decided, however, not to read it till he was alone. As he was returning, he stopped in a path in the dense forest, and opened the letter, nerving himself against weeping. He thought he was succeeding finely as he read down through the main body of the letter, as he restrained all his tears. At the bottom he saw a postscript, in something like the following words: "My dear son, it is late at night, and your mother is sitting by my side, bathed in tears, weeping over you." His manliness, as he falsely styled it, gave way, and he sank down by the path and wept like a child. Immediately he rose up, and resolved, "I will go home to my father and mother." This illustrates the right change of heart when the sinner resolves to turn and go home.

The balance of the history of the case, illustrates the mercy and goodness of God in receiving the sinner when he turns. As early as possible, he started homeward, and reached his father's house one morning at eight o'clock, and rapped at the door. The father, not knowing that his

son was within three thousand miles of home, opened the
door, and saw his son. The young man stretched forth his
hand and exclaimed, "O, father, can you forgive me?"
The father's heart melted; he sprang forth and embraced
him, replying, "with all my heart, I forgive you, my dear
child." In a moment he was brought into the house, and,
looking into another apartment, here was the mother,
who wept while that letter was being written, approaching, when he cried out, "O, mother, can you forgive me?"
You know how a good mother can forgive! Young man,
your mother stands next to God. If you do so badly that
your mother can not forgive you, there is but one more
you can go to. Your mother will forgive you when no
other human being will forgive. The mother, in an ecstasy,
sprang forward and clasped her boy in her arms, exclaim-
ing, "With all my heart, my dear child, I forgive you." "So
there is joy in heaven among the angels of God when one
sinner repents," says Jesus.

How kind and compassionate is our heavenly Father,
against whom we have sinned, not only one year, but
every year of our life, till we turned to the Lord, to forgive
all our sins — blot them from the book of remembrance
and remember them no more forever — not even permit
them to be mentioned; and how wonderfully ungrateful
must man be to refuse to come and accept this most gracious pardon, when freely and mercifully offered! And
when we remember that He stands all the day long
stretching forth His hands to a gainsaying and disobedient
people, the ingratitude is heightened if men and women
refuse. By all His tender mercies, then; His goodness, His
great love; His wonderful compassion; by the value of
your precious souls, by the sufferings of the bleeding,

dying Savior; the shame and indignation heaped on Him, when He bore our sins on the cross; by all that is lovely and endearing, be persuaded to turn to the Lord and live forever.

NOTES

1. From Z.T. Sweeney's *New Testament Christianity*, Vol. III. Columbus, Indiana: New Testament Christianity Book Fund, Inc. 1930.

10

"The Prodigal Son"

CHARLES REIGN SCOVILLE[1]

Before beginning the sermon proper, the following letters were placed on the blackboard: F-A-T-H-E-R

F-Freedom
A-Adieu
T-Trial
H-Hunger
E-Extremity
R-Reception.

The Scribes and Pharisees saw Jesus at a feast eating with publicans and sinners, and they said, "This man receiveth sinners and eateth with them." Many things were said about Jesus which were not true. But if there ever was a true thing said about the character of Jesus remember this is one. We are told that they wagged their heads at him; they made light of him; spit upon him; rejected him; put upon him a purple robe, and a crown of thorns upon his head. They pierced him; they mocked him; they reviled him; they crucified him. They did all they could and yet he reviled not again. All of this Jesus bore, and he bore it so meekly, so kingly, so beautifully. Not a single time did the Lord answer them scornfully. And now notice, please, while he is sitting here at the feast, he understands that they are saying these scornful things about him; he knows what is in their hearts and he hears them without a reproachful word. How lovely he begins saying the beautiful things recorded here. The bruised heart of the Man of Sorrows here gave the world's literature its masterpiece. He paints three pictures.

He first gives them the picture of the lost coin and in this picture or parable he is answering the murmurings of the Scribes and Pharisees.

Here is a woman that has lost a coin. Possibly the woman is a mother that has been working over the washboard all week, or possibly it is a woman in a sweatshop, or it may be she is a widow — a woman with three or four little ones all too small to even sell papers or shine shoes; — and so the mother has to provide. It represents their bread for over the Lord's Day; it represents possibly their winter's clothing; it represents it may be, the coal, gas, or fuel to keep them warm over the Lord's Day; and on the way home the woman has lost the money some way. Or, it may be she took it home and possibly put it on a shelf and the children accidentally knocked it off, and it is now lost. Now Jesus says, this woman began to hunt for that coin diligently. Can you imagine how a mother would hunt for a coin that meant bread for her babies or clothing for her little ones? That meant that they might have warm beds, or bread over the Lord's Day; that meant that their little shivering limbs, with blood already too thin, might be frozen before the Lord's Day is over, if it were not found. Can you imagine how a mother would hunt for a coin that meant all this? Ah, friends, she searched until she found it!

Did you ever see a mother who had lost her child? In the streets of New York City one day a cry went up, "A baby is lost!" "A baby is lost!" Business stopped and the cars stopped, people thronged everywhere, even on Wall Street; and the cry went up and down that street also. "Baby lost! Baby lost!" — and it was not long until that baby was found. Just like that, was the way the woman searched for that coin until she found it. Notice the children's joy; see the smiles on their faces; soon they are satisfied with food. What is the satisfaction of the mother when the babies are asleep and she looks down upon them with all the fond love that a mother has, and she sees the little ones sleeping quietly in the cradle? Is there not satisfaction there? So Jesus says like this, like this is the joy there is in Heaven over one sinner that repenteth, even more than over ninety and nine just persons that need no repentance.

Here is another picture. Jesus paints this picture thus: A certain man had a hundred sheep. Do you know how the sheep are counted? As they go into the fold the shepherd holds up a rod like this, and when the first comes along, it will jump over the rod and all the other sheep will jump just as high as the first one did. You know they say that sometimes men are like sheep. We are; many men are like sheep in that particular way. We will do so much like the sheep that precede us, especially if we think they are lambs of the Father's fold. So the shepherd holds up that stick and counts them. "Ninety-nine. Only ninety-nine! This, (he says) won't do. Drive them out." So they send in the shepherd dog and drive them out again, and as they come to the stick which is held up they will jump. After awhile they jump whether the stick is there or not. You can train a whole flock of sheep just in that way. That's true; it isn't only theory; its an actual fact. The man counts the sheep again and there are only ninety and nine. He sees there is one gone. There is one thing evident, either that sheep has been killed, or it is a poor sheep and a weak sheep, one not able to follow the others home. Either that, or it may be fast in the thorns. In either case it is not very complimentary to the sheep. But the shepherd counts the sheep as they go back into the fold again; counts up to ninety-nine and the hundredth sheep is not there. This time the shepherd takes his dog and crook, and is soon off for the search.

> None of the ransomed ever knew
>   How deep were the waters crossed;
> Nor how dark was the night the Lord passed through
>   Till he found the sheep that was lost.
>
> Away on the mountain he heard its cry;
>   It was sick, and helpless, and ready to die;
> But the angels echoed around the throne
>   Rejoice, for the Lord brings back his own.

I have this from a minister who was in Scotland. He was walking along one day and met a man with a sheep on his back. He said to the man, "Where did you find this sheep?" The man replied, "On a rock." It must have been there many days. Didn't you know where it was? "Oh yes, but I couldn't get it." How was that? "Well, you see it was like this; the sheep was on a high rock, and down here was another one where the grass was nice and tender. But there was a crevice between, and when it jumped down it could not get back. I hunted for it the same night it was gone, but I couldn't find it." The man asked him what he did when he couldn't find it; and he said, "Oh, I hunted for it until I did find it. I knew it could live as long as the grass was there, so I waited; and finally, I went there one day , and the grass was eaten off the little rock. I went back again and it tried to get up. I went back the next day, but the sheep made no attempt to get up. That was today, and I climbed down and put the sheep on my shoulder and am now carrying it home." Many men are just like that sheep.

Your pastor told us last night of a man over here on a splendid avenue who a year ago intended to obey the Gospel of Jesus. He listened to Brother Newman, but obeyed not; and during this year that man passed away. Last night a little boy came down that aisle at the invitation; the pastor told of his sister who last year obeyed the Gospel, and now is on the other shore.

Since I began the meeting in Allegheny with Bro. Lhamon, two of my nearest and dearest friends have passed on to the other shore. And while that is true, some others who heard the word, and who might have been gathered into the Father's bosom — just like that sheep — refused to do it, and jumped to a lower life. They went to a place where the good pastor could not come; if he did come, they went farther from God. If the pastor even calls

211

to see them, they are like that sheep; they say they will go away where they can't hear him. If the mother says a word, they go farther away. On your death-bed you call for mother and for the pastor and beg all to pray unto the Lord. How like that sheep! Why wait until you go so low?

Now you see the shepherd as he comes home. True his sheep is sickly; is a poor one; his sheep is nearly dead, but it is his and is found, and he is happy, and the shepherd says, "Rejoice with me for I have found my sheep that was lost," and Jesus says "Likewise I say unto you there is joy in heaven!" Oh that I might speak of that joy to-night! What joy? The joy of the mother that got her child off the track just as it was near to being killed. The joy of the mother that took her child off the boat that was sinking! Just as a mother stands over her sick child; as my mother stood over my body when I was nine years old, — that joy! "Likewise, I say unto you there is joy in the presence of the angels of God over one sinner that repenteth." Over one sinner! I tell you, my friends, we lose sight of the units. I praise God for twelve and thirty seven, but I don't forget the one soul; and I want to say to some good men here tonight (and you are here with your wives and daughters) if every man in Pittsburgh should give his heart to Jesus and you should not, you are one for whom the Saviour died, and the only one who can make your wife happy. Please remember that to-night, and then say, as the Prodigal son, "I will arise and go to my father."

There on the left side is the picture of the Lost Coin, and over there the picture of the Lost Sheep, then here over the pulpit let us hang the master-painting, the Lost Son. If there are any of the Master's works greater than others, then this is the greatest. The Lord's pictures are marvelous. Here is the master-piece of the Master's — the master-piece of all masters. Here is the grandest thing in literature, or in any of the world's art galleries. It is the picture of the Prodigal Son and the Wonderful Father. Tonight I am not going to talk about the Prodigal Son alone, but I am going to divide my sermon and speak also of the Wonderful Father. The Scotch people don't call this the Parable of the Prodigal Son; they call it the parable of the Wonderful Father, and I like that better.

The first thing is the son's *desire for freedom*. The first suspicious thing the father noticed was one night when his son had come in from the fields, and the horses were put away and supper ended, the boy instead of going to bed, was walking back and forth in his room; or, perhaps, out in the barnyard. There is something on his mind. The father knows there is something on his boy's mind, and the next night he watches him very carefully; and as the boy comes in with his sleeves rolled up the father sees him anxiously looking over the hills as though he expected to meet somebody. There is a little town over on the side of the hill, and the father understands. The son comes in, combs his hair, shines his shoes and starts off for the city. That is his first taste of freedom. He feels how fine it would be to be his own master. After awhile the boy makes up his mind that he will break away from the old man. I beg your pardon for using that term, "old man," but that is what so many boys say. Or, he doesn't want to be under the watchful care of the "old lady." You remember the night of the mother's meeting, I said God is our father and the Church is our mother, and some people don't want to be under the care of father or mother, and they steal away from God and the Church.

So the desire to be one's own master is the beginning of all sin. If you have a son or daughter in your family, if you have a boy in your school, if you have a clerk in your office, or a man in your employ who is not satisfied and not trying to do his duty or his work, it is because he wants to be his own master and free from all restraint. So, I say the desire for freedom is the beginning of all sin. So, possibly some morning after the father has been weeping nearly all night the good man says, "Wife, there is something going to happen; I fear our boy is going to the bad very rapidly; we must do something." Maybe he does just as a father did in New Jersey: he places himself in front of the door and says, "If you are going down town to-night, my son, you must go over my body. You are killing me now." He says, "You are drifting away from the influences of your poor mother and sister. My son, you must not go; I can't stand it to have you go." The boy has had too much of a taste of the other side, and like the cows or sheep or the goats that have once been over the fence, so it is hard to restrain a person who has had a taste of the other side. And as the father in New Jersey placed his form before the door, his young son with a curse stepped over his father and went down town. I need not tell you how that father went to a premature grave, nor follow the boy out into the darkness.

I cannot understand how a boy can nerve himself up to such a pitch that he can go home and kill his father and mother. One of my old classmates did this. I saw him in Michigan City when I went there to study prison life. One day I looked through the bars and there was Dwain Webster. I turned white, and so did he. My mother had written me about him; — a boy with whom I had skated and played ball, and with whom I studied my first lessons. That boy was there for shooting his father and mother. I said to him "Dwain, I cannot understand this"; but my friends, tonight I have as much respect for Dwain Webster as I have for that boy who will openly and carelessly go forward and crush a father's or mother's heart, and bring disgrace upon the name of a sister; upon the family name; upon his own home and upon those who are his dearest friends. It would not be so bad in this world if a man could go to condemnation alone. I know angels could weep over this loss, but I know something else, there are always many hearts that bleed with burdens angels would shudder to bear. Brother Lhamon said to me one day, here is a young girl going to ruin, and she is bringing her family to ruin, too. Here is a crushed heart, that of a sweet-heart, perhaps, or of a father or mother, a brother, or sister; one for whom Jesus died. Oh, God! help us realize that one can't go to condemnation alone. You can't say bad words in this world alone; you can't live a bad life, and live it to yourself. You must not say, "I can do as I please." You must not say, "I am my own boss." You must not say, "I won myself." That can't be. Around you are thousands of influences; around you are thousands of people to be influenced; around you is the fragrance of the loveliest flowers of the whole family, and you will not only ruin the bouquet of today, but you will bring the whole plant to wither. God help you, my brother, as a father, husband, or son; God help you my sister as a mother, wife, or daughter, to remember no soul goes down alone.

If I could say but one word tonight, it would be, my good friend, that the greatest sin in the world is ingratitude — a man who lives out of gear with God and man, dead both to the life that now is and to the world that is to come.

The boy is fretful; he wants his freedom, wants to be his own master, just as the father said the night before in his tears, "I'm afraid something is going to happen." So it did happen. The boy says, "I might as well make bold of it, first as last;" and so he nerves himself and goes up to his father and says, "Give me the portion of goods that falls to me." No love there; not an adjective, or adverb, not a single participle, not a word that expresses anything but the basest ingratitude. I want the portion of goods that falleth to me. He used one good word and that was "Father," but it was necessary to say something because it was his father who was addressed. So you see the father in starting out, foolishly grants his request and divides unto him his living. It is grand for us that God does not always give what we ask; we would all be prodigals if He did. I know a man in an Ohio town who says he is not a Christian simply because God doesn't give him what he says he ought to have. He is comfortably situated, is making two or three dollars a day; but that isn't enough and he is far from being a Christian. I baptized his wife and daughter, and he lives drifting away from God.

Professor Wakefield, who was a bosom friend of President Garfield's says God loves our souls more than our bodies, and God gives the thistles and thorns and heartaches in order to save souls. And this is his illustration: He says that it is the idler who steals; it is the idler who murders; it is the idler who does all sorts of mean things. He says that if we were all idlers, society would soon be rotten. God loves our souls more than our bodies, and God knew it was better to place us where our bodies would be busy, and God knows they need to be busy in order to be pure.

When Eve saw the tree in the Garden of Eden, that it was good for food and one to make one wise, she partook of it.

Henry Moorehouse tells us a story of his own home. He was a great English evangelist who possibly turned as many Englishmen to Jesus as any other man except Spurgeon. Henry Moorehouse had a brother who was ungrateful; ingratitude was in his every look, word and act. One Christmas time, the father, who had been worrying about the boy, called to his daughter and said, "My daughter, what shall I do with your brother tomorrow? I have pleaded with him, entreated him, and done everything I can for him, but he is crushing my heart; what will I do?" And the sister turned to the parable of the prodigal son and read it, and then said, "I believe I would let him go to the husks." The sister didn't mean to be unkind, but they had tried to do all they could for him and it all had no effect. The father then came to Henry, the older brother, and he gave him the same advice. That evening a neighbor came in to dine with them. When dinner was over the father took down the old Bible and read the story of the Prodigal Son. When he had finished he told the story of his own son as near as he could. Then he turned to his neighbor, his good friend, and said, "I have asked my daughter what to do, and she says turn him out. I have asked my son, and he says the same thing, but neighbor, if he were your son, not your servant, what would you do; what is your advice?" You know Englishmen are a little bit slow. He rubbed his head and sat meditating a little while, and finally said, "I believe the advice of your son and daughter is the best. Let him go out into the world; let him see what the far country is like; let him go and taste of the husks. Let him find out what riotous living means, and maybe he will come back and understand what it is to be a son and have a father. I would turn him out for awhile." The father went to the son and put his hands under the son's chin and said, "My child, thou hast heard what thy sister has said; thou hast heard what thine only brother has said; thou hast heard what thy father's best friend has said. What hast thou to say for thyself? Shall I turn thee out?" Then the father began to sob, and cried bitterly. "Turn thee out, my child, — turn thee out! My dear child, I never will. You are mine; you are my baby; I love thee; if thou shouldst be lost, I would die. I cannot let thee go, my child, I will not turn thee out." The son got up and put his arms around his father's neck, and father and son wept together, and the boy said, "Father, I will never be a prodigal." Oh, fathers! Don't give the portion of goods, but give all of a father's love.

Next I shall speak of his *adieu*. Adieu. I don't suppose he left a watch for his mother or a ring for his sister; I don't suppose he left a single thing for his brother, for he "gathered all together." Did you ever know how an ungrateful person gathers all the time? A spring ever gives up pure water, hence it never becomes impure. But his boy gathers all together, and then he takes his journey into a far country. His heart has already gone into the far country; and when a man's heart is gone his head will soon follow. You show me in the Central Church, in the East End Church, a man whose heart is in the world, and I will show you a man whose head will soon be out too. Notice that, please. Wherever a man's heart goes his head will follow. Jesus knew that and said "Do not lay up for yourselves treasures upon earth where moth and rust doth corrupt and where thieves break through and steal, but lay up for yourselves treasures in Heaven where moth and rust do not corrupt and where thieves do not break through and steal, for where your treasure is there will your heart be also." Notice, please, that God asks for our hearts. So the boy's head follows his heart. May I be excused for saying something about myself tonight? I am talking to the boys and I am so glad they are here. Do you know what I believe saved me? I will tell you what it was. The day I was twenty-one years old I said, I am going home (I never told this at all until I told it in Allegheny;) I was in college at the time; I wanted my father and mother one more day. Some way I got the idea that when I got to be twenty-one I was going to be my own boss but I wanted to be a boy yet and to have parental advice, and so I went home. That night I walked around through the house, but I didn't have much to say. When all was dark I went out beyond the barn under a tree to pray, and while this may sound silly to you, I believe as much as I believe I am standing here, that my Heavenly Father heard my prayer. I asked him to be my father, — for my responsibility to my earthly father (according to the laws of this country) ended next day, and I didn't want to be without a father. I tell you a ship can't get along without a pilot or without a helm. A railroad can't get along without two tracks. God's spirit must bear witness with man's and I wanted to have a guide. You might say I was a silly boy, that I am a weak man, but I can't help that; but I say with all my heart, I love that spot; and I am conscious of this fact, the fact that has helped me through more difficulties than all else in the world, "The Lord is my Shepherd." I may be a fanatic, I can't help it; I believe that if any young man or woman in Pittsburgh, no matter what your circumstances are — I believe with all my soul if you will cast all your care upon Him, not a part of it, that He will care for you. "Commit thy ways unto him and he will direct thy paths." I believe this also that, All His ways are ways of pleasantness, and His paths are paths of peace. That "The path of the just is as a shining light that shineth more and more unto the perfect day." Don't get scared when someone comes around and tells you you ought to be perfect today. Don't feel disheartened because you are tempted, for the greatest attack is directed against the strongest fort, and the greatest guns are aimed at the strongest points, and the devil does the same thing; and so remember this and follow the shining path "Until the perfect day."

Certain influences affect us tremendously. People like the prodigal go by stages. Every man will get to the end of his journey but some men go faster than others. Some take a through train, some take a sleeper, and sleep all the way (even in church); you know there are some people, practically speaking, who go through the world asleep, without God and without hope, taking a sleeper for life; even taking a sleeper through to death, and it doesn't take them long to get to their journey's end.

I have often wished that when the first day ended the boy had turned around; I wish that he might have "come to himself" the first Lord's Day. I wish he had said to his companions, "I will arise," before he had gone so low. He didn't do it; the first Lord's Day ended, but he went on.

It is his adieu. Don't say anything to him; he will not

listen. He knows his father is crying. Go into the house, and see the dear old mother; see her weeping; her bosom heaving; hear her sobs, — only a mother can know how her heart aches. See those eyes that once looked so deep into the soul of that baby boy. Oh, her bleeding heart! Her unutterable grief over that child for whom she has suffered so much! Look at that, and when you get through looking at that, look at the cross and think how that life is being crushed and pierced by sin, those hands and feet pierced by nails, that head crowned and pierced by thorns, that body bruised for our iniquities, that heart bleeding for our sins! Think of that, young man, father, husband, brother, and then "gather all." Can you forget the cross? Can you forget the cross? Oh, man! Can you look at that cross, and then go away and say, I will do as I please?

He went into a far country. One of our great men says a man can go to the Lord's Table, and yet be in a far country. They have fixed their eyes on a house and lot. Set your affections on things above; center them not on things in the earth. "Lay up for yourselves treasures in Heaven where moth and rust do not corrupt." Don't say the world is better than the church. Some are like the children of Israel; they begin to complain; they said to Moses, we remember the good things we had to eat down in Egypt. Listen! They said, "Who shall give us to eat? We remember the fish we did eat in Egypt; we remember the cucumbers and the onions and the garlic, but we have nothing to live upon." There are pastors pleading in churches and tiring their bodies and almost going to rack trying to interest some members who sit in the church, but whose hearts are away back in Egypt. They are hearing but not heeding, the pastor's sermons. They are eating manna, but they complain. So these people said, "Don't you remember the melons and the onions?" There are some people who think more of melons on the devil's side than of manna on the Lord's side, who would rather be filled with garlic than be thrilled with the gospel, who prefer the onions of Egypt to the incense of Heaven. You say that man is making fun of the Bible. I am not. He says "you remember the fish?" Yes. "Do you remember the cucumbers over on the other side?" Yes. "Remember the melons?" Yes. "We remember the onions and the leeks; the onions and the garlic, and loved that. It was good; it was good compared to this old manna," and so they complained to Moses and God. I tell you my brethren that there are some people here in Pittsburgh (they don't belong to the East End Church or the Central Church, or to the First Church, of course) but some of them say they belong to the Lord, and if I speak my heart tonight I am afraid that sometimes their desires or appetites are for onions, garlic, cucumbers, melons and leeks, more than for the leaven of Heaven; they drink oftener from the wells of sin than from the fountain of salvation. These people are remembering those things back in Egypt but have forgotten the land of promise. I tell you, my friends, they are just like the Prodigal Son. They say to their Heavenly Father, "Give me the portion of goods that falleth to me," and they take their adieu. So I say, it is possible for a man to be an elder in the church, a deacon in the church, if you please, possibly an evangelist, a pastor, a singer, a Sunday school superintendent, or teacher; I believe it is possible for a man to be all that and yet his heart be fixed in the world. The Prodigal Son was that way, so he went into the far country. Self indulgence.

My third point is his *trial*. And in his trial he failed. He wasted his substance. Every boy will be tried some time. The time will come when the father or mother will say, "Stand up, my boy, you must stand up alone." The Bible says, "He wasted his substance in riotous living." Sensual pleasures. Notice, please, his cup is full; full of wine, but when the wine is gone nothing but the serpent remains. First it is the honey, then the sting; first the wine, then the delirium; the meat, then the bone; first the father's heart, then the stranger's husks. Completion or self-condemnation. This is what you see. Solomon said, "Young men, rejoice in the days of your youth, but remember for all these things God will call you into account." The Prodigal Son found it so. He reaped what he sowed. "He wasted his substance," his time, his years. I find idle girls in the church who would make good kindergarten teachers, wasting their substance. I see people in churches who would make as good singers as anybody, only they won't sing in the chorus choirs. Wasting their substance.

> If you faithfully use every talent
> And with it do ever your best,
> He will greet you 'Well done, faithful servant,
> Enter into the joy of thy rest.'

> Then how faithful should be our whole service,
> In using the talents God gives,
> For who thus has obtained the Lord's favor
> In his presence eternally lives.

"And when he had spent all." I want you to notice next that he "spent all." Young man, your voice; young lady, your voice, your influence, your years; for I say to you tonight you are wasting your years; you are either in

Satan's or the Saviour's army. You may love your wife, but you are against her; you may love your child, but you are against it. If you are not helping your wife to bring the children into the church, you are helping Satan to keep them out. "If you are not for Me you are against me."

"And when he had spent all." Over in Georgia a young man and woman married. They were as wealthy as anybody in that part of the state, but that man began to drink and went down, down, down, until finally he lost his store; lost his business and all his property. Finally pawned his watch, pawned his overcoat, and everything in his house went. The last thing to go was the old clock that the woman had received from home. That night when he came home and the broken hearted wife had gotten him sober, she put her arms around his neck and said, "See here, John, let us start over again. Let us start all over again." He looked at his wife and said, "That's good, but my dear companion, why didn't you say that to me before I had gone so low; before we had spent all?" I tell you there are some men in Pittsburgh and Allegheny, if they don't change their ways, or practices, they will soon have spent all. That is the point, and I wish I might say this tonight with the power of an archangel of God, or with the power of Paul on Mars Hill, or John the Baptist at the River Jordan. "Whatsoever a man soweth that shall he also reap." The Prodigal Son had spent all; but men, tonight hear the words of that dear wife and man down in Georgia, as he said to his companion, "Why did you not say stop before we had spent all?" So let me say it. Stop now! Oh, the prodigal son returned, but he had spent all.

And when he had spent all, he began to be in want. Then another thing, he began my friend, to feed swine.

When he began, does it say there arose a mighty famine of swine? Not at all; the devil never has any famines. There are always evil places, evil associates and evil games. But he began to be in want, and they sent him into a field to feed swine. That was the worst thing a Jew could be asked or compelled to do. If there is anything a Jew hates it is a pig. Shakespeare causes Shylock to say in the "Merchant of Venice," where the merchant invites Shylock to dine with him, "Yea to smell pork! I will walk with you, I will talk with you, but I will not dine with you." Jesus says they sent him to the lowest possible work. There was no work under heaven; there was no work in all the earth, no calling so low to the Jew as to go down where the swine were. This boy had one trait of character that I love. He would work, and as long as a man works, there is some hope for him, but for a lazy person there is no room on the earth, and I know there won't be any on the other side. I have no respect for a man who won't work.

I want you to notice next his hunger. First. Hunger for what he had lost. He left his father's house for the stranger's swine. He left his father's table where he could eat, to go where he couldn't eat. He left as the son of his father, to become the slave of a stranger. This is what he hungered for, his home, for the food that was there. He hungers not only for the food, but for something else; he hungers for the work. Look at the work he might be doing for his father. There are his father's sheep; there are his father's straying cattle; nobody to look after them. The farm is going to waste; the horses are growing old and are of no account, only an expense to his father. There is a fine farm of 200 acres with nobody to work it for this father; you see it is all going to waste. Just like the Sunday school over there, like those little Juniors down there. Oh, that you might help your father! People, it seems to me today, as I said before, the sin of the earth is ingratitude. A boy who breathes pure air and doesn't thank God for it; the man who drinks pure water and doesn't thank God for it; a man or woman who sits down to a well provided table three times a day and does not thank God for the things they eat; I tell you, my friend, there is ingratitude somewhere in your heart or life.

The boy lost his opportunity; lost his testimony. Mr. Moody says that the boy is feeding the swine, and three fellows ride along in a carriage, and they began to say, "Look at that fellow! Isn't he a fine fellow down there among the swine?" and they laugh and wag their heads at him. "Oh," he says, "you needn't laugh at me; my father is just as wealthy as yours; my father is just as good as yours." They say, "yes, you look like a rich man's son, don't you? You look as if your father had plenty: had as much as our fathers." That is why I say:

Rescue the perishing, care for the dying;
Snatch them in pity from sin and the grave.
Weep o'er the erring one, lift up the fallen;
Point them to Jesus, the mighty to save.

Or,

Down in the human heart, crushed by the tempter,
Feelings lie buried but grace can restore.
Touched by a loving hand, quickened by kindness,
Chords that were broken will vibrate once more.

I met a boy who was one time with us in Chicago, and he was down so low that he had no confidence in himself and none in anybody else. That's the reason I pity a sinner; many a man has gone so far away from home and so far away from God, that he has no confidence in himself any more. So, my friends, I want you to notice one thing; you can be a child of a king if you wish. I want you to notice I have said tonight that he lost five things, his home, his food, his influence in his father's house, his father's work, his father's testimony. But there is one thing he never lost. Do you know what it is? Who can tell me? What does that spell over there? Father! If there is a man in this building tonight, a husband, a young man, a son; if he is a hard working man who has fallen; if he has been a wealthy man; a great man in the field of art, and if he has failed in everything else, remember one thing — you have a father. I want you to remember that. If friends, earthly friends forsake you, your father remembers you; there is one thing, — he calls you friends tonight.

We have next his *Extremity*. He has gotten to his extremity. Now he comes face to face with two facts. He says, "In my father's house there is bread enough and to spare, and I perish." Lo, I perish! But will he perish? The Bible says that he came to himself, and as soon as he came to himself, he came to his father. I tell you there isn't a single man in New York, or Chicago, or anywhere in the world, but who, if he comes to himself, will come to his father. Ask these business men; ask these husbands; ask these enthusiastic people in your city tonight. They will say if you come to yourself, you will come to your Father. He thought about his father, and he said, "come home." He thought about his mother, about the old trees and the barn, and they all said to him, "come home." Then he thought about his elder brother — no he didn't; if he had, he wouldn't have come home, and I want this point to stand out. I have met men in every city who say, if certain people were not in the church, if there weren't certain people there, I would go in; but I won't as long as they are there. I won't say anything about the man in the church, for he has tried, you haven't. As when Moses lifted up the serpent in the wilderness. May be it was an old crooked pole; but Moses said, don't look at the pole, look at the serpent. And Jesus says, "And I, if I be lifted up, will draw all men unto Me." The church may be crooked, but it upholds Christ. If the Prodigal Son had reasoned about his brother, he would have stayed down among the swine. Oh men! Take your eyes off the brother and fix them on the Father; take your eyes off the church and fix them on Jesus, and then arise and come to the Father.

I met a young lawyer from Indianapolis one night who said, "Mr. Scoville, I would like to be a Christian, but I can't decide." I said, "You have your choice to go up or down. There are other young men going up. Will you go up or will you go down?" He just reached out his hand and said, "I will arise." The Prodigal Son said I will arise. I like that decision, "I will."

I met a young lady in Michigan who was a principal in one of the schools; and I said to her, "You have been standing undecided for years; will you still stay down there in undecision, or will you rise higher before God and men?" And she said, "God helping me, I will," and she did.

There was a man at Noblesville, Indiana, who had been drinking. His wife and little girl gave themselves to God and he said he would give his life if he could be a good man, and I said to him, "You don't need to give your life, you can save your life and just give your influence if you will," and he said, "I will." That night that man stood up there, and said to the audience, "Years ago I was in good standing in this community. Then I lost this friend and that friend, and I can see that I must face about, I must face about and go to my Father, and God helping me, I will." There are three hundred and forty-seven people in that city who gave themselves to Christ. I went back there afterwards and met that good man. Now that man is one of the strongest there. Wasn't it well he turned that night? My brother, just say, I will. It isn't because you can't; it is just because you won't. Though you may be among the swine tonight with ten thousand devils, with as many thousand tongues, to hiss you back, remember the Father calls you and all Heaven is pledged to help you just say "I will."

The last point is the *reception*. The Prodigal Son says, "I will arise," and he starts — goes home. Do you see that cross? I have seen people hold on to the seats until they couldn't stand any more, and when I took an old man in Ohio by the hand, he cried like a child and said, "Brother Scoville, I just couldn't stay away any more." Isn't it strange how people stay just as long as they can stand it? Just like the Prodigal Son; he stayed until he had lost his coat, his character, his ring, his substance, had spent all, then he said, "I will." Men! men! men! Hear me! Before God, are you going to wait until you come to the dying moment of your life? When your influence is gone; when wife and father have gone to premature graves because of your sin, will you then stand up and say, "I will?" Will you do like that poor sheep, and allow the Lord to pick you up from the gutter of sin or indifference? Will you come tonight? I am asking you a plain question. The prodigal said, "I will," and he did. There is not a man in this house tonight but who, if he says "I will," he will.

Finally he comes to his native country. Oh, that thrill of joy! Who can describe it? He comes where he can see his own hills again. All at once he comes in sight of the house and as he comes to where he can see the house he walks faster. Let us look on the scene from the house. What is the old father doing? Just like the father in Illinois whose boy ran away from home. See that father standing there at the depot waiting for his son. Nine years he went to the depot every day. I have this from a traveling man. Then six years more, but no son. Still the old man stood there, with his cane in one hand and a crutch in the other, until fifteen years had gone. Think of that! You say, did the boy know his father was coming to the depot every day? Yes he did. You say he must have been the most ungrateful of sons. Finally one day a man with a broad brimmed hat got off the train, and the old gentleman ran forward and embraced his son. Bosom came to bosom, heart to heart; and the old man cried out aloud, and that traveling man says there was not a dry eye among any of the traveling men, business men, railroad men, or hackmen there. Oh, Sir! How long has the Lord Jesus waited for you? fifteen, twenty-five, yea forty years. Will you ever come home?

Finally one night the father said, I want to have one more prayer. So the old gentleman takes the Bible and reads and when he gets through he kneels down and prays; prays for his servants, for his elder son, and when he tries to pray for him his lips tremble and tears come. He is beyond expression; he can't speak. He has waited all these years. Poor man, he is almost home. Poor old father, his life is about finished. But still he says, "I am a sonless father and I cannot give him up." He gets up from his knees without an amen, and goes out of the house and the servants get up and wipe their eyes also. The old gentleman has gone up on the flat roof and he sees someone coming. He quickly wipes his eyes. Oh! he says, is that my child? Down from the roof he comes, he pushes one servant one way and another, another, and fairly leaps into the hall; down over the steps he goes and says, "Yes, yes, this is my child!" The Bible says he ran to meet him, the only time in all the Bible that God is represented as running. He had been a bad boy; he had spent all. No shoes, poor clothing; "Spent all." "Wasted his substance in riotous living." Lost everything but his father. And that father ran until he fell. Did you ever hear of anybody running and then falling? They go so fast that when they get to the end they just give away. And the Bible says, "He fell upon his son's neck and kissed him." Joy unspeakable. He said to one servant, run and get a ring for his finger, and to another, get shoes for his feet. Go and get the best robe and put on him; to another, kill the fatted calf, for my son was dead and is alive, was lost and is found. And the Bible says they began to make merry. The Bible doesn't say it ever ended, and it never will. Friends, like that is the joy there is in Heaven over one sinner that repenteth. That is the joy that can be in your heart if you will say tonight, God helping me, I will arise and go to my Father.

There's rejoicing in the presence of the angels,
  Over sinners coming home;
All the heavenly harpsters with a mighty chorus,
  Now are praising round the throne.

Then rejoice, all ye ransomed;
  Let your praises reach to heaven's highest dome,
For the dead's alive, the lost is found and wanderers
  Now are coming, coming home.

NOTES

1. From Charles Reign Scoville's *Evangelistic Sermons* delivered during the Great Meetings at Pittsburgh and Des Moines, as taken down by Mary M. Swaney, stenographer. Des Moines: Christian Union Publishing Co., 1902.

11

"What Think Ye of Christ?"

J. V. COOMBS[1]

"What think ye of the Christ? whose son is he?" — Matt.
22:42.

The Jewish Passover was the most matchless assembly
that ever met on earth. Josephus says: "Between the
hours of three and five in the afternoon, by actual count,
256,000 lambs were slain for the sacrifice, and
2,700,000 people partook of the feast." Yonder they
come — from the banks of the historic Euphrates, from
the classic shores of the Dead Sea, from old, dried-up
Egypt; the Orient and the Occident are all here. Yonder
come mothers and fathers, greeting the children after long
absence; strangers looking for the first time upon the
wonderful temple. Yonder come one thousand priests,

singing their hymns, fluttering their banners and waving their plumes.

All day long Jesus mingled with the maddened multitudes. He went about healing the sick, cleansing the lepers and encouraging the despondent; yet the Sadducees and Pharisees conspired to destroy him. They tried in every way to trap and confuse him. The Sadducees asked in regard to the woman who had seven husbands, "Whose wife will she be?" Jesus answered that in the resurrection there is neither marrying nor giving in marriage. Seeing he had put the Sadducees to flight, the Pharisees asked, "Which is the greatest commandment in the law?" The Master replied: "Thou shalt love the Lord thy God with all thy heart, with all thy soul and with all thy mind. The second is like unto it, Thou shalt love thy neighbor as thyself." He had defeated both. Trying to entangle him, the Pharisees formed a combination with the Herodians and asked, "Is it lawful to give tribute to Caesar?" If he had said "Yes," all the Jews would have abandoned him. If he had said "No," he would have been in rebellion against Rome. Say "Yes" and have no friends. Say "no" and be put to death. He replied, "Whose image and superscription is on the coin?" They replied, "Caesar's." Then he sent the dagger of criticism to the heart, "Render unto Caesar that which is Caesar's, and render unto God that which is God's." Pay your taxes and don't complain, then do your duty toward God. They were silent. Jesus then became the questioner. He asked, "What think ye of the Christ? whose son is he?" They gave the schoolboy's answer. Every Jewish boy was taught that the coming Lord would be the son of David, so they said, "The son of David." Then the question,

"How then does David call him Lord?" They dare not answer according to their own prophets, and from that day they asked him no more questions. They attempt argument no more, but will now resort to force. From that time till his death upon the cross Jesus was constantly under the eyes of spies.

What think ye of Christ? What do the historians say? Jean Paul Richter says: "The life of Christ concerns Him who is mightiest among the holy, and holiest among the mighty." Napoleon says: "Jesus has builded a kingdom upon love that shall survive all other empires." The centurion said: "Surely this is the Son of God." Pilate says: "I find no fault in him." Thomas said: "My Lord and my God." Peter declared that Jesus was "the Christ, the Son of God." I am interested in what historians, his enemies and his friends have to say of Christ, but what do you think of him?

The story of Christ comes to us not by tradition, but by the historical evidence of faithful witnesses. Marcus Dods says: "In point of fact, the majority of events of past history are accepted on much slenderer evidence than that which we have for the resurrection. The evidence we have for it is of precisely the same kind as that on which we accept ordinary events; it is the testimony of persons concerned, the simple statement of eye-witnesses and of those who were acquainted with eye-witnesses. In short, the evidence can be refused only on the ground that no evidence, however strong, could prove such an incredible event. It is admitted that the evidence would be accepted in any other case, but this reputed event is in itself incredible. This seems to me quite an illogical method of dealing with the subject. The supernatural is rejected as a preliminary, so as to bar any consideration of the most appropriate evidence of the supernatural. So long as the miracles of our Lord are not recognized as an essential part of his revelation, so long will they be felt to be a hindrance, and not a help to faith. But Jesus evidently considered miraculous works of healing an essential element in his work, and whoever feels uneasy about the miraculous, and fancies that perhaps it would be well to yield the point and surrender miracles, must be looking at the matter with very different eyes from which our Lord viewed it."

These men — Peter, James, John, Luke and others — were witnesses to be trusted. They had no inducement to tell a false story. They could not have been mistaken. Professor Orr says: "It is to be remembered that the apostles, with numerous other eye-witnesses, lived for years together at Jerusalem, continuously engaged in the work of instruction; that during this period they were in constant communication with each other, with their converts and with the church which they founded; that the witness which they bore necessarily acquired a fixed and familiar form; and that the deposit of the common tradition which we have in the Gospel, has behind it, in its main features, all the weight of this consentient testimony — is therefore of the highest value as evidence."

Joseph of Arimathea, Nicodemus, Mary Magdalene, and many other infallible witnesses, bore testimony of the resurrection of our Lord.

A. N. Gilbert gives a very excellent summary of the appearances, which follows: "The tomb was opened by an earthquake, and the rolling away the stone Sunday morning (Matt.), visit of the women (all four). Mary Magdalene receives the message for the disciples (Matt., Luke and John). He appears to other women (Matt., Mark and Luke). Peter and John visit the tomb and find it empty (Luke and John). Mary Magdalene sees Jesus (Matt., Mark and John). Mary Magdalene tells the disciples (Mark and John). The guards report to the chief priest (Matt.). He appears to Peter (Luke and I Cor.). The walk to Emmaus (Luke). He appears to the ten after the return from Emmaus (Mark, Luke and John). Seven days later he appears to the eleven (John). He appears to the disciples in Galilee (Matt. and John). And again in Jerusalem (Luke and Acts). The appearance of his ascension (Mark, Luke and Acts). And last of all, he appeared to Paul (I Cor.). Although no one saw his resurrection, the circumstantial evidence is so complete that no room is left for doubt."

Men have their lives written after they die. The life of Jesus was written fifteen hundred years before he was born; written in prophecy; read by Greek, Roman and Jew. Five hundred prophecies refer to Jesus. About 105 times the Old Testament tells us what Jesus would do; 105 times the New Testament tells us that these things were done. The one — the Old Testament — was prophecy. The other — the New Testament — was biography. Prophecy is history before it occurs.

PROPHETIC ARROWS

Suppose five men would stand here to-night, each with a quiver of ten arrows. They desire to shoot the arrows into the center of the target. They do not know where the target is. It may be here, yonder or there. Man No. 1

stands at a station fifteen hundred yards from target. He sends his ten arrows out into the darkness. Man No. 2 advances and stands at a station one thousand yards from the target. He sends his arrows out into the inky blackness. No. 3 stands eight hundred yards, and No. 4 six hundred yards from the target. No. 5 and last, advances and stands but four hundred yards from the target. They send their arrows forward. You call for lights, and all fifty arrows are in the center of the bull's-eye. What would you say about such an occurrence? You would say such a thing could not take place by chance. Let us call up a few prophetic arrows.

Moses stands fifteen hundred years from the coming of the Lord. He sends his arrows into the future, which is inky blackness. He tells us that Jesus will be a prophet like unto Moses.

David advances, and, standing yonder one thousand years from the birth of Christ, sends forward three hundred prophecies. What wonderful things he says! He tells us that while on the cross Jesus would cry: "My God, my God, why hast thou forsaken me?"

Then Isaiah, Daniel and Malachi, at different stations, send their arrows into the future. We call for lights, and there are five hundred prophetic arrows centered in Jesus. No skeptic has ever tried to answer this argument. Christianity is the only religion that appeals to prophecy for its authenticity. Remember, these prophecies were read not only by the Jews, but by Roman, Greek and barbarian. The place of Christ's birth, the manner of his life, and the suffering on the cross, were all read long before he walked the earth.

What do you think of Christ as a helper? When here

on earth he went about aiding people. He fed five thousand, and encouraged the despondent and had compassion on the needy.

What do you think of him as a comforter? When he sojourned on earth he comforted Mary and Martha in their sorrow; he said, "Weep not." He is the same great comforter. He will comfort you with his promises and with his word.

While in California a little girl was killed by a horse running away. Bro. H. D. Connell was asked to conduct the funeral. He said to me: "I just can not preach that funeral. These are very dear friends and this is the only child. It will break the heart of the mother. You must preach; I will just read the lesson." I consented. Brother Connell had read but a few verses when the mother's mind gave way. The glare of the eye showed that the mind was wavering. She rushed to the coffin, took the dead child in her arms, and said: "Pearl, I can not give you up. They must not take you away." Brother Connell said: "Mother, that is not Pearl. That is only her dead body. Pearl lives in heaven." "Who said my darling would live again?" "Why, Jesus himself." "Well, then, I can go to her." She quietly returned to her seat, comforted by the promises of Jesus.

He is the good Shepherd and he will care for us. A minister went to the bedside of a dying mother. She said, "Oh, brother, I am afraid to die." "Why, I thought you were a Christian and not afraid of the future." "I know I am saved, and that I will go to heaven, but the fear of the agony of death." A few days later the minister called again, and she said, "I am not afraid now; I have read the promises of Jesus and he will go with me through the valley." In a few hours she went to be with Jesus. A month passed, and the same minister met the husband, who said: "Come with me at once. My little girl Allie is dying of diphtheria. She wants to talk with you." What will she want to talk about? In our worldly affairs we talk of everything, but when we come to the time of death we talk of Jesus. The minister hurried to her bed and found her gasping for breath. He said, "What do you want me to talk about, Allie?" "Talk about heaven and where mother is." "Well, Allie, heaven is a glorious country. Your mother is there. Jesus is there. No little girls have sore throats there." Her eyes sparkled. "If I die, I will go to mother. She will be at the gate to meet me." Just then the physician come in and said, "Allie, I must burn your throat again." "Papa, don't let them burn my throat again; I want to go to mother. Papa, take me in your arms." He took the poor little, dying creature in his arms. "Now, hold me just a little higher; hold me nearer mother and heaven." There, just as high as he could hold her, her spirit went home to Jesus and mother. Skeptic, what have you to offer to that dying girl? You blow out the light and leave her in darkness.

NOTES

1. From J. V. Coombs' *The Church of Christ: Sermons, Lectures and Illustrations.* Cincinnati: Standard Publishing Co., 1916.

12

"The Blood Atonement"

JAMES EARL LADD[1]

INTRODUCTION

Of all the damnable pictures ever etched against earth's midnight, I thing the most terrible is of sin; the fact of sin. Fools laugh at sin, and philosophers explain it away, but brethren, we cannot bury our heads ostrich-like in the sand, and by wishful thinking dismiss the fact that sin is with us.

I believe the existence of sin in the world can be demonstrated in three ways. The first way is by way of observation. I stood on the front steps of one of the greatest asylums for the insane, and the head of the institution made this statement: "Preacher, 80% of the people who are in this institution are here because of sin — their sins, or their parents."

I am told by the medical circles that 50% of the blindness is directly attributable to people's background of moral delinquency; passed on even to the tenth generation.

Sometimes I allow myself to become involved in foolish arguments. A few years ago in the town of Lakeport, California, a little man engaged me in a silly discussion. We spent about 15 or 20 minutes discussing the existence of sin. He was a contractor by trade. He said there was no sin in the world, and while we were talking we were standing in the shadow of a concrete jail that he was building. He tried to tell me nobody ever did anything wrong. Every motorcycle officer that you have; every jailhouse that you have; every law that you are forced to pass, takes cognizance of the fact that sin is. All you have to do, sir, is to read the daily newspapers, and you can see the slimy track of the serpent in the lives of individuals.

I have a second reason for believing in sin. It is based upon personal experience. I can illustrate it like this: A few years ago a little boy went out to go swimming. It was a little bit cold, and he stayed in the water too long. He was weakened and enervated. On the way home he passed by an apple orchard where there were some green apples. Now mind you, he was in a bad condition to begin with. Then he climbed over the fence and ate fourteen green apples. Immediately, from the standpoint of bureaucracy, there was a great upset in the department of interior, and while he was doubled over rubbing the cramps out of his stomach muscles a very good, sweet, gracious and lovely lady, like they have in story books, came by and said: "Little boy, what is wrong?"

He told her he had a "tummy" ache. She smiled sweetly and proceeded to disabuse him of his hallucination.

She said, "God is good; God is love, and pain is an error of the mortal mind, and you are simply laboring under an illusion that you are experiencing pain."

The boy looked up at her for a minute, felt of his "tummy," and said: "Lady, it's all right for you to talk that way, but I've got inside information."

Now I know there is sin for the same reason the boy knew there was colic. I have inside information. I have sinned.

What is sin? The Bible gives three definitions. The first is this: "Sin is the transgression of the law," (I John 3:4, King James) and I know I have sinned because I have done things contrary to God's will. The Bible has a second definition of sin: "To him that knoweth to do good and doeth it not, to him it is sin" (James 4:17). Good things left undone become sins, and I know there are good things I have left undone, therefore I know I have sinned. The Bible gives us a third definition of sin: "Whatsoever is not of faith is sin" (Romans 14:23). In other words, if a person does something that is questionable, if you and I do something with a question in our minds; if you and I do something and you and I know the church frowns upon that thing, whether it's right or wrong, it's SIN. "Whatsoever is not faith," God says, "is sin." "...Faith cometh by hearing, and hearing by the Word of God" (Romans 10:17, King James). Oh, my, experience! I know there is sin because of experience.

I know there is sin in the world because of God's Word. The Bible says there is sin. Romans 3:23 — "ALL have

243

sinned." That's what God Almighty says, and that should settle it. Matt. 1:21 — "...thou shalt call his name Jesus; for it is he that shall save his people from their sins." Mark you, He will not save them IN their sins; He will save them FROM their sins. And here is the $64 text in I John 1:8 and 10 — "if any man says he is without sin, he makes God a liar, and the truth is not in him." I want to say that again, brethren, so it will soak in. If any man says he is without sin, he makes God a liar, and the truth is not in him. Brothers and sisters, it is a dangerous thing going around calling God a liar — it is dangerous, dangerous!

Recently on the radio I heard a very skillful speaker. He was so skillful he kept me at that radio until I was late for an appointment. But, brethren, I just couldn't turn the radio off because he had my curiosity aroused. Perhaps, I shouldn't say curiosity — just women are curious, but we men have "inquiring minds." That's the scientific approach, you know. Anyway, I wanted to hear what he had to say.

Just about the time I was ready to dial off he would say, "Don't dial off, because just before I close, I'm going to tell you what sin is." Well, I thought I would stick around and find out what sin was. I got tired in a minute and reached for the dial to cut myself off again, when he said, "Don't dial off," just as if he had been watching me. "Don't dial off, I'm going to tell you what sin is." Well, I stayed with him.

Just at the time to sign off, he said, "Now listen. Listen carefully. Listen closely. I'm going to tell you what sin is. Sin is anti-social." Then he signed off — Uggg! The most conservative statement I've heard.

It reminded me, brethren, of a lady who described a skunk. She said a skunk was "a sachet kitten." Negative aromatics, you know. A very conservative statement, if you ever had any experience with a skunk. Sin is anti-social! Of course it's anti-social, but it's more than that, sir, it's transgression of the commandments of God.

When you and I sin whom do we offend? I can illustrate that with the story of David. David committed adultery with a woman named Bath-Sheba, and then to cover up his sin, he murdered her husband. King David, when he came to his senses — when he repented — under inspiration made this statement: "Against thee, and thee only, have I sinned." Now since sin is a violation of God's commandments; since sin is deliberate and stubborn rebellion in the face of God; since God is the aggrieved party; then only God has the right to write the terms whereby sins might be forgiven.

Beginning back in the Old Testament you will find the story unfolding. You will find it in that blessed Book, in the 17th chapter of Leviticus, verse 11, "I have given it (the blood) to you upon the altar to make atonement for your souls: for it is the blood that maketh atonement...."

Go with me back to the Garden of Eden. Before I make this observation, may I say this? I will write it down so you can see it — the word atone means "to cover" or "to conceal." A secondary meaning is "to cancel." With that thought in mind, let's go back to the Garden of Eden. Do you hear it? I hear a cry. Out there in the Garden of Eden a lamb is dying. God is killing that little beast, and God is taking the skin from that little beast to make clothes for Adam and Eve. Do you know, brethren, that the first drop of blood shed on this planet was shed by a little lamb, that that lamb's skin might cover the bodies of Adam and Eve? What a picture, as years later God provides a covering for sin.

I hasten on down the Old Testament picture, and I come way down to the land of Egypt. There comes a great Passover day. Here we have the commandment — God said wherever there was blood on the doorpost His angel would spare, and where there was no blood the first-born baby should die. The children of Israel take the branch of hyssop, they dip it in blood, they paint the side-post, they paint the top of the door. That night when God's great death angel, with his hand on his black sword-hilt, comes zooming across the land of the Pharoahs, wherever God's death angel sees the blood-smeared doorpost, and the blood-smeared lintel, He "passes over." Another picture given to us in advance of the Blood Atonement.

I. THE BLOOD OF JESUS

Then comes the Jewish theocracy of the great day of atonement. The seventh day of the tenth month the high priest went into the outer place, he scrubbed his body scrupulously clean, he put on either new linen that was never before worn, or freshly laundered. Then he went up to the altar of the sacrifice, and took one goat and one lamb, without spot or blemish, he put that goat or lamb, as the case might be, upon the altar. He put his right hand to the lamb's head. He put a knife between his teeth, he raised his right hand like this and threw back his head and between his clenched teeth he prayed. He took

246

the knife and he cut the lamb's throat. If he missed on the first strike he turned and they brought a second lamb. And brethren, an orthodox Jew today won't eat meat unless a man of the Tribe of Levi has prayed through his clenched teeth and killed the beast with his left hand. They call that meat "Kosher meat." You have seen it advertised. The High Priest took the blood of the Lamb. He walked across the holy place toward the Holy of Holies, and as he approached the Holy of Holies where God dwelt, God pulled the curtain and the High Priest placed the blood upon the horns of the altar, and the sins of the people were shoved ahead for twelve months. A year passed. Again, at dawn, the High Priest got up, bathed himself scrupulously, put on white linen, prayed to God through his clenched teeth, killed the lamb, walked into the Holy of Holies, the sins of the people were shoved ahead for another year. This took place, brethren, for over a millennium. For twelve centuries the sins of the people were shoved ahead, farther, bigger, higher, and blacker the cloud became — then once for all, in the fullness of time — hear me — an Infinite number of sins of an infinite number of people demanded an infinite sacrifice, and God sent His Son!

What killed Jesus Christ in six hours on the Cross? If you were to nail me to the side of that wall I should probably live for three days, because God gave me great physical resistance. There have been some exceedingly tough men who have lived five days, after being crucified. History in Rome showed that some criminals lived on a cross for five days. Jesus Christ was a powerful man. He carried His cross for Himself from the Praetorium out to Golgotha. As near as I can figure it was a mile and three-quarters. The regulation Roman cross had to weigh two hundred seventy-five pounds, and He carried it. What killed that mighty Man in six hours? They nailed Him to the cross, and the Bible says Jehovah God "laid on him the iniquity of us all" (Isaiah 53:6). That big, black cloud of sins that had been shoved ahead at the Jewish sacrifices, just shoved ahead, never covered — your sins — my sins — the sins of Hitler — the sins of Stalin — the sins of Genghis Khan — the sins of Tamerlane — the sins of Napoleon — God laid the sins of the world on Jesus Christ, and that mighty Man of the Cross said, "My God, my God, why hast thou forsaken me?" (Matt. 27:46). His heart broke.

I mean that literally — I mean the muscles ruptured. When a man's heart breaks, the auricle tears, the plasma and the corpuscles pull apart. Christ's heart ruptured, this I know because when they lanced His side, what flowed out? "Blood and water" (John 19:34). The plasma had separated from the corpuscles.

Christ, just before He died, said, "It is finished." The Greek word for it is finished is "tetelestai." This is an interesting word. I found when teaching my classes in New Testament Greek, and in doing some research in Koine papyrus, that this was a banking term, and when a man had paid his bill in full the banker wrote across the back of the bill "tetelestai." There's the sins of the world stacked up, and Jesus, when dying, said, "Tetelestai" — paid in full. The Blood Atonement.

Consider these blessed texts: Rev. 1:5 — "Unto Him that loveth us, and loosed us from our sins in His blood;" and that great text in Romans 5:9 — "Much more then, being now justified by his blood...." Take that great text of the Apostle Peter: "Ye were redeemed, not with corruptible things, with silver or gold, from your vain manner of life handed down from your fathers; but with the precious blood, as of a lamb without blemish and without spot, even the blood of Jesus Christ" (I Peter 1:18-19).

I was preaching in Hollywood, and a Christian Church preacher came to me. We have all kinds of preachers in the Christian Church. This fellow said to me, "Ladd, I believe God could have forgiven our sins if Jesus Christ had never died on the cross."

I said: "Brother, so do I." That took all the wind out of his sails because I agreed with him. He wanted to argue. Why of course God could do anything. God could have forgiven us if Christ had never died. Why, bless your heart, God could have made Long Beach bigger than Los Angeles. But he didn't. God could have made the Los Angeles River as big as the Amazon. The point is, He didn't. God could have made each one of us fourteen feet tall, and given us three pairs of arms, but bless your heart, God didn't do it. LISTEN! God COULD save people without the blood, but the point is, God is not going to. God said: "Apart from the shedding of blood there is no remission" (Hebrews 9:22). Oh, I like those texts.

Twenty-five times in the book of Revelation Jesus is called the Lamb of God; the Lamb of God that takes away the sins of the world. "What can wash away my sins? Nothing but the blood of Jesus."

So many folk ask me if my sermons are in print. Well, I have three books under way, but I brought along a copy of my biography tonight. It has only three pages. Look at the first page (black) — that was my heart to begin with — I had sinned. Look at the second page (red) — there's the blood of Jesus Christ that cleanseth us from sin. Look at the third page (white) — "wash me and I shall be whiter than snow." Just three pages, praise God, to Earl Ladd's biography, because life begins at Calvary.

II. HOW IS THE BLOOD APPLIED?

Now, brethren, the unfortunate thing about it is this — the most of our good Bible preachers, preaching on the Blood Atonement, preach just like I have preached so far, and they hold up their Bibles and say: "Now, brethren, we are through." But I am just getting ready to begin. I have heard sermon after sermon on the Blood Atonement. I checked one year, and I think I heard thirty-two sermons on the Blood Atonement over the radio, and not one sermon told me what to do to get under the Blood. Friends, if you are dying of cancer, and someone tells you there is a remedy, if they don't tell you how to get in contact with it you will die the same as if there wasn't a remedy on earth. We must appropriate the shed blood of Jesus Christ. All right! How can we do it?

I'm going to draw a rough circle on the blackboard, and it will represent something. Where was Jesus Christ's blood shed? Tell me. Yes, in His death. So I will write D-E-A-T-H. Now the psychologists tell me there is no impression without expression, so I'm going to make an impression. Christ's blood was shed in His death. There's His blood, shed in His death. Now, if I'm going to come in contact with Christ's blood, I'm going to have to come in contact with His death. That's obvious isn't it? I'm being very slow here because I want to be sure I'm not being misunderstood. In Romans 6:3 — "Or are ye ignorant that all we who were baptized into Christ Jesus were baptized into His death?" All right, when I was baptized into His death, what did I contact there? Why, His blood, of course. I quoted five or six texts tonight which showed our sins are washed away in blood.

I can quote two or three texts on baptism — Acts 2:38 — "...repent and be baptized for the remission of your sins...." Acts 22:16 — "And now why tarriest thou? Arise, and be baptized, and wash away thy sins...." All right. There's a text which says sins are washed away in baptism. Isn't that horrible? It contradicts itself. It says sins are washed away in blood, and it says sins are washed away in baptism. Which is true? Why, they are both true. We learned in high school that things equal to the same things are equal to each other. Then if sins are washed away in blood, and if sins are washed away in baptism, then, the blood, the cleansing blood, the saving blood, is applied where? Why certainly, in baptism.

To make it foolproof, God, in I John 5:6-8, said "...For there are three who bear witness, the Spirit, and the water, and the blood: and the three agree in one."

I will illustrate that so you can remember it. Brother Frey, may I borrow your baton? Imagine that is a ball bat. I like to play ball. I still play baseball. I made my letter in three lines of sport back in school, and here I am a grandpa in my 40's, and I pitched three games this last summer, and we won all three of them. One of them was a two-hitter. I remember what one kid said. I would rare back on a high, hard one, and put my 240 pounds back of it, and this boy said: "Grandpappy, that ball looks oblong." I like to bat, too. I bat left-handed just like Babe

Ruth, and there the resemblance stops. There are three things it takes to make a successful hit — a ball, a bat, and a batter. Put all the bats in Peru. Put all the balls in Ecuador, and put all the batters in Missouri, and you've ruined baseball. Now, here on the mound the pitcher winds up, and follows through, and here's the batter. He sets himself. The ball comes down the groove, he brings the bat like that, the wrist leads, and when the wrist comes out like that in the wrist action, they call that "cowtailing the bat." And he walks away from that pitch, and when you hit 'er square on — Oh, it's a grand and healthy feeling to see that thing rise, and rise, and rise, and go over the fence. It doesn't happen very often, but when it happens you remember it. Three things have to get together to make a successful hit.

Now get my terrific application. God says these three things go together — The Spirit, the water, and the blood. You take the Bible texts on baptism and break them up and you will find they break up in three parts. Let's take two or three and see what happens.

Titus 3:5 — "... He saved us, (that's blood) through the washing of regeneration (that's water) and renewing of the Holy Spirit (spirit)." Titus 3:5 has three parts.

Take Acts 2:38 — "... repent ye and be baptized (water) ... unto the remission of your sins (blood); and ye shall receive the gift of the Holy Spirit (spirit)."

Christ was baptized. Jesus walked sixty miles to Galilee to be baptized at the hands of John the Immerser in the Jordan River. What happened? The water was there in the Jordan (water), His unshed blood was still in His veins (blood), the Spirit of God came down when Christ was baptized in the form of a dove (the spirit). You saw your minister a few moments ago take three folk and bury them in water. You heard the splash of the water (water), the blood of Jesus Christ cleansed their sins (blood), and the Holy Spirit of God entered their hearts (spirit). Oh, brethren, hear me! I'll give one thousand dollars in cold cash to any man on the face of God's green earth who can show where the cleansing blood is applied to an alien sinner outside the waters of baptism.

Let's take the Book, and let's believe it. "Oh, Mr. Ladd, you have got to repent." Surely! "And confess." Of course! "And believe." Certainly!

I like to perform marriage ceremonies. I have performed a lot of them. I have the famous Ladd non-skid, fool-proof hitch that I apply. I have taken the Episcopalian high ceremony, and the Episcopalian low ceremony, and the Methodist ceremony and the Presbyterian ceremony, and the ceremonies of four or five Christian preachers, and I have put them all together. When I marry them they are married.

It starts something like this: "Dearly beloved, we have gathered together in the presence of God and these witnesses to join this man and this woman in the bonds of holy matrimony. If any person present knows why these two should not be so wed now is the time to speak or forever hold your peace." Then I stop and glance around. So far nobody has ever spoken up. What would you do, brethren, if some disgruntled suitor jumped up and said, "Please, sir, I object." About all you could do is give them rainchecks and say come back Thursday.

So I go on throughout the various parts of the ceremony and I come to the ring part — "from time immemorial the circle has been the symbol of eternity. As the ring is in the shape of a circle, as it has neither beginning, nor middle, nor end, I trust that throughout the years your love for each other will be everlasting. As the alloys which compose this ring are precious, I trust that throughout the years your love shall become increasingly precious. As the alloys which compose this ring are pure, I trust throughout the years your love for each other shall remain untarnished." Are they married yet? We are more than half way through and they are not married yet.

I ask the boy in question and say, "So you take this girl for better, for worse, to have to hold, etc., etc." You know the ceremony, how it goes.

This reminds me of the fellow who divorced his wife and was asked why. He said she was too fat. They asked if he didn't promise to take her for better or worse." He said, "Yes, but not for thick or thin." There's a difference. You ask why I am telling this tomfoolery? Because some of you folk are getting sour and when I hit you on baptism in 20 seconds I want you in a good humor.

Are they married yet? I ask her if she takes this man to be her lawfully wedded husband, etc., etc. She says she does. Are they married yet? Not yet. Not yet. Then I say, "Join your hands," and they join their hands, and I say, "By the authority invested in me by this State as an officer authorized to solemnize marriages, and as an ordained minister of the Church of Christ, I now pronounce you husband and wife. What God hath joined together, let not man put asunder." Are they married? Why certainly.

Get my application. Were all the parts of the ceremony important? Yes or no? Were those questions necessary? Certainly.

Now get this application. A man walks down the aisle. He stands in front of the congregation and takes the minister by the hand and says, "I believe that Jesus Christ is the Son of God."

Is he under the blood? Not yet. He repents of his past mistakes, "Oh, God in Heaven, I am sorry, I repent, I repent."

Is he under the blood? Not yet. He makes a public confession of faith. Is he under the blood? Not yet.

But he has believed, and he has repented, and he has confessed, and then a minister takes him into the watery grave of baptism where he comes in contact with the death of Jesus Christ; he is buried in the watery grave; he rises from the watery grave. Is he under the blood now? Why certainly. I don't understand how it is that preachers can stand in front of congregations and tell people what to do to be saved and leave out the Bible platform for doing it.

I think that an atheistic teacher led me into the ministry. It was an atheistic professor who thought she was being smart. She was assigning book reviews in a class in English at the University of Oregon. A student suggested before the book reviews were assigned, that they assign a review on the Bible. The teacher turned to me with a laugh and said, "Ha, Mr. Ladd, that will be a good one for you. You write a book review on the Bible, and be sure to tell us what the plot is. Ha! Ha!" I believe that led me to Christ.

Well, I felt like a fool because I didn't know the Bible had a plot. To me it was just chapters and verses with no more plot than the dictionary, but I went to work, and she forced me into saving my soul. I found the Bible began in

255

Paradise, in the Garden of Eden. I found the Bible ended as a great musical composition, on the same note on which it began. The Bible ends in Paradise. The plot of the Bible is this: Man through sin fell from Paradise, and through the shed blood of Jesus Christ on the Cross, man was restored, and Paradise lost became Paradise regained. Your modernist has done two things — first, he has missed the entire plot, and second, he has left out the main character. Otherwise he knows the Book.

Someone said to me, "Mr. Ladd, is there anything God can't do?"

"Yes, there is. There's one thing God can't do. God, with all of His power, can't see my sins through the blood of Jesus, Praise God."

Across a big cathedral in a certain place they had a big cross. A little boy came in. He didn't know much about crosses, but he looked up and said, "Gee, what's the big plus sign for?"

It is — plus redemption, plus God's eternity, plus everything — the cross of Jesus.

Years ago during a rebellion in India a hundred and twenty British officers were placed in a horrible, stinking, loathsome dungeon. Waist deep were they in viscous mud that sucked them down. Finally, due to some kind of political phenagling one hundred and twenty Sepoys were exchanged for the men who were in prison. They said we will get these fellows out of the mud. They threw ropes to them, but the mud stuck so they couldn't get loose. They fastened the ropes around them and put sacks under their arms so the ropes wouldn't cut and they pulled them out. Four or five men had their arms dislocated. The Sepoys lined them up and put the leg irons on them, two anklets with fifteen pounds of iron ball, thirty pounds of steel on each leg. Each man dragged sixty pounds of metal.

One of the officer's name was Baird. Baird was a little man. He had had the fever, and he was weak. He was rocking back and forth on his heels. A big Highland major named MacGregor turned to the Sepoy Colonel and said to him: "For the sake of God in Heaven, don't put those leg irons on Baird, he can't drag them ten mile, let alone to Keta."

The Sepoy said, "Well, my orders say to put one hundred and twenty pairs of leg irons on one hundred and twenty British officers and march them to Keta."

MacGregor said, "May I see your message?"

He looked at it and said, "It says one hundred and twenty leg irons, and one hundred and twenty prisoners. It doesn't say each one of us has to have leg irons. Put Baird's on me and I will stake two sets."

This appealed to the sporting blood of the Sepoy. He turned to the blacksmith and said, "Take the leg irons off this man and put them on the big man."

They put them on above his own, and they bit into his muscles. Three miles out the big man was rocking and rolling as he walked, blood came down and filled his puttees. Seven miles out he could stand no longer, and big Malcolm MacGregor dropped in the sand. The temperature was 120 degrees. The Sepoy Colonel spoke to a man next to him, and he picked up his rifle, raised it, and brought the butt down, mercifully putting MacGregor out of his misery. In the distance the birds came circling into their feast. Baird, walking unimpeded, kept up with the caravan. Baird reached Keta.

After the war was over, Captain Baird came back to

India, and because he was rich he hired beaters to go out on that desert. Seven miles out from that prison town, out alongside of an old watercourse where men hardly ever went they found the skeleton of a giant man, with one hundred twenty pounds of steel on his legs. Carefully and tenderly they picked up that skeleton. They placed it in a sealed casket and they brought it back to Scotland. My folk are Scotch, you know. I'd like to have you stand with me in Glasgow and view a monument. It's a beautiful monument, as tall as the front of this building. It says this on it: "Major Malcolm MacGregor." It has this epitaph: "Greater love hath no man than this, that a man lay down his life for his friends" (John 15:13).

Do you see my picture? I had sinned. Earl Ladd had sinned, and Satan had his shackles on me. I was bound hand and foot, and I cried out and said, "Oh, miserable man that I am, who will deliver me from the body of this death?"

Jesus said, "Earl, I'll wear them for you. I will take your sin-weight." And my blessed Lord died on the cross, with my sins upon Him, and your sins upon Him. Jesus said, "Tetelestai" — "It's paid in full."

Tonight who will come under the blood? Tonight who, believing in Jesus, will take these steps by which the blood of Christ can cleanse him from every sin? Tonight who will come and place his membership with the Church? Tonight who will say thank you to Jesus?

NOTES

1. Ladd, James Earl, *"As Much as In Me Is" and Other Sermons*, Portland, Oregon: Bealthe & Co., 1951.

13

"Seven Detours on the Road That Leads to Hell"

A. B. McREYNOLDS[1]

Text: Matthew 7:13, 14

There are only two roads in this world upon which people may travel: one is the straight and narrow trail that leads to the city of gladness and eternal joy, the other is the broad way that leads to destruction. Jesus says we can occupy no neutral ground. "He that is not with me is against me," are his own words. All of you people are traveling upon one of these two highways at this very moment. These two roads run in opposite directions and you cannot travel on both of them at the same time. You are either on the road that leads to the city of God, or you are on the road that leads to eternal destruction.

Are you traveling day by day toward the city of light, or

are you traveling toward the city of darkness? Hell is an awful place! It is a place of haunting memories, remorse and everlasting regrets. It is a place of unutterable shame and sorrow. It is a world without hope. Over a dark prison door someone has written these words: "All who enter here leave hope behind." These same words can be written in letters of blazing fire over the gates of hell.

Before we go any further let me impress upon your minds this fact: God did not make hell for you. God made hell for the devil and his angels. Jesus says very plainly in Matthew 25:41, "Depart from me, ye cursed, into everlasting fire, prepared for the devil and his angels." God did not make hell for you. God did not have you in mind when he made hell. Hell was created for the disobedient angels who were not satisfied in heaven, and if you insist on breaking into a place which was not made for you, you cannot blame God.

God plainly says in II Peter 3:9, "The Lord is not slack concerning his promise, as some men count slackness; but is longsuffering to us-ward, NOT WILLING THAT ANY SHOULD PERISH, but that all should come to repentance." "For God so loved the world that he gave his only begotten Son, that whosoever believeth on him should not perish, but have everlasting life," and "Him that cometh unto me I will no wise cast out," are the Master's own words.

God has done all within his power to keep you from plunging headlong down the trail that leads to eternal destruction. Some folk say that God could not be a kind and merciful heavenly Father and permit his children to be lost. In this message tonight I think you will discover that God has done all within his power to prevent us from deliberately and willfully going on and on down this broad highway that leads to destruction. God does not wish us to be lost. He desires that we repent and accept salvation.

If you go to hell you will go with the heavenly Father and Jesus Christ, the crucified Savior, standing there beside the highway pleading with you to turn round about and accept salvation. Heaven is a prepared place for prepared people, and if you refuse to repent and if you refuse to become a citizen of Christ's kingdom, you have no one to blame but yourself.

Some people say that the Christian life is hard. It is not hard. Christ's yoke is easy and his burden is light (Matt. 11:30). It is the way of the transgressor that is hard (Prov. 13:15). The broad way that leads to destruction is the hard way.

I want you tonight to see these two highways leading through the world, running in opposite directions. There is the straight way with the narrow gate that leads to eternal life and few there be that find it. There is the broad way with the wide gate that leads to destruction, and many are they that enter therein. I wish you could see that great vast throng, that great multitude of men and women who are hurrying on and on down this broad trail that leads to eternal destruction.

I want to take time to call your attention to a very important fact concerning this broad way. This road is wide enough for all kinds of people. Thieves, murderers, liars, adulterers, and folk who are living vile, wicked lives are not the only ones who are traveling down this broad trail. You have seen highways, with a white mark running along the center, dividing the traffic into two groups, the slow traffic and the fast traffic. Down this broad trail that leads to hell there is a line which divides these travelers into two classes. On one side of this line are the malicious, unrighteous, vile characters we have already referred to, but on the other side of the line are people whose lives are above reproach, good fathers, good husbands, good citizens, men and women who are living lives as pure and commendable as those who travel the straight way that leads to the city of God. What is wrong with these people? What is it that they are doing that is sending their souls to hell? They are not doing anything. Some day when you and I stand before the judgment bar of God, we will learn that people are going to hell by trainloads, not because of things that they are doing, but because of the things that they are not doing. It is my firm conviction that for every man or woman who is lost because of sins of commission there will be a hundred lost because of sins of omission. You are going to hell, my friend, because of what you are not doing. Read the twenty-fifth chapter of Matthew carefully, and see what the Great Judge says about it.

These people on the broad way who are going to hell by the thousands in spite of their clean, moral lives, have never accepted Jesus Christ as their personal Savior. They have never repented of their sins, and Jesus says that unless you repent you shall all perish. Anybody knows that without repentance there can be no forgiveness of sins. Those people have never confessed Jesus Christ before men, they have never been baptized, sprinkled or anything else. They are going through this world without God and without Christ. They are members of nobody's church. They don't even claim to be Christians. So when they die, their bodies are placed in Christless caskets, they are lowered into Christless graves, and their souls go out yonder into a dark and Christless eternity without God and without hope.

These people on the broad trail that leads to destruction need to turn around and go the other way. "Repent ye therefore, and turn again (turn around), that your sins may be blotted out" (Acts 3:19). They need to turn around. They are on the wrong trail, they are going in the wrong direction.

Let us consider tonight a few of the detours that God has placed across the broad trail that leads to hell. As we travel down our splendid highways we often come to a detour sign placed across the road which makes it impossible for us to proceed any farther on our journey. Our heavenly Father has placed across this broad way many of these detours, but we shall take time to consider but a few of them.

The first thing that God has placed across this broad trail as an obstruction to head off people and turn them around is the Bible. It is the only book in the world that reveals God's love, that tells us about a life beyond the grave, that tells us how we may reach the city of eternal joy. It is a book that warns us against sin and reveals to us the consequences of sin. It is filled with beautiful pictures of heaven, and with awful pictures of hell. No man can go very far down the trail that leads to hell without meeting the Bible, and if he plunges on and on, he goes into perdition in spite of the efforts God has made through his Holy Word to turn him back. A single verse in God's Holy Book has turned back thousands, yes hundreds of thousands. John 6:37, "Him that cometh to me I will in no wise cast out," is one of these verses. Amos 4:12, "Prepare to meet thy God," is another. Romans 6:23 and John 3:16 are others. We shall never know until Judgment Day how many men have been turned back by a single verse in God's Holy Word.

I was called out to the county poor farm near Athens, Texas, one afternoon to see an old man who was dying. He told me the doctors said that he had but a few hours to live. "Brother Mac, I want to tell you the story of my life," he said. He then told me how he had been guilty of almost every sin in the catalogue of crime. He had come to Texas from a northern state where he had even been guilty of murder. He had forsaken his wife and six children, and told me that it was booze that had wrecked his life. After telling me the story, how he had been guilty of murder, he said, "Brother Mac, when my light goes out and my soul goes out yonder into the darkness of eternity, there will not be much hope for me, will there?"

All I could do was read to this dying man these words found in John 6:37, "Him that cometh to me I will in no wise cast out." I read them to him again and again. "That can't include me," he answered. But I continued to read this verse to him, and it seemed to relieve his mind. I was compelled to leave him and return to the city, but the next day the superintendent of the poor farm told me that the old man died muttering these words, "Him that cometh to me I will in no wise cast out."

At the conclusion of a sermon, in a revival in a large city, a prominent business man came forward to accept Jesus Christ as his personal Savior. It created quite a sensation, and the next day the evangelist visited this man's office and said to him, "I am so proud that you took the step that you did last night, and I am anxious for you to tell me what it was in the sermon that caused you to make the decision." The business man answered, "My dear sir, do not be offended when I tell you that I do not remember a thing you said in your sermon last night. All during your message I was thinking about something else; I was thinking about a text I heard thirty-five years ago. That text was this: 'If a righteous man is scarcely saved, where shall the sinner and the ungodly appear?' I had been thinking for many years about that verse, if a righteous man who has lived for God throughout his entire life, has been faithful and true, a loyal and profitable servant of the Master, if he is scarcely saved, what is going to become of the man who doesn't even claim to be a Christian? Those words have been ringing in my ears for several years, so I must say to you in all frankness that it was this one verse from the Word of God that caused me to take that step last night."

I wish I had the time to tell you how a soldier boy, dying in a shell hole in France, was converted by reading a portion of the twenty-seventh chapter of Matthew. When he was carried to the hospital that night a Red Cross nurse asked him if she could do anything to ease his pain. He asked her to read the twenty-seventh chapter of Matthew, from his khaki-covered Testament. As this Red Cross girl — God bless the Red Cross nurses — read to this soldier boy the twenty-seventh chapter of Matthew, she began to choke until she could not finish the chapter. Falling on her knees beside the army cot she, too, gave her heart to Jesus Christ. What did it? One chapter of God's Holy Word.

You can't go very far down the trail that leads to hell without coming face to face with God's book, placed there to head you off and turn you around in the right direction.

A Christian mother's teachings and a mother's prayers is another detour which God uses to head men and women off as they go plunging toward destruction. There are not fifteen people in this audience tonight who were not, very probably, brought to Jesus Christ through a Christian mother's influence. In the few years I have spent in the evangelistic field, I have seen hundreds who have been won to Jesus Christ by a Christian mother's prayers.

In the first meeting I ever held a great big man, whose wife and child were sincere Christians, was spending his time and his money in a frivolous manner. His wife and child tried so hard to persuade him to become a Christian; in fact, everybody was interested in him and when the last night of the meeting came it was a beautiful sight to see him come forward on the last invitation. I shall never forget the expression upon his face, and the tears rolling down his cheeks, as he said, "Brother Mac, won't my mother be happy when I write and tell her what I have done?" That old boy became a Christian at last because of a mother's prayers.

Years passed before I was permitted to visit this little town again. But when I drove into town and inquired for my friend, I found that he had moved out of the little shack in which they used to live over into the better residence district. The husband was not home but the wife said to me, "Brother McReynolds, I shall never forget you, I often speak of you and tell folks that if it hadn't been for Brother McReynolds we would not be so happy today. Just think of it, we own our home now. B. owns his own truck, and he is a deacon in the church. He even prays. I tell you life sure means more to us now, since he has become a Christian, and I tell folks every week that Brother McReynolds is the one who did it all." But she was mistaken in giving me the credit, for back of it all was a Christian mother and her prayers.

I could stand in this pulpit tonight and tell you of instance after instance where a mother's prayers turned the boy around in the right direction. It was in Hill County, Texas, that a young man was leaving home to go up North. After packing his suitcase, his old mother with a trembling hand, wrote on the inside of the lid these words. "My boy, wherever you go, remember that I am praying for you." That boy, like many boys, had been born in a Christian home, rocked to sleep in a Christian mother's arms, and taught to pray at a Christian mother's knee. That same prayer that your mother taught you and my mother taught me:

> "Now I lay me down to sleep,
> I pray thee, Lord, my soul to keep.
> If I should die before I wake,
> I pray thee, Lord, my soul to take."

This young man did not open his suitcase for several days. When he did he saw these words written on the lid: "My boy, wherever you go, remember that I am praying for you." It made him very angry, and with his own pencil he wrote beneath his mother's message these words: "May God damn your prayers."

Several years passed and that young man was living in Oklahoma City. He married a Christian girl but even her efforts to get him to go to church were in vain. One evening he sat on his front porch looking toward a little tent which had been erected across the street. In this tent a revival service was being conducted. In the quiet evening the words of the evangelist carried across the street and seemed to pierce his very soul. Under the spell of the sermon he got up off the porch, walked across the street and stood by the tent pole outside listening. Although he had on his working clothes when the invitation hymn was sung, this young man went inside the tabernacle, walked forward and took his stand for Jesus Christ. Today he is a Sunday school teacher in one of the largest churches in Oklahoma City. What did it all? A dear Christian mother back in Hill County, Texas, praying for her boy.

I, myself, am a preacher today because of a mother's prayers. I left my home in Jamestown, Indiana, a boy fifteen years of age, went out West to the Pacific coast never to return. Five years of my life were spent traveling through every state west of the Mississippi River. I worked as a cowboy in the Blue Mountains south of Pendleton, rode the line for the Porter Ranch near Pilot Rock, worked as a harvest hand on the Umatilla Indian Reservation, worked in the logging camps, and hoboed through many states. For five years I went to nobody's church, read nobody's Bible and prayed to nobody's God. I was teaching school in the Willamette Valley south of Portland, Oregon, preparing to enter the University of California to study law. I was boarding with a man and woman who were not even church members, and I was living in a community where there was no church. I was going with a young lady who did not belong to any church. Nobody said anything to me relative to my life plans. I did not hear any heavenly voices and I did not see any heavenly vision.

No angel came down in the middle of the night to almost choke me to death trying to convince me that I ought to be a preacher. Without any of these influences I suddenly changed my life plans. I decided that instead of studying law I would go to a Bible college, study that instead of studying law, and prepare myself to be a preacher.

My mother was at that time living in Oregon City and I went home each Friday night to spend the week-end with her. After making this change in my plans I wondered what my mother would say when she learned that instead of being a lawyer, as I had always planned to be, I was going to be a preacher. When I arrived home late Friday night, I did not tell her of my plans. I did not tell her the next morning before breakfast, because she was not strong and I knew it would be a shock to her. After breakfast as she sat in a little sewing chair crocheting or tatting, I do not remember which, I said to her, "Mom, I am not going to be a lawyer." "What are you going to be?" she asked. I expected to see her faint as I answered, "Mother, I am going to be a preacher." Instead of looking surprised she did not even miss a stitch as she answered, "My boy, I have always prayed that you might be a preacher."

While I was out there working in the harvest fields my mother was back in Indiana praying that I might be a preacher. Night after night as I slept in a box car or on a pile of ties beside the railroad track, my mother was praying that I might be a preacher. I had not been to church in five years, but my mother was still praying that I might be a preacher.

Across the trail that leads to hell, God has placed many detours, but one of the strongest walls that he has erected between the sinner and hell is a Christian mother's love and a Christian mother's prayers.

God has also placed across this trail another great influence which has turned back thousands — the sermons that we hear. They do not always seem to bring about the desired reaction in the lives of people, but nevertheless the sermons that have been preached through the ages have been instrumental in turning millions back from the inevitable fate waiting for those who continue down a broad way. In our evangelistic meetings sometimes we see hundreds accept Christ, sometimes fifty or sixty, sometimes only a few, but does this mean that the only results obtained by these sermons are the conversions we see each night? I have seen tabernacles filled with hundreds of people, people of every type, class, and character. I remember one meeting in which there were cowboys from the ranches, lumberjacks from the mountains, Indians from the reservation, gamblers, bootleggers, girls from the streets, girls from the dance hall, people from every walk of life, jammed in the tabernacle. Night after night scores came forward to confess their sins and accept Jesus Christ as their personal Savior. But night after night hundreds left the tabernacle without giving any evidence whatever of the sermon having made any impression upon their hearts, but I know by the lives of many of them afterward that they were deeply impressed, and that the sermons they heard had brought about great changes in their lives.

One day in Jerusalem, Saul of Tarsus, then a young man, heard a sermon preached by Stephen. It is true that this sermon apparently had no effect upon the young Jew, but we know that it was only a matter of months until this same Saul enlisted as a soldier for Jesus Christ.

Who can say that the sermon preached by Stephen, with his dying breath, did not serve as one of the obstructions placed across the broad trail that helped to turn Saul of Tarsus around?

Then when I think of the influences that God uses to keep men and women from going on and on to ruination, I think of the Sunday school teachers. I am thinking of Mrs. Houk, a beautiful lady, now living in Nashville, Tennessee, who taught our class of boys in Jamestown, Indiana. I am thinking also of old Brother Emmert, now gone to his reward, both of them Sunday school teachers who had a real influence in turning me around in the right direction, when I, a reckless lad, was hurrying down the broad trail that leads to destruction. Thank God for the Sunday school teachers who have been instrumental in saving boys and girls. You Sunday school teachers will never know until Judgment Day how many children have been saved from hell through your efforts.

As I think of the Sunday school teachers I want to take time to mention the ladies who give their time so faithfully to the Junior Endeavor Societies. I remember how as a little boy I used to ride my bicycle two miles each Sunday to the Junior Christian Endeavor Society. The dear old lady who worked so faithfully with our little crowd of mischievous children did not realize then that she had a golden chain fastened about our hearts which helped to hold us back as we were attempting to go plunging down the broad trail that leads to hell.

God pity the Sunday school teacher or Junior Endeavor superintendent who says to the little boy who is asking for information in regard to the Christian life, "You will have to ask the minister." Any Sunday school teacher or

271

Endeavor superintendent who cannot show the boys and girls the way to heaven has no right to hold such a responsible position.

The Sunday school teachers have responsibilities equally as great as their privileges. The members of their classes look to them as the leaders and patterns for their lives. What a shame that in our Sunday schools we find young ladies, young men, fathers and mothers, as teachers whose lives are a disgrace to the name Christian. No man or woman will ever teach a Sunday school class in a church where I am pastor, unless they are at least striving to live a Christian life. No boozer, gambler or dancer can ever hold any official position in my church. Neither will I permit anyone to teach in my Sunday school who does not remain for the church services each Lord's Day. We need preachers in America who have enough cement in their backbones and enough sand in their craws to demand a Christian life of the teachers in Sunday schools.

There are many other detours which the Lord God has placed across the broad trail that leads to hell, but I am going to mention but two others. I want to pause for a moment to pay tribute to the one person who has a greater influence upon a man's life than anyone else. There is no influence in the world that can contribute as much to the character of a man, that can contribute as much toward keeping him on the trail that leads to the city of God, as the guiding hand of a Christian wife. A woman can lead a man to heaven or drive him to hell. "You made me what I am today," is a statement that most husbands can truthfully make to their wives. Back of almost every successful man you will find a successful wife. I am not forgetting a Christian mother's influence when I say that the wrong kind of a wife can tear down and undo in a man's life, in twenty months' time, the things that a good mother has been trying to build during the past twenty years. No influence in the world can contribute as much toward keeping a man on the straight and narrow trail that leads to the city of God as the guiding hand of a Christian wife.

Last of all, let us consider the greatest influence of all. Across the trail that leads to hell, God has placed many detours. There is the Bible, the Christian mother's prayers and influence, the sermons we hear, the Sunday school teachers, Christian friends, Christian wives and many other walls erected by God to head men and women off as they go plunging to damnation, but the greatest influence of all is the one that I am going to mention at this time. If you can pass this obstruction, then you are indeed hopeless. I am referring to the old rugged cross. There by the side of the highway that leads to hell the cross is planted, and hanging upon it with blood trickling down his face, Jesus Christ the Savior, with pity in his eyes, is pleading with you to turn around and go the other way. You may pass all of these other obstructions, and there is still hope, but if you pass by the crucified Savior as he hangs upon the cross, then you are gone. "The preaching of the Cross is to those who are perishing foolishness, but to those who are being saved, it is the power of God."

The road that leads to hell is a broad way, it is a steep way, and the farther you proceed the greater becomes the momentum, and the harder it is for you to turn around. So tonight I plead with you in the name of God, if you ever intend to turn around and start in the right direction, do so at once. Do not put it off until tomorrow, until next week, or next year. You have put it off too long already. Do you know that only one man out of a hundred accepts Jesus Christ after reaching the age of twenty, only one out of a thousand after reaching the age of thirty? Thousands of people have taken me by the hand as they come forward in my meetings to accept Jesus Christ, but only a few of these have been past the age of fifty.

The road that leads to heaven is a long, old trail, and if you ever expect to get there, you are going to have to start pretty soon. As we close tonight, I am pleading with you. If you have been on the wrong trail, my friend, turn around and take your stand for Jesus Christ, right about face, and let us sing together:

> "I am bound for the Promised Land,
> I am bound for the Promised Land,
> Oh, who will come and go with me?
> I am bound for the Promised Land."

NOTES

1. McReynolds, A.B., *Soul-Winning and Stewardship Sermons.* 2nd edition, St Louis: CB of Publishing, 1931.

EVANGELISTIC SERMONS
FROM THE PRESENT

Introduction to Part Three

Certain aspects of evangelistic preaching change. This truth is illustrated well by the sermons that are included in the following section of this volume. Here are six sermons by six different contemporary preachers. All are different in both content and style, yet all lift up the basic evangel, the Gospel.

Interestingly (yet typical of evangelistic preaching of today), only one of these preachers is in general evangelism. The others come from a variety of backgrounds, but their major contributions have been in local churches or as teachers of preachers in college or seminary. Some, like Harvey Bream, Olin W. Hay and Alger Fitch, have combined both. Yet, these six men have held hundreds of evangelistic meetings among them. Some of them have meetings scheduled three to four years in advance.

One is also struck by the relative brevity of these sermons. Again, this reflects the present age and the generally accepted pattern of evangelistic preaching. Sermons are shorter and subjects are not so broadly thematic. Sermons are generally textual or topical. Illustrations are profuse but often brief (as over against the involved illustrative stories of a past age).

Other preachers and other sermons could have been included. No value judgement is being made by the particular selection of these six men. However, the editors are aware of the dearth of published sermons, evangelistic as well as other types, among those within the Restoration Movement of the twentieth century. Perhaps this volume will stimulate greater production from those who are committed to the Ancient Gospel as well as the Ancient Order.

14

"Three Appointments With God"

O. GEORGE STANSBERRY

"But I don't believe in a life after death," he said. "Why should I prepare for a life in which I do not believe?" He was the manager of a local soft drink company in Michigan City, Indiana.

As I sat in his home that afternoon I thought of an old illustration that I heard years ago. "Suppose you are right," I said. "Death ends it all. There is no heaven, no hell, and no day of judgment. I live for Christ and you do not live for Christ. What will I have lost?"

He replied, "You will not have lost anything but neither will I have lost anything."

"But let us suppose that the Bible is correct and that there is an eternity where there will be a day of judgment and both a heaven and a hell. I live for Christ and you do not live for Him. In that case what will I have lost?"

"In that case you will not have lost anything either," he replied.

"And you, sir?" I asked.

He said, "I think I see what you are saying. Either way it goes you will not be a loser but if I'm wrong I will lose."

If there were nothing more than the mere mathematical possibility that there is an eternity like the Bible describes why wouldn't a man be willing to make preparation for it?

In Hebrews 9:27, 28 the writer mentions three appointments that we may have with God. The first two are mandatory and the third one involves a choice. "It is appointed unto men once to die, and after this the judgment: so Christ was once offered to bear the sins of many; and unto them that look for him shall he appear the second time without sin unto salvation."

The first appointment with God is at the time of our death. But we do not need the Bible to inform us that we shall die. Every time we have passed a cemetery, attended a funeral service, looked at a tombstone, read an obituary in a newspaper, noticed a funeral home, or passed a hearse we have realized that death is a reality.

To show that you believe in death let me ask you this question. How many of you in this audience, by the raising of your hand will indicate that you have some form of life insurance? Thank you, Now, quickly take your hand down before some insurance man noticed who did not raise his hand.

Thomas Edison is known as the world's greatest inventive genius. Yet he was unable to perfect an invention that could save him from the hour of his own death. Today there is a grave for Thomas Edison.

Albert Einstein is known as the world's greatest mathe-matician. It is said that only thirteen men could understand his theory of relativity. Yet Einstein was never able to for-mulate a theory by which he could escape the moment of death. Today there is a grave for Albert Einstein.

Alexander the Great is known as the world's greatest military genius. He cried at the age of thirty because he said, "I have no more worlds to conquer." Yet Alexander was never able to amass an army great enough to save him from death. Today there is a grave for Alexander the Great.

John D. Rockefeller is known as the world's greatest financial genius. He gave away most of his fortune before he died. In the last five years of his life he took a few hun-dred thousand dollars and turned them into more than five million dollars. The man was a financial genius. But he was unable to amass a fortune large enough by which he could buy his way from the hour of death. Today there is a grave for John D. Rockefeller.

Houdini is known as the world's greatest escape artist. He would be handcuffed, placed into a sealed wooden box and thrown into a body of water. Within two minutes he would emerge a free man. But Houdini was not able to escape the bonds of death and he died.

Here are five of the greatest men who have ever lived on this earth. If they could not escape death do you think that you shall?

The Bible informs us why we must die. I have often heard people say, "Oh, we don't understand it now but someday we shall." There should be no mystery about the ultimate cause of death. "Wherefore as by one man sin entered into the world, and death by sin; so death passed upon all men, for that all have sinned" (Rom. 5:12).

Because Adam sinned, physical death has passed upon all men. We die today because of this sin. One may die as an infant, in the prime of life, or in old age. But whenever death occurs it has come as a result of the sin of Adam.

Sometimes we are prone to blame God for the death of a loved one. But God did not bring death into the world. If you want to place the blame somewhere, place it at the feet of Satan. He brought sin and death to the human race.

God is the giver of life. The recipient of the gift has no right to make demands upon the Giver. Whether we have life for one hour, one day, or one hundred years we shall still say, "Thank you, God, for giving me life in this body."

It isn't enough to merely recognize that we are going to die. The great question is what will happen to us after we die.

I like the old story of the man walking through the cemetery reading the epitaphs on the tombstones. He came across one that said,

> Remember friend, when passing by
> As you are now, so once was I.
> As I am now soon you will be.
> Prepare for death and follow me.

But the town joker came by and scribbled two additional lines in chalk:

> To follow you I'm not content,
> Until I know which way you went.

Though the Christian knows that heaven lies beyond

the door of death, he should never treat death as a friend. Death is not a friend. It is an enemy. The apostle Paul says in I Cor. 15:26, "The last enemy that shall be destroyed is death."

On certain occasions I have heard I Cor. 15:55 quoted as though it were already a reality for the Christian. "O death, where is thy sting? O grave, where is thy victory?" But this verse has not yet been fulfilled for us.

Look at verse 54 which precedes it. "So when this corruptible shall have put on incorruption, and this mortal shall have put on immortality, then shall be brought to pass the saying that is written, Death is swallowed up in victory. O Death, where is thy sting? O grave, where is thy victory?"

Paul is saying that it is in the future, at the second coming of the Lord Jesus, that death will be destroyed. Verse 55 is true only of the Lord Jesus since he overcame death and was raised from the dead never to die again. Otherwise, your body would never be placed into a grave and there would be no tears, heartache and heartbreak or separation of loved ones.

But the day is coming when all of this shall be changed. Satan shall be defeated. Death will be destroyed. The graves shall give up their dead. Christians shall receive the new body of perfection that shall be fashioned like the glorified body of the Lord Jesus.

However, the Christian does not fear the enemy of death. He knows the One who holds the future in His hands. The Bible has clearly revealed what will happen to the Christian when he dies. There is no clearer teaching in all of the Bible regarding the destiny of the Christian than II Cor. 5:8. "We are confident, I say, and willing rather to be absent from the body, and to be present with the Lord."

"I am torn between the two: I desire to depart and be with Christ, which is better by far" (Phil. 1:23 NIV). So the Christian goes to heaven immediately upon his death.

We often speak of a loved one having "departed." Some of the African Christians use the term, "arrived." I like that. The Christian does more than merely depart this life. He has a destination. That destination is heaven. He has finally "arrived" at his goal.

But if we face God in death without a Savior then Jesus says, "Fear not them which kill the body, but are not able to kill the soul: but rather fear him which is able to destroy both soul and body in hell" (Matt. 10:28).

Again Jesus told of the rich man who had excluded God from his life. "The rich man also died, and was buried; and in hell he lift up his eyes, being in torments ...and he cried...send Lazarus, that he may dip the tip of his finger in water, and cool my tongue; for I am tormented in this flame" (Luke 16:22-24).

She was the frail wife of a prominent physician in their town. Many had said that if her physician-husband preceded her in death that she would not be able to stand the shock. But they didn't know the faith of that little child of God. He did precede her in death. She took the sign from her husband's office and put it on her front door. It said, "Gone out. Back soon." Yes, gone out of this body and life for a little while, but back soon in the return of Jesus to receive a new body.

The second appointment with God is at judgment. "But after this the judgment" (Heb. 9:27). Again, you have no choice about this appointment as it also is mandatory.

Judgment is a forgotten subject from many of the pulpits across the world. Bishop Chelmford, of the church of England, has said, "The Christian Faith seems to be dying out. In the days of our grandparents there was a gravity, a solemnity about religion which has completely vanished.... God has become a tolerant, easy-going deity who is certainly not 'extreme to mark what is amiss' but can always be relied upon to let everybody off in the long run, and if there is a heaven — of course there is no truth whatever in hell — we shall all muddle into it somewhere."

Judgment is a recurring theme throughout the Bible. "We shall all stand before the judgment seat of Christ" (Rom. 14:10). "...who shall judge the quick and the dead at his appearing..." (II Tim. 4:1). "He hath appointed a day in the which he will judge the world in righteousness by that man whom he hath ordained..." (Acts 17:31). "And I saw the dead, small and great, stand before God; and the books were opened: and another book was opened which is the book of life: and the dead were judged out of those things which were written in the books, according to their works " (Rev. 20:12).

There are three reasons why, out of a moral necessity, the God of this universe must have a coming day of judgment.

First, there are individuals who walk the streets of this land who should be behind prison bars. Some are free because of a legal technicality. They have actually committed the crime, not only against the state and fellow human beings, but against God. But they cannot be convicted and punished here. Who will judge these sinners? God will.

Others are free because the "long arm of the law" will never know who they are or where they are hiding. You have heard the old adage, "The perfect crime has never been committed." Humanly speaking this is not true. There are many crimes that have been committed for which there will never be found a human solution. But that proverb is true if you believe in a coming judgment.

Secondly, some have been falsely imprisoned for crimes they did not commit. A man in Michigan spent several years in prison for a murder he did not commit. Another man confessed to the murder as he was dying. Who is going to straighten out a mess like this? God will in the coming day of judgment. This does not mean that our system of justice is wrong. It only points out that it is administered by fallible, human beings who can err in their judgments. God cannot and will not make any errors of judgment in that hour.

Thirdly, God has some laws for which there can be found no counterpart in human law. Jesus said, "But I say unto you, That whosoever looketh on a woman to lust after her hath committed adultery with her already in his heart" (Matt. 5:28). Who is going to judge this broken law of God? There is no court in these United States that can convict a man of lust. But God will.

The apostle John says, "Whosoever hateth his brother is a murderer" (I John 3:15). Do you know of a court that will convict a man for hating his brother? There is none. But God will.

The fate of the sinner who dies without Christ is foretold by Jesus himself in Matthew 25:41. "Then shall he say also unto them on the left hand, Depart from me, ye cursed, into everlasting fire, prepared for the devil and his angels."

But the Christian will have no fear of the day of judgment because he is in Christ Jesus. "Herein is our love made perfect, that we may have boldness in the day of judgment....There is no fear in love; but perfect love casteth out fear" (I John 4:17,18).

The Christian will not stand in judgment to give an accounting for his sins. He does not have any sins at that moment. They have all been forgiven through Christ. "The blood of Jesus Christ, his son, cleanseth us from all sin" (I John 1:7).

The word that is translated "condemnation" in your Bible is the same word for judgment. Thus in Romans 8:1 we read, "There is therefore now no condemnation (judgment) to them which are in Christ Jesus." You can substitute the word "judgment" for the word "condemnation."

Jesus said, "He that heareth my word, and believeth on him that sent me, hath everlasting life, and shall not come into condemnation (judgment); but is passed from death unto life" (John 5:24).

The sinner will stand in judgment for condemnation. The Christian will stand in judgment for commendation. "Well done, thou good and faithful servant." This will not be said because of any inherent goodness on the part of the Christian but because he has been "made the righteousness of God" in Christ (II Cor. 5:21).

> When the great plants of our cities
>   Have turned out their last finished work,
> When our merchants have sold their last yard of silk
>   And dismissed the last tired clerk,
> When our banks have raked in their last dollar
>   And paid out their last dividend,
> When the Judge of the earth says, "Closed for the night,"
>   And asks for a balance — WHAT THEN?

When the choir has sung its last anthem
   And the preacher has prayed his last prayer,
When the people have heard their last sermon
   And the sound has died out on the air,
When the Bible lies closed on the pulpit
   And the pews are empty of men,
When each one stands facing his record
   And the Great Book is opened — WHAT THEN?

When the actors have played their last drama
   And the comedian has made his last fun,
When the film has flashed its last picture
   And the billboard has displayed its last run,
When the crowds seeking pleasure have vanished
   And gone out into darkness again,
When the trumpet of ages is sounded
   And we stand up before Him — WHAT THEN?

When the bugle's call sinks into silence
   And the long marching columns stand still,
When the captain repeats his last orders
   And they've captured the last fort and hill,
When the flag has been hauled from the masthead
   And the wounded afield checked in,
And a world that rejected its Savior
   Is asked for a reason — what THEN?

The third appointment with God is found in Hebrews 9:28. "So Christ was once offered to bear the sins of many...." You have the choice, the privilege of meeting God at Calvary.

Between us and God there stood the barrier, the burden, the mountain, the river, the swollen ocean of our sins. But by His death on the cross, Jesus removed that barrier, He lifted that burden, He tunneled that mountain, He bridged that river, He split that ocean. In agony, in

288

loneliness, in shame, in travail, in blood, Jesus died for the sins of mankind.

But God demonstrates his love for us in this: "While we were still sinners, Christ died for us" (Rom. 5:8 NIV). "...Christ died for our sins according to the scriptures" (I Cor. 15:3). "In whom we have redemption through his blood, the forgiveness of sins, according to the riches of his grace" (Eph. 1:7).

Never has there been such a love given to those who were so far from loving the Lover. Never has there been such a love that has been expressed in such declaration, deeds and the death of the Lover. Never has there been such a love bestowed upon those who were so degraded by sin and filth. "We love him because he first loved us" (I John 4:19).

Do you want to go to heaven when you die? Most people do. But heaven is a place without sin. You and I have sinned. How can people with sin go to a place that has no sin and stand in the presence of a sinless God? We can't — unless we have a Savior to forgive us of all our sins.

One sin is enough to keep you out of heaven. "Whosoever shall keep the whole law and yet offend in one point, he is guilty of all" (Jas. 2:10). One broken law makes you a lawbreaker. One sin makes you a sinner. I can hear you saying, "Then no one can go to heaven." That is correct — if you are depending upon your own goodness. But if you depend upon Christ who has died for you then heaven can be your final home. Jesus said, "I am the way, the truth, and the life; no man cometh unto the father, but by me" (John 14:6).

What must you do to be saved? In Mark 16:16 Jesus

says, "He that believeth and is baptized shall be saved." In Acts 2:38 several thousand people wanted to know what to do to go to heaven. Peter replied, "Repent and be baptized every one of you in the name of Jesus Christ for the remission (forgiveness) of sins, and ye shall receive the gift of the Holy Spirit." Put these two verses together. A dynamic faith plus a genuine repentance plus your baptism into Christ equals the forgiveness of all your sins. Isn't that wonderful?

Some years ago I was in the home of a young expectant mother in northeastern Ohio. After I pleaded with her to become a Christian she said, "I just can't do it now." "Why?" I asked. "I'll tell you why," she replied. "I'm expecting a child in about three months. I'm being very careful as I have lost two previous children since I was unable to carry them full term. I just know my husband would never approve of my being baptized now. But after my baby is born I would be willing to become a Christian."

I said to her, "God would never ask you to do anything that would harm you or your unborn child. But if you were to die tonight do you believe that you would go to heaven?"

She began to cry. "No, I know I couldn't go to heaven because I'm not a Christian."

That night she came to the evangelistic crusade. When the invitation hymn was sung she walked down the aisle for Christ. With faith and repentance in her heart she was baptized into Christ. All went well.

Three months later her baby was born. The local minister went to visit her in the hospital. Later he told me what she said. "I'm so glad that you came to visit me in my home during the revival and that you urged me to become a Christian. You see, I don't know whether I'm going to live or not. But if I'm not permitted to live I want you to know one thing. I'm not afraid to die because I know I'm a Christian and can go to heaven."

That twenty one year old mother only lived for thirty-six hours and then passed into eternity. But she had met God at the foot of the cross. And when she met God in death there was no fear. And when she shall stand in judgment there will be no fear because she died in Christ.

Have you been intending someday to become a Christian? Then let today be the someday in your life. You do not go to heaven by taking a chance. You go to heaven by making a choice. Make your choice for Christ right now as we sing the invitation hymn.

15

"You Must Be Born Again"

HARVEY C. BREAM, JR.

A birth is a joyous and momentous occasion. None of us are too old but that we cannot fondly recall the birthday parties we used to enjoy with the brilliantly candled cake and ice cream and birthday presents.

As the years pass by with an increasing rapidity, we look with less eager anticipation to each approaching birthday. I understand that the female of the species is particularly vulnerable at this point.

However, I recall the occasion when a grand old lady in our community was celebrating her birthday. Her home was directly across the street from the church building. I left the church office and made my way over to congratulate her. In response to my knock, she opened the door and graciously invited me in. She had me seated in a big old-fashioned rocking chair. As we conversed together, I suddenly broached the question. "Auntie Addie," I asked, "just how old are you today?" And then suddenly I realized that I had been guilty of a terrible breach of etiquette — asking a woman her age. So I immediately began to apologize. She threw up her hands in a gesture of mock horror and said, "Why, brother Bream, don't you even think of apologizing. I would be the one who would have to apologize if I were ashamed to tell you how many wonderful years with which the Lord has blessed me. Today I am 85 years old!"

As I made my way back to my church office, I thought, "What a beautiful outlook on life. Praising God for all the wonderful years He had given her."

But there are those wags who tell us, "Life begins at 40!" I have long since become a disbeliever in that little old cliche. The grand revelation of the Bible is not that life begins at 40, but that life begins in Christ!

And that is what our text is all about. It is a strange scene which we witness. A religious leader of the Jews is coming to Jesus under cover of darkness. There are some commentators who affirm that the reason for this is that, basically, Nicodemus was a coward at heart. He was afraid of being seen by his colleagues in the presence of Jesus.

Others, however, insist that this is not true, for Nicodemus was a sincere inquirer after truth and he was seeking the type of an audience with Jesus which could not possibly be had in the midst of the press of the huge day-time throngs. I am personally inclined to agree with the latter because of what we read later on in the Gospel narratives.

But Nicodemus' statement was accurate as far as he

went. He stated, "Rabbi, we know that thou art a teacher come from God: for no man can do these miracles that thou doest, except God be with him." And that was a true assessment. The miracles that Jesus performed proved that He had God's favor and power.

But Nicodemus had come to learn about the nature of Jesus' kingdom. So Jesus came straight to the point. He said, "Verily, verily, I say unto thee, except a man be born again, he cannot see the kingdom of God."

I can just visualize the expression that must have crossed Nicodemus' face. If Jesus had been talking about Gentiles who had been proselyted to Judaism, perhaps he could have understood why in some fashion they needed to experience a rebirth. But the idea that he, a good Jew, one who had Abraham, Isaac and Jacob as his forefathers — the idea that he needed a rebirth? That was absolutely incomprehensible!

But before we become too critical of Nicodemus, let us note that there are a host of people who stand at a different vantage point than did Nicodemus, who have all the Scriptures and ample examples to show them what Jesus meant when He talked about the necessity of a new birth, but who are nonetheless just as mystified and confused as was Nicodemus.

Our text tonight leads us to two inescapable conclusions. The first, whatever the new birth is, Jesus said that without it no man would get to heaven. This leads us then to the second conclusion: the New Testament teaching on the new birth must be plain. For if without it no man can get to heaven, God would not be a just God nor a loving God if He made it so confusing that a man could not possibly understand or so difficult that no man could possibly comply.

So we ask the first question: "What is the new birth?"

You might respond: "Don't ask me. Here was Nicodemus, a religious leader of the Jews, and he did not even understand what Jesus was talking about."

Why was Nicodemus confused? Because he was thinking in terms of a physical birth. This was evidenced in his response to Jesus when he said: "How in the world can a man when he gets as old as I am be born again? Do you mean that in some mysterious fashion I have to get back inside my mother's womb and go through the process of birth all over again?"

But Jesus was talking about a spiritual birth, which is expressed in His response in these words: "That which is born of the flesh is flesh; and that which is born of the spirit is spirit. Marvel not that I said unto thee, ye must be born again."

There are some who in immediate response to this question would say: "Well, the new birth is some kind of a mysterious, inexplicable inward action; some type of a mysterious spiritual regeneration."

I would be the first to affirm that without some type of an inward action, the new birth would be an impossibility. But this experience which many are quick to equate with the conversion experience, is what the Bible accurately refers to as repentance. It is in repentance that a man experiences the change of mind, the change of heart, and the change of his will. And without this inward action, without repentance, the new birth is impossible.

In His endeavor to clarify this subject to Nicodemus, Jesus cited two elements. However, I hear Jesus quoted in two different ways in John 3:5.

There are those who have Jesus saying: "Verily, verily, I say unto thee, except a man be born of water, he cannot enter into the kingdom of God."

You might respond by saying: "I never heard anyone quote John 3:5 that way." You haven't? You know where I hear it quoted that way most frequently? In churches of Christ or Christian churches.

You might say: "Why I have been a member of the church of Christ all my life and I have never heard anyone quote John 3:5 that way." You haven't? Here is the way I hear it most usually expressed when I visit in many homes and communities where I hold revival meetings. "Why, brother Bream, haven't you heard of old brother so and so? Why, years ago he held a protracted meeting in my home church. There was a great ingathering of souls. We had a great baptismal service. We even had to break the ice to have it. And I tell you I used to win bars every year for perfect Bible school attendance. I used to win white Bibles for bringing the most people to the revivals. I used to sing in the choir. I was a Bible school teacher. I was a deacon. I was an elder." I finally come to the conclusion that this person is nothing but a "usta-wuzzer." He "usta" do this, he "usta" do that, he was this, was that. Somewhere along the line such individuals have been led to believe that just as long as they were baptized at some point in time, that the fact automatically gives them a guaranteed entrance into the pearly gates.

Listen, my friend, nowhere does the Bible teach that baptism alone will save any man. With that concept, it is no wonder that many conclude that we believe in water salvation or baptismal regeneration.

As a reaction to this posture, there are those who then

297

quote John 3:5 thusly: "Verily, verily, I say unto thee, except a man be born of the spirit he cannot enter into the kingdom of God." This is the way you will hear 99 per cent of the media evangelists quoting John 3:5, as I have heard them do it on frequent occasions.

Why is John 3:5 quoted in such a fashion? Because of an instinctive desire to get rid of any water in connection with God's plan of salvation.

There are those who would affirm that when Jesus mentioned water, He was referring to the physical birth. This could not be the case for that had been Nicodemus' misunderstanding and Jesus was now endeavoring to clarify that, and He was citing the things that were prerequisite to entrance into the kingdom of God.

There are others who affirm that Jesus was here speaking figuratively and that He did not mean literal water, but rather He was referring to the Word. They say this because of the Scripture's reference in other places to the role that the Word of God plays in conversion.

And again there are those who affirm that it is figurative and that Jesus really meant spirit, instead of meaning water. They would have our Lord guilty of a gross redundancy by saying that "except a man be born of the spirit and the spirit he could not enter the kingdom of God."

I may not be much of an English scholar or grammarian, but I do know enough English to realize that that three-letter word "and" is a conjunction. And a conjunction always joins together two things of equal importance. And one thing is never figurative and the other literal. Jesus said what He meant, and He meant what He said.

My proposition is this. If we can find out how a person becomes a Christian, if we can find out how one is saved, how one becomes a part of the church, then we will know what Jesus was talking about when He mentioned the necessity of the new birth.

The New Testament will reveal to us that it is not a mysterious event. To illustrate this fact Jesus used the most commonplace illustration known to man — a birth.

We are all aware of how conception takes place — of man's role in the birth process. The thing that we all stand in awe about, including medical science, is the mystery of life. Where does this life come from that animates this little flesh and blood body? Life is of God!

So also it is with the new birth. The New Testament Scriptures do not leave us mystified as to man's role in the process of the new birth. We find a number of examples of this in the book of Acts of the Apostles. The thing that causes us all to stand in awe and marvel is the mystery of the new life that animates this babe in Christ and makes him a new creation! Because life is of God!

In any birth, whether it be physical or spiritual, when man does his part, God does his part.

That leads us to a second question: "How is the new birth accomplished?"

In immediate response to this there are those who assert that the new birth is accomplished by some type of a mysterious, supernatural, inexplicable operation of the Holy Spirit upon the naked soul of a man apart from the Word of God.

In response to this, I ask the question: "Do you affirm that a man can be saved and become a Christian without faith?" "Oh, no," is the answer: "A man must believe because the Hebrew writer says in Hebrews 11:6, 'without faith it is impossible to please God, for he that comes to him must believe that he is, and that he is a rewarder of them that diligently seek after him.'"

I ask another question: "How does faith come?" The apostle Paul answers that in Romans 10:17 when he says: "Now faith cometh of hearing, and hearing of the Word of God."

Also, the apostle Peter affirms the role of the Word of God in conversion when he states in I Peter 1:23: "Being born again, not of corruptible seed, but of incorruptible, by the Word of God, which liveth and abideth forever."

We read almost the same thing in James 1:18: "Of his own will begat he us with the Word of truth, that we should be a kind of first fruits of his creatures."

To affirm that a man is born again, is saved, becomes a Christian by some alleged working of the Holy Spirit apart from the Word of God, would make God guilty of gross discrimination. It would make Him a respecter of persons.

To illustrate — if at the conclusion of this service I was to extend what in some circles is called "an altar call," and would urge you to come forward and kneel and to pray for this experience, and I should kneel by you and pray with you for the same thing and indicate my willingness to stay with you until the midnight hour until you would experience it, and while we were doing that, your neighbor should step out from his pew and come down and kneel beside you and pray just as earnestly and tearfully for the same thing, and suddenly you would get it and he would not get it, that would make God guilty of gross discrimination. Because, you see, Holy Spirit baptism was a promise and not a command. Jesus has promised His disciples in John 14:26: "But the Comforter, which is the Holy Spirit, whom the Father will send in my name, he shall teach you all things, and bring all things to your remembrance, whatsoever I have said unto you." In the same conversation He said in John 16:13: "Howbeit when He, the Spirit of truth, is come, He will guide you unto all truth: where he shall not speak of himself; but whatsoever he shall hear, that shall he speak: and he will show you things to come."

And just ten days before Pentecost when Jesus was with His disciples we read in Acts 1:4: "And, being assembled together with them, commanded them that they should not depart from Jerusalem, but wait for the promise of the Father, which saith he, ye have heard of me. For John truly baptized with water; but ye shall be baptized with the Holy Spirit not many days hence."

Ten days later when the disciples were together in the upper room and the day of Pentecost dawned, the promise was fulfilled when "suddenly there came a sound from heaven as of a rushing mighty wind, and it filled all the house where they were sitting. And there appeared unto them cloven tongues like as of fire, and it sat upon each of them. They were all filled with the Holy Spirit, and began to speak with other tongues, as the Spirit gave them utterance."

When accused of being drunk by some mockers in the audience, Peter cited Old Testament Scripture when he said: "But this is that which was spoken by the prophet Joel: and it shall come to pass in the last days, saith God, I will pour forth of my Spirit upon all flesh...."

He affirmed this again later on in His sermon in Acts 2:33 when He said: "Therefore being by the right hand of God exalted, and having received of the Father the promise of the Holy Spirit, He hath poured forth this, which you now see and hear."

Since the baptism of the Holy Spirit was a promise and not a command, and if the new birth were this experience, then you and I would be alleviated of any moral responsibility with regard to our salvation, and God would be responsible for whether or not you and I were saved or lost, or went to heaven or went to hell. Because nothing that you and I could do could affect such a determination. You cannot obey a promise, you can only wait for it. So if God would give it to one and not another, He would discriminate and be a respecter of persons.

So we come back to my original proposition. If we can find out from the New Testament Scriptures, from the Word of God, how man is saved, becomes a Christian and a part of the Lord's church, then we will know what it is to be born again.

There is only one intellectually honest way we can affirm this, and that is by turning back to the infallible and inspired record, the New Testament Scriptures.

The first such instance of persons becoming Christians is found in the second chapter of the book of Acts. The Holy Spirit came upon the apostles in fulfillment of Jesus' promise. The apostle Peter stood up and preached the Word. This is that "incorruptible seed, the Word of God, which liveth and abideth forever," that Word of truth whereby we are to be begotten again so that we might be a kind of first fruits of His creatures.

As Peter preached, and with irresistible logic and irrefutable evidence proved the deity of Jesus Christ, he summed it all up by saying in Acts 2:36: "Therefore let all the house of Israel know assuredly, that God hath made that same Jesus, whom ye have crucified, both Lord and Christ.

Being conscience-smitten, the multitudes cried out and said: "Men and brethren, what shall we do?"

And what did the Holy Spirit lead Peter to say? What was the response of this Word of truth that they had heard proclaimed and by which they were to be begotten again? Listen to Acts 2:38: "Then Peter said unto them: "repent (that change of a man's mind, heart, and will — that prerequisite to the new birth) and be baptized every one of you in the name of Jesus Christ for the remission of sins, and you shall receive the gift of the Holy Spirit." Born of the water and the Spirit!

And what was the audience's response? Acts 2:41: "Then they that gladly received His word were baptized: and the same day there were added unto them about 3000 souls."

And this thrilling Pentecostal record concludes on this note in Acts 2:47: "Praising God, and having favor with all the people. And the Lord added to the church daily such as should be saved."

So the new birth is simply obedience to the Word of truth in faith. That which saves a man, grants him remission of sins and the gift of the Holy Spirit and makes him a part of the Lord's church, is the very same thing which enables him to experience the new birth and to become a child of God, a part of His family.

It is a physiological fact that that which gives birth must be larger than the object to which birth is given. The parent body, of necessity, must be larger than its offspring. There is only one thing in the Christian religion which makes this possible — that is baptism into Christ. That is why in the eighth chapter of Acts you have the Ethiopian eunuch, after the confession of his faith in Jesus

Christ as the Son of God, going with Philip, the evangelist, down into the water, being baptized, and coming up out of the water.

That is why the apostle Paul so beautifully describes it in Romans 6:3 and 4: "Know ye not, that so many of us as were baptized into Jesus Christ were baptized into his death? Therefore we are buried with him by baptism into death: that like as Christ was raised up from the dead by the glory of the Father, even so we also should walk in newness of life. For as we have been planted or united together in the likeness of his death we shall be also in the likeness of his resurrection."

But we now come to the most beautiful part of the new birth by asking the question, "What does it do?"

This is the question that is asked by the good moral man. He asks: "What is baptism going to do for me? I am a good man, I don't drink smoke, or curse. I am not an adulterer. I don't lie, cheat, or steal. I pay all my debts. What is baptism going to do for me?"

And herein does he err as do many people in our churches. Nowhere does the Bible teach that baptism has as its purpose the changing of a bad man into a good man. This is accomplished in repentance. It is in repentance that a man changes. He changes his intellect. He changes his affections. He changes his will, and having repented, he is then baptized. Why? To bring him into a change of state.

Those of you who are married can recall some years ago when you stood beside that sweet, pretty, young thing, and exchanged your vows. And then you heard it said: "I now pronounce you husband and wife."

You may have even pinched yourself to see if it was

true. But I tell you a mighty big change had just taken place. Whereas you had been single and your pockets did jingle, now you are a married man. Now you have taken unto yourself a wife. Now she wears your name. Now you establish a home and a family. By the fact of that pronouncement you had entered into a completely new and changed state!

And so the Lord used this simple, beautiful, and most commonplace of all illustrations to convey the lesson of the new birth. That baby that is carried for approximately nine months in its mother's womb is exactly the same baby that is eventually given birth. But through the process of birth, it suddenly and drastically experiences a changed state.

So also is a man when he is born again. He is brought from being a sinner to a saint, from being lost to being saved. He is brought from Satan to God, from hell to heaven, from the world into the church. He experiences a changed state!

That is why Paul says in II Corinthians 5:17: "Wherefore if any man is in Christ Jesus, he is a new creation: the old things are passed away, behold all things are become new."

But the new birth also does something else very beautiful. It bestows a parental likeness. The apostle Paul affirms in Galatians 3:26 and 27: "For ye are all the children of God through faith which is in Christ Jesus. For as many of you as have been baptized into Christ, have put on Christ."

I sympathize with young unmarried preachers. I was 26 years of age before I married, and I recall some of the embarrassing situations in which I occasionally would find myself.

When I would visit in the home or in the hospital right after a baby had been born, I would often be confronted with the question: "Who do you think the baby looks like?" I would take a long thoughtful look. I knew it was a baby. But even after I had had four of my own, I could not dogmatically say of any of them: "Well, this one looks like its mother and this one looks like me."

It is true, when you see a newborn babe, you may not be able to see any parental features. But give that youngster five years, and some of the parental features begin to appear. Wait until he is 12 years old and stands along side of his dad, and you say: "Why, he is a chip off the old block." Of course, in my situation, with my father only being 5' 8" and my being 6' 3", they would always say of me: "he is a splinter off the old chip."

And then when you see that fine looking 21 year old man standing shoulder to shoulder with his dad, you say: "he is the spitting image of the old man."

And so it is, when a man is born again. Whether he be 8 or 80 years of age when he experiences the new birth, he is referred to in the Scriptures as a babe in Christ.

At first you may not recognize any Christ-likeness in this new babe. Here is a man who has been profane all of his life and after his conversion may thoughtlessly, let slip an oath. It has been the only language and vocabulary he has know for years. And some Christians would be thrown into a state of shock and would advocate dismissing him from the church immediately and branding him as a hypocrite.

Or here is a man who has been an alcoholic and is struggling to live the Christian life perhaps even more so than many who have been Christians for years and years.

But one day he slips and indulges in a drink which immediately leads to another and he becomes drunken. Again there would be some people who immediately would be thrown into a state of shock and brand such a fellow a hypocrite and would advocate calling the elders together and voting to excommunicate such a person.

I recall in one of my former ministries being called by a distraught wife who had already had several separations from her husband and was frantically looking for him because he had gone off on a drunk and she had not seen him for days. She asked if I would help to find him. After a week I finally found him in a bar in one of the suburbs and succeeded in getting him out and back home. We went through the ordeal of drying him out. Shortly thereafter he started attending our services and about six months later became a part of the family of God in that community.

He did remarkably well for a while and then one day as a result of a dispute with his wife, he went out and got drunk again. I immediately went to the bar where I had found him the first time and found him there.

What should we have done under such a situation? Should we have chastised him? Should we have threatened him with expulsion from the church? Of course not. We put our arms of love and compassion about that man and restored him, heeding the admonition that: "Ye who are spiritual restore such a one in the spirit of meekness." And with the passage of time, that man became a Bible school teacher, a deacon, and then an elder.

Do you married men recall the occasion when your wife with a sweet tone reminded you that it was your time to change the youngster? Did you take him and hold him out at arm's length and say: "Whew, you little stinker. You don't belong around our house." And then open up the front door and kick him out and say: "You don't belong in our family, you dirty little hypocrite. You clean up your act first before you come back around this place" and then slam the door after him? Of course not. You take that youngster and clean him up, though distasteful it might be. You love him and you teach him and train him until finally as years pass he becomes a fine young lad and then grows up into young manhood.

And so with a babe in Christ. You do not expect instantaneous maturity. The Christian life is a growth process. That is normal.

I recall when my wife was carrying our first youngster. I accompanied her to the doctor's office. The first thing he did was to put her on the scales. He then made this observation. "Mrs. Bream, I want you to let that baby do its growing after it is born."

If we demanded of a babe in Christ that he be full grown at the point of birth, it would be absolutely abnormal. Physically it would be fatal to child and mother. It is no less unreasonable spiritually to expect such a thing.

There is a time to be born. One never wants to procrastinate with regard to the matter of birth. And when one has heard the Gospel and believed on the Lord Jesus Christ with all his heart and repented of his sins, it is time for that person to be born again. Delay could be eternally fatal.

And then comes the beautiful process of growth. The Scriptures admonish us to "grow in the grace and knowledge of our Lord and Savior Jesus Christ" (II Pet. 3:18).

They admonish us to "as newborn babes desire the sincere milk of the word that we might grow thereby" (I Pet. 2:2).

And there is where you have to begin. With the milk of the word. You do not feed a newborn babe beef steak and mashed potatoes unless you want to choke it to death. You do not start out a new babe in Christ on the book of Romans or Hebrews or Revelation unless you want to choke him to death. But on the sincere milk of the Word until he develops his spiritual molars and then you can feed him the meat of the Word. This is for mature men and women in Christ.

I was helping establish a new church in Johnstown, Ohio, northeast of Columbus. There was a nucleus of Christians who wanted to start a New Testament church in that community. They learned of an old historic church building on the outskirts of town that was going to be sold at public auction. The farmers in the community were also interested in that building. Some of them wanted it for a hay-barn, some of them for a stock-barn.

The bidding began. But when the farmers heard that there was a band of Christians who were interested in purchasing that building to preserve it for its historic purpose as a house of worship, they all withdrew their bids and that group of Christians purchased it for $900.

There was a lot of work that had to be done. The building had to be painted inside and outside. It had to be rewired. The floors had to be refinished.

People in the community passing by and seeing this work, would stop and give us $5, $10, or $20. One woman wrote us a check for $50 with which to buy materials.

The revival began several weeks before Christmas.

There were 8 inches of snow on the ground. The weather was sub-freezing.

One of the first persons in the church building for the first service was a little, 83-year-old lady, by the name of Aunt Tillie Glynn.

During the early days of the revival at the conclusion of an evening service, she drew me aside and explained that when she was a young lady she had taught a class of junior girls on the platform of that building.

It was the last Saturday of that two-week revival when in my house-to-house calling throughout the community, I finally arrived at Aunt Tillie's house. When I walked into the living room, I found her seated in a big chair with an open Bible in her lap and another one open on the end table under the lamp.

I walked up to her and shook her hand and said: "Aunt Tillie, that is a grand book isn't it?" She replied brightly: "It certainly is, and I can't begin to tell you all the blessings I have received from it across these many years."

I asked: "Aunt Tillie, have you done all that God has asked you to do?" Immediately a change came over her. The tears welled up in her eyes and down her cheeks. At last, regaining her composure, and with tremulous voice, she said: "I don't know. I have read the Bible all my life, but had never studied much in the book of Acts. Since attending the revival, I have read it through several times and have found that I was never baptized the way they were baptized in the Bible. Do you think it is necessary?"

I paused for a few moments not knowing exactly how to answer, for I certainly did not want to offend this grand lady. And then I answered her question by asking a question. I said: "Aunt Tillie, do you believe that God ever asked anything of us that was not necessary?" Immediately she responded: "Oh, I don't think so. And I would hate to think that in a short time I would have to stand before my Lord and not have done what He asked me to do."

It was the last Sunday night of the revival. The largest crowd was in attendance. The building was packed out. As I came to the conclusion of the message and gave the invitation appeal and had the audience stand to sing, on the very first word there stepped out into the aisle, leaning heavily on her cane, and slowly coming to the front, 83-year-old Aunt Tillie Glynn. The invitation broke down completely. You could hear sobbing all over the audience. The pianist could not even play because of her tear-dimmed eyes. After further exhortation, I had the audience seated and Aunt Tillie reaffirmed her faith in the Lord Jesus Christ.

We did not yet have a baptistry in that building but had made arrangements with the Utica Church of Christ, about fourteen miles up the highway, to use their facilities.

Almost everyone joined the long car caravan that made its way fourteen miles up the highway through snow and subfreezing weather to the church building at Utica. It was about 10:30 o'clock that Sunday evening when I stepped into the baptismal pool with 83-year-old Aunt Tillie Glynn. She was a short, little woman. If I had held my arm stretched out, her head would not have touched it. And there before that audience, I said: "Aunt Tillie, upon the profession of your faith in Jesus Christ as the Son of God and your Lord and Savior, it is now in accordance with His own example and by His authority that you are being baptized into the name of the Father, and of the Son, and of the Holy Spirit." And then I slowly lowered her into the waters of baptism into union with her Lord in the likeness of His death, burial, and resurrection. And when I raised her up out of the water, I was not ready for what happened next. There before that audience, she turned around and faced me and stood on her tiptoes and threw her arms around my neck and gave me a great big hug and said out loud: "Oh, brother Bream, I am the happiest woman in all the world!"

How can a man be born when he is old? Jesus answered: "Verily, verily, I say unto thee, except a man be born of water and of the spirit, he cannot enter into the kingdom of God."

My friend, have you been born again? Are you a child of God? Have you become a part of His family? By His grace, through faith, you can become so tonight through your loving, faithful obedience to the Word of the Lord. Come now and be born again that you might have the promise of being a part of that glad family reunion when Jesus comes and share in that blessed eternal family fellowship. "Jesus is tenderly calling thee home."

16

"The Ultimate Alternatives: Heaven or Hell"

OLIN W. HAY

INTRODUCTION

Tonight we have an almost impossible assignment. We come with our limited intellect to measure a limitless eternity. We come with our inadequate vocabulary to describe the awful, awesome abode of the damned and the eternal glory of the home of the saved, the terror of hell and the comfort, joy and beauty of heaven.

Difficult as the assignment may be we do not shrink from it, God forbid. Time is running out. In fact, for many time has already run out.

Somehow, we the saved, must be stirred to a deep agonizing unrelenting concern for the lost because of the eternal realities that rest upon the ultimate alternatives. We pray what we say tonight will stir us to this end.

I. HELL IS ACTUAL

Many there are who ridicule the idea that hell is real. Some quotes: "Hell fire is a riot of imaginative genius." "The concept of hell is inconsistent with the character of God revealed in Jesus Christ — an insult to the name of the very being we are taught to love." "Hell is a state and not a place." "To live in harmony with what we understand to be God's law is truest heaven, to live out of harmony with that law is hell."

Even Origen thought that hell was not material fire but an internal fever, self-kindled, a figurative representation of the moral process by which restoration shall be effected.

If there is no actual hell, the Bible is a bundle of blunders, a myth, a book of fairy tales, the prophets are perverters, and the apostles deceivers. If there is no actual hell, Jesus deserves to wear the label, imposter. He said "If thy hand offend thee, cut it off: It is better for thee to enter into life maimed than having two hands to go into hell into the fire that shall never be quenched; When their worm dieth not and their fire is not quenched."

If there is no hell, Calvary with all its agony is a colossal mistake. I can not imagine God going to such lengths, if hell is not real. It is incredible that Jesus should become a man and endure such extreme suffering and die to save men from a short temporal consequence.

In the light of the Bible hell is actual. Awful as the thought may be, there is no other conclusion. It is the only book in the world where we learn about hell. The same Bible that speaks about heaven and all its glories, speaks just as clearly about the woes, pains, and miseries of hell.

And who in the Bible spoke most clearly about hell? None other than the Lord Jesus. You say it is cruel to preach about hell, then Christ was cruel. You say it is narrow, then Christ is narrow. Listen to Him: "Then shall he say also unto them on the left hand, depart from me, ye cursed, into everlasting fire prepared for the devil and his angels" (Matthew 25:41). Again: "Fear not him who can destroy the body and not the soul, but rather fear him Who can destroy both body and soul in hell" (Matthew 10:28). His teachings are as clear as sunlight, and plain as words can make it.

Common reason dictates that there must be a hell. Where there is law there must be penalty, else law has no leverage whatsoever. In fact this is our greatest problem today. Reason dictates that some day the scales must be balanced. Wrongs must be punished. Pay day some day. If there is no penalty, law becomes null and void. For illustration, if there was no penalty for murder and no man was ever punished, the law is of no effect.

Yes, hell is for real. But some will say that scholarly preachers no longer preach an orthodox hell. Well, they do not give up because of Greek or New Testament scholarship. But suppose they have: Many times the scholars have been wrong. No scholar except Noah believed a flood would come, but it did. No scholars except Abraham and Lot believed fire would fall on Sodom and Gomorrah, but it did. No scholars except Jeremiah and Baruch believed Jerusalem would be destroyed by Nebuchadnezzar, but it was. The scholars of Jesus' day scoffed at

Jesus' prediction concerning the coming destruction of Jerusalem, but 40 years later Jesus' prediction came true. Hell is actual; Jesus again and again confirmed it; I don't care what wishful thinking the scholars may say.

II. HELL IS AWFUL

Hell is away from God. Revelation 20:6 speaks of the second death. Death is separation. Physical death is separation of the spirit from the body, the second death is the separation of a man's spirit from the presence of God to "outer darkness where there is weeping and wailing and gnashing of teeth." It is enough to make a sinner's blood run cold.

Hell is a real place. It is not just a condition. We quote Jesus again, "Fear him who can destroy both body and soul in hell" (Matthew 10:28). "A place prepared for the devil and his angels" (Matthew 25:41).

A place of everlasting fire so Jesus says in Matthew 25:41. Now we are not going to split hairs whether the fire is literal or not. The terrors of hell are not minimized, but they would rather become a thousand times more terrible. For physical pain is never so severe as soul anguish. If the fire of hell is figurative, then the streets of gold are figurative too. Hell will be no less unendurable and heaven no less beautiful — But whatever, remember Jesus said, "The fire is not quenched."

A place of vile companionships. "But the fearful and the unbelieving, and the abominable, and the murders and whoremongers and sorcerers and idolaters and all liars shall have their part in the lake which burneth with fire and brimstone, which is the second death" (Revelation 21:8). Please note that listed along with all these vile souls is the unbeliever. And along with these will be the devil with all his demons. The fellowship of the damned.

A place with no exit. There is a great gulf fixed from the day of death on. No escape.

III. HELL IS ALWAYS AND FOREVER

"Then shall He say to those on His left hand, depart from me, accursed ones into everlasting fire prepared for the devil and his angels." There are those who believe that after a time of torment the sinner may be purged of his meanness and will then enter the realms of glory. Hell is not a reform school but a penalty attached to law. Hell is not a place to get ready for heaven. The man who dies rejecting God's pardon goes into eternity guilty, forever guilty and forever punished.

The expression "Eis tous aionos ton aionon" occurs twelve times in Revelation. Correctly translated it means, "unto the ages of the ages." Eight times it is used expressing the duration of his reign. One time it is used expressing the duration of the blessedness of the righteous. In every remaining instance it is used to express the duration of the punishment of the wicked. It is the strongest known expression for endlessness. Hell is always and forever.

IV. THE GLORIOUS ALTERNATIVE

In days like these how we ought to cherish hope. As

Paul says, "That we sorrow not as those who have hope." "We are saved by hope." So Paul reminds us in Romans 8:24. Hope kept Paul going. By our hope we can face the daily trials that come.

Abraham looked for a city which hath foundations whose builder and maker is God. That kept him going.

Stephen looked unto heaven and died beautifully.

May we lift our eyes to the glorious things God has in store for his family.

Heaven is a place. There has been a great deal of fallacious talk about heaven being merely a state of lovely abstraction. Jesus called heaven his Father's house. And he promised to prepare a place for us. Hebrews 11 calls heaven a city with foundations, built and made by God. O blessed happy beautiful place, future eternal reality.

Long ago the devout Jew had an expression strikingly significant, "Let Jerusalem come into your mind." No matter where the Jew went, nor what his battles, burdens, or pressures, that expression aroused and inspired him. So in these uncertain and pressure days, O Christian brother, let the New Jerusalem, the heavenly city come into your mind.

Let her beauty come to mind. John said, "I saw the New Jerusalem coming down out of heaven adorned as a bride for her husband." I love beautiful church weddings, especially that climactic moment when with the swelling organ, the bride steps into view. A number of times I have heard the groom gasp at the sight of her. Behold the bride, the Holy City coming down from God, streets of gold, gates of pearl, walls of jasper, sparkling in divine light, the foundation flashing the rich colors of many stones. There the clear flowing waters of the river of life flow from God. There the most glorious trees, all along the river. In heaven beauty will have reached perfection. There is nothing with which to compare it.

Let her purity come to mind. There will not enter anything that defileth. How man has defiled the earth, polluting the rivers, cutting the forests, scarring the mountains. The air heavy with toxic gases. How man's sin has polluted the world. Are we not weary of the defilement of our day? It seems to be seeping in at the cracks. I think of nearly 180 murders in Atlanta this year, of the gay rights movement, of Hollywood spewing our sex, horror and violence on the TV screen. We are driven to cry out, "O Lord, how long? how long?" In heaven, praise God, we will be done with it, "there will not enter in anything that defileth or anyone who does what is shameful."

Let heaven's rest and comfort come to mind. On earth we become so weary, the brain grows tired, the head bows with heaviness, the limbs drag and the spirit cries out in exhaustion. There shall be none of this in heaven. Rest from labor, from sorrow, from pain. "And God shall wipe away all tears from their eyes." And above all else, NO DEATH.

Let her blessed fellowship come to mind. John says a great multitude, more than could be numbered, gathering about the throne, everyone of them a beloved brother or sister in Christ. Imagine what a song service that will be. Imagine the warm greetings of friends and dear ones long separated by death. The great Bible heroes will be there. It will take the first one thousand years to visit with them all: Moses, David, Elijah, Isaiah, Beloved John, and heroic Paul. For a hero worshipper like I am that will be heaven enough. There will be my preacher, B. W. Carrier, who so inspired me into the ministry. W. C. Sayers, the saintliest man under whom I ever studied, R. C. Foster who kindled fires in me that have never gone out.

Let her glory come to mind. She is the Holy City and she will glow with the light of divine presence. There will be no temple there, because the Lord God almighty and the Lamb are the temple. The city does not need the light of the sun or the moon to shine on it, for the glory of God gives it light and is the lamp thereof. Yes we shall see Him in all of His holiness and glory. But John excites us even more when he says "and we shall be like Him, for we shall see Him as He is." His holiness, His glory will be ours.

Let her endless day come to mind. There will be no death there to put that big bold period at the end of life. We shall live forever. There will be no night, nothing to mark the passing of time. Heaven is forever, Home at last, never more to roam.

Time does not permit more. There are the great dimensions of heaven 1500 miles square and every foot of it permeated by the atmosphere of love. No wonder John prayed — "Even so come Lord Jesus."

CONCLUSION:

As of this moment, the alternatives are still open. Friend outside of Christ, think on your way. Broad and crowded is the way that leads to death in Hell, away from God. Reject Christ and your decision is made. God will not have sent you, you will have gone to hell in spite of all He could do to prevent it. Choose Christ, choose heaven.

Preacher friend, warn men. Some will say, it is cruel to

preach about hell. Is it cruel to label poison with a skull and cross bones? Is it cruel to arouse sleeping people when the house is on fire? Better be called cruel for being kind than be called kind for being cruel. But preach heaven too, and take all with you who will go.

Christian friend, give an answer to everyone who asks you about your hope — share it whereever you go.

17

"A Trembling Sinner"

ROBERT C. SHANNON

Court is in session at Caesarea. Across the bar of justice two men face each other. One is a governor and judge, the other a prisoner. One is free, the other in chains. One represents the Roman government and its power. The other represents a ragged, religious sect without power or influence. One trembles in fear. The other is confident and at ease. But it is not the prisoner that trembles! It is not the man in chains! It is not the representative of a despised religious minority. No, it is the representative of Rome who trembles. The governor! The judge! The free man! The man with the might of Caesar behind him!

What makes him tremble? Is it a hint of a political coup? No. Nor is it the sound of an invading army, or even the thought of a fatal disease. It is a sermon. Words, only words. I wish we could listen to those words. We have only the briefest summary of them, as indeed we have only a brief summary of the whole encounter.

And after certain days, when Felix came with his wife Drusilla, which was a Jewess, he sent for Paul, and heard him concerning the faith in Christ. And as he reasoned of righteousness, temperance, and judgment to come, Felix trembled, and answered, Go thy way for this time; when I have a convenient season I will call for thee. He hoped also that money should have been given him of Paul, that he might loose him: wherefore he sent for him the oftener, and communed with him. But after two years Porcius Festus came into Felix' room: and Felix, willing to shew the Jews a pleasure, left Paul bound.

Acts 24:24-27

Two words attract our attention: FELIX TREMBLED. Who is this man?

He began life as a slave. He sees the chains on Paul and thinks how once they felt about his wrists and ankles. He knows what it means to have every move dictated by another, to be unable to call your life your own. His brother, however, was a friend of Caesar. He got him his freedom and he finally got him his job. It is a good job. Caesarea was a pleasant place. On the shores of the blue Mediterranean, where the soft breezes temper the hot summers and the cool winters as well. The view is superb. There is little to do.

Felix has come a long way, but he can take no pleasure in it. It is not a personal accomplishment nor a mark of the talent men saw in him. He is indebted to two — his brother and his sword. It was the efforts of his brother that started him on the upward road. The rest of it he paved with violence. Hired assassins cleared the way before him. At this very moment there is a band of them ready to snuff out any threat to Felix.

His wife, Drusilla, is at his side; the woman he stole from Aziz, the king of Emeza. He even hired a sorcerer to help him seduce her. He sits uneasily on the throne. Will someone else prove more appealing to Drusilla than he? Will someone else get the job the same way he got it? He whose security rests on the whims of Caesar rests uneasily indeed. Here is a man uneasy politically and uneasy personally; but neither of these makes him tremble.

Paul makes him uneasy spiritually. Someone said that the preacher's job is to comfort the disturbed and to disturb the comfortable. Certainly Felix needed to be disturbed.

What was the message Paul preached? He seems to be defending Christ more than himself. Beyond that, he takes the offensive. To Paul, every encounter is an evangelistic opportunity. Isn't it strange that we never see one?? Most church members will say they never really have much chance to witness for Christ. Paul, a prisoner, saw every encounter as such an opportunity. You find what you are looking for!!!

Men ought to tremble at the Word of God. Look at its source. If I came to you today with a message from the governor, what would be your reaction? Indifference or interest? If I came with a message for you from the President, would you anxiously gather to hear it? If I came to you today with a message for you from God, would you wish to receive it? I have never met our governor. Neither have I seen our President face to face. The third incident has occurred. God gave me a message for you.

I am not vain enough to believe that I am God's confidant, that He whispers His secrets in my ear and not others'. No, the message God gave me for you is the same He gave to every other faithful preacher of the gospel from the first day until the present hour. That should not dim for us the glory of it. Jehovah God, the almighty, the eternal, the Lord God of hosts has sent a message for you. I have it here. Can you possibly be indifferent to such a message?

At Sinai there was thunder when God spoke, and lightning and a thick cloud "so that all the people who were in the camp trembled." It was thus that God spoke. And in the Revelation it is "with a voice of thunder" that God speaks! On the mount, Christ was transfigured and His garments shone as the light; and in the bright, bright glory God spoke.

The written word must be received with the same awe and reverence. It isn't that we worship the book. Our worship is reserved for Christ, the Living Word. But we honor the record by which God spoke. We respect it.

He reasoned of righteousness. That does not mean holiness. That comes in the next world. Righteousness means right relationship with God. Now, Felix knew something about relationships. He had been a slave; and he knew how important it is to please a master. His relationship with his brother put him where he is. He knows how important relationships are. His relationship with Caesar is crucial.

Paul calls to his attention a forgotten relationship! It is not with a brother but with a Father in heaven. It is not a king but the King of kings — mightier than Caesar, whose wrath is more to be feared. No wonder he trembled at his relationship to God.

And what of us? We are concerned about other relationships in life. We worry over business relationships, social relationships, family relationships. What of the divine relationship?

The word "judgment" means "condemnation." It is not a judgment of deciding but a judgment of sentencing. Here Paul directs his mind to another courtroom — a courtroom where bribes will not buy off the judge. Many times Felix has pronounced the death sentence on a man. Often he has seen the look of horror that his words brought. Never did Felix dream that his name would be called. But now he considers that it will be called — by God — and that the verdict will be "guilty as charged."

The judgments of scripture ought to make us tremble. The word "woe" appears 102 times on the pages of scripture, Old Testament and New. "Woe to thee, Moab!" "Woe unto thee Jerusalem!" "Woe unto Nebo!" "Woe unto them that call evil good and good evil!" "Woe to the shepherds who scatter the sheep!" "Woe to them that are at ease in Zion!" "Woe to her that is rebellious and defiled!" So cried the Old Testament prophets Isaiah, Jeremiah, Ezekiel, Amos, Micah, Hosea, Nahum, Habakkuk, Zephaniah, and Zechariah.

So cried Jesus. "Woe unto thee, Chorazin!" "Woe unto thee, Bethsaida!" "Woe unto you Pharisees!" "Woe unto you scribes!" "Woe unto you when all men speak well of you!" John, in Revelation, sees an eagle flying through the darkness and crying out, "Woe, woe, to those who dwell on the earth."

It does no one a favor to pretend that it is not so. Judgment is as much a part of God's message as forgiveness, or love, or hope, or grace. Indeed, it is only against the dark backdrop of judgment that the glory of forgiving grace is truly seen. Thank God, the message is more than judgment. We can escape the penalty. We do not have to bear the woe.

In this country, if a man is paroled it means that he no longer must bear the penalty for his crime. If that was all God did for us it would be something to praise Him for; but He did more than that. If a man is pardoned it not only means he no longer bears the punishment but that the record is cleared. God does that for us and more.

It is not parole or pardon that is received but justification. That means we are found innocent. We are not innocent, but God treats us as if we were. Imagine! We are guilty but God finds us not guilty — treats us as if it never happened, forgets it! That's God's forgiveness. What good news!

As men tremble at God's Word because of its source and because of its judgments, they tremble also because of its hope. The outcome for Paul was that he went back to prison. Felix hopes for a bribe. How unjust for Paul to be in jail and Felix to be free. How does Paul bear such injustice? Perhaps he recognized that the world is always full of injustice, that it is, after all, an unfair world. Perhaps Paul comforted himself in the knowledge that he was free in a way that Felix never would be — free from the pangs of a guilty conscience, from the blood of innocent men, from the regrets that turned Felix's dreams to nightmares. It was not that Paul had always been free from such things. Paul had shed innocent blood. Paul had condemned the guiltless. But the blood of Christ cleanses and the grace of

Christ forgives.

As for Felix, he was recalled from his post beside the sea and sentenced to die. Did he think of Paul's words about judgment to come? As he sat in his lonely cell, did he recall that other prisoner who seemed too confident while he, the judge, trembled? He trembled all the more now. Every step in the corridor brought fear to his heart. Is this the day? Are they coming for me now?

Happily, his brother intervened again, and Felix escaped execution. He was set free to live and die in obscurity. Doubtless, history would have heard nothing of him except for a chance meeting one day with the Christian preacher Paul.

He might have gone down as a hero, freeing Paul or speeding him on to Rome so that the case might be tried quickly and the matter resolved. More than that, he might have turned to the Christ Who forgave Paul and been, himself, forgiven. God could have forgiven a murderer like Felix. He had before. He has since. "THE BLOOD OF JESUS CHRIST HIS SON CLEANSETH US FROM ALL SIN." On Pentecost, the men who murdered Jesus were offered forgiveness of sins. Think of the influence he would have had. Who knows? Perhaps Caesar himself might have been so astonished that he, too, would have given the gospel a hearing. Truly, of all sad words of tongue or pen, the saddest are these: "It might have been."

But now, learn one more vital lesson. It is not enough to tremble. Men who merely tremble at the preaching of the Word are no better off than before. Indeed, they are worse off. Their lives are not only filled with sin but also with dread and fear. Men must do more than tremble.

They must turn. That is the grand Biblical word for repentance, turn. That is the grand Biblical word for conversion, TURN.

"Turn ye," cried Isaiah. "Turn, oh backsliding children," said Jeremiah. "Turn from iniquity," said Daniel. "Turn thou to God," cried Hosea. "Turn unto the Lord," said Joel. "Turn from your evil ways," said Zechariah. "Turn from these vanities," said Paul. "Repent and turn again," said Peter. Turn! Turn! So say they all!

So say I! What say you???

18

"By Grace Are Ye Saved"

ALGER M. FITCH[1]

SALVATION by the grace of God is a theme meant to be preached! It is a theme meant to be understood, accepted, and enjoyed by every man, woman, and child upon the face of the earth.

Do you know that salvation by grace is a theme found only in the Christian religion? It is only in the Book of the church that one may read such a verse as "by grace have ye been saved through faith; and that not of yourselves, it is the gift of God" (Ephesians 2:8, ASV). The law came through Moses; grace and truth came through Jesus Christ. But Jesus himself never used that particular word as far as the Biblical account is concerned. The word grace occurs about 156 times in the New Testament. And 101 of those times, it is a word used by the apostle

331

Paul. Some have called it Paul's signature in all his letters.

The book of Ephesians emphasizes salvation by grace through faith. Chapter one might be explained as the nail-scarred hands of Christ reaching out to all men in grace; chapter two then shows the empty hands of men reaching up toward God in faith to receive the gift of salvation that God has to offer.

In Ephesians 2, Paul contrasts our B. C. and our A. D. condition. By B. C., I mean "Before Conversion, and by A. D., "After Deliverance." What a contrast Paul draws as he describes our state before and after "salvation by grace through faith."

Ephesians 2:8-10 is recognized universally as the greatest of doctrinal summaries. The evangelical truth condensed in these few verses is hung upon four meaningful prepositions: "by grace," "through faith," "for good works," "in Christ." "By grace" is the source, "through faith" is the channel, "for good works" is the consequence, and "in Christ" is the place.

To properly understand this summary and the historic reformer's great cry, "Grace alone, faith alone, Christ alone," we need to see the single word "grace" standing for all God has done to save man and the single word "faith" representing all man is to do to receive that salvation. If you don't recognize Ephesians 2:8-10 as an evangelical summary, you will take it out of context to your misunderstanding.

One day many years ago I was looking at a tract which had on the cover of it the title "Salvation." The tract interested me because, as I turned the pages, each page had on it only three, or maybe four, words. "Salvation" said the cover, so I turned to page one which read "God thought it." The next page said "Christ bought it"; the third, "the Spirit wrought it"; next, "the Bible taught it"; again, "the devil fought it"; and on the last page, "But, praise God you can get it!"

God thought it — As we begin to make an acrostic on the word "grace," consider first Ephesians 1:3-6. Especially look in that paragraph for the words "chose," "foreordained," and "will," because the foundation of all evangelism is this goodwill of God. Note the word "foreordained," or "predestined" in some versions. Do not think, as many people do today, that God has chosen certain ones to be saved and others to be damned. This foreordination is not the foreordination of a particular man, but a particular plan. If Jesus had planned, in eternity past, to save all the physical sons of Abraham, Isaac, and Jacob, that might be salvation by race, but that could never be called salvation by grace. If Jesus had determined, in eternity past, that the person on your left be eternally saved, that might be salvation by fate, but it would not be salvation by faith. What is being determined here in the mind of God is that all men who will come into His Son shall know salvation. It matters not what the clime, it matters not what time, God has never willed the damnation of any baby ever born (Matthew 18:14).

The grace of God is amazing and abundant, but not irresistible (Matthew 23:37). It is God's will for all men to be saved and come to the knowledge of the truth" (I Timothy 2:4).

Peter said amen to Paul when he wrote, God "is not wishing (or willing) that any should perish, but that all should come to repentance" (II Peter 3:9). The will of God — that which is foreordained — is that every man who will come into Jesus Christ can be saved. Redemption bought it — Ephesians 1:7-12 talks about the incarnation time. There was a time when the Creator was not yet the Redeemer of man. Grace must be more than an abstract idea. Grace must become concrete. The invisible God has to become material, human, so He can die. This is the theme of the apostle Paul in Philippians 2:6-8. Jesus has to come down to earth. That is the incarnation. He had to die on Calvary. He had to rise physically from the grave. God thought it, redemption bought it.

We sing, "Mercy there was great, and grace was free." But it was not free to God. After planning salvation, the price of Calvary had to be paid. So, after God thought it, redemption bought it, and then the Spirit of God was ready to work it in our lives.

Anointing wrought it — In Ephesians 1:13, 14, we read that God's Spirit seals the Christian. Paul had written, "If any man hath not the Spirit of Christ, he is none of his" (Romans 8:9). God gives the Spirit to all who will obey Him, as Acts 5:32 teaches.

In the words of Acts 2:38, if believers will repent and be baptized, something will be taken away and something will be given.

What will be taken away is sin. What will be given is the Spirit of God. He will be the seal of one's redemption.

One book I like to study is the book of Revelation. In it John says that those who follow the beast have a mark. They are marked on their forehead and they are marked on their hand. That means simply that if you follow the devil, you will think like him and act like him. But if you are filled with the Spirit of God, you are not only marked, you are sealed. You will think with the mind of Christ. You will do His bidding. The Holy Spirit of God will work within you the miracle of Heaven.

Christians taught it — God's grace must include some agency to let the whole world know about His grace. Consider verses 15-23. The church is called the body of Christ, the extension of the incarnation. Read this section in light of what Paul will say about the church's place in bringing salvation to the world. In Ephesians 3:10,11, God's plan for man's redemption includes the church as the single channel for bringing this message to man. The truth of God's grace is to "be made known through the church" and this is "according to the eternal purpose which he purposed in Christ Jesus our Lord."

The fact makes us ready to understand the burden of Paul's prayer. The request is for "wisdom," "revelation," "knowledge," "enlightenment." Paul is interceding so that Christians will know and understand the resurrection facts concerning the Christ, so they can share them with others, so the world can be redeemed.

Evil fought it — In Ephesians 2:1-3, you will find that evil fought it. It mentions by name the "prince of the power of the air." Satan has touched every life so there is none righteous. What a dilemma for our world!

After Paul describes that dark, dark picture, you see that the gospel is good news. We are sinners, but God specializes in saving sinners! Praise God we can receive salvation through faith. Once afar off, we can be near. Once dead, we can be alive in Jesus Christ. Next we must move from salvation by the grace of God to salvation by the responsive faith of man.

The other side — What was in the mind of Paul just

before he wrote this summary statement of Ephesians 2:8-10? Will you agree with me that he would remember his own salvation by grace through faith? According to Acts 9:6, Jesus told him that in the city of Damascus he will be told what he must do. Paul would not reply, "But, Jesus, if there is something I must do, it would no longer be salvation by grace through faith — that would be salvation by works."

What did Ananias tell Paul to do? "Arise, and be baptized, and wash away thy sins, calling on his name" (Acts 22:16). Would Paul protest and say, "But, Ananias, if I have to be baptized it will be salvation by works, not by faith." You would never convince Paul, by such modern jargon, that his baptism would be salvation by works. It was salvation by grace through faith.

Paul thinks this way: If the grace of Christ demands the baptism of suffering on the part of Jesus — the cross — then the responsive faith of man demands the baptism of submission on the part of the convert. While exalting the beauty of Christian immersion, John Paul Pack said, "Christian immersion is the total surrender of a total man to the total will of God." That is salvation by grace through faith.

Paul did not study in Athens; he studied in Jerusalem. He did not think like the Greeks that one must separate anything physical from anything spiritual and that only the spiritual is good. (That is the way Plato thought.) Hebrews were holistic. They had a Bible filled with stories where God graciously acted on the part of Israel, and Israel believed and obeyed. So when I read in Acts about repentance and baptism, they are simply faith gone audio-visual.

336

After Paul's first missionary journey, he returned from Galatia and wrote (Galatians 3:26,27), "Ye are all sons of God, through faith, in Christ Jesus. For as many of you as were baptized into Christ did put on Christ." His second missionary journey started in Philippi and ended down in Corinth. Up in Philippi, Paul preached salvation by grace through faith. He baptized Lydia and her household, as well as the jailer and his household. Down in Corinth, we find the same thing. Acts 18:8 says, "The Corinthians hearing believed, and were baptized."

So what is in Paul's mind as he writes Ephesians 2:8-10? Certainly his own conversion. Certainly his own ministry. Certainly every letter he ever wrote – and let us not dehydrate the epistles. The book of Romans (which tells us what is justification by faith alone) contains a full chapter on baptism (chapter 6).

As Paul writes Ephesians 2, he is also thinking of something Jesus said about the grace of God. He remembers Jesus' story of the prodigal son and his gracious father. When the son came home to the father, he was considered alive again. Look at Ephesians 2:1,5. The dead are alive again. That is the conversion experience. The story of Luke 15 states that the prodigal son went into a far country. What do Ephesians 2:14 and 17 say? That those who were afar off are now made nigh. And if the prodigal son, coming home, finds music and dancing in the father's house, Ephesians 2:19 says that those back home are now in the "household of God."

Found by the love of Christ – This leads us to a brief acrostic on faith, starting in Ephesians 2:4. In the mind of Paul is the story of the love of God. The faith that saves includes the assurance that prodigals can be found by the love of God. Notice that verse 4 mentions both the mercy and the love of God.

Do you believe "once a child always a child"? Once a child of the devil, always a child of the devil? No! Men can be saved. While everyone of us — like prodigals — are depraved, we do not suffer a depravity so total that we cannot be reached. This man of a far country had a mind capable of thinking how good his father was. He knew that if he would come home, he would be accepted at least like a servant. It turned out a lot better than he ever dreamed. So, as prodigals, we can be found by the love of Christ.

Awakened by the life of Christ — We can also be awakened by the life of Christ because He wakes us up to live (2:5). By grace we have been saved. In sin, Jew or Gentile are stone dead. From the baptismal waters, converts rise to "walk in newness of life" (Romans 6:4). Colossians 2:12, 13 compares God's raising of Christ from the dead and His raising believers to life at their baptism.

Included in the reign of Christ — We are awakened to live and to be included in the reign of Christ. We are made to sit with Him in heavenly places (Ephesians 2:6). We can share in every victory that is won. I know that some congregations don't quite understand the grace of God. They know that sinners out there in the real world of sin can be forgiven, but they assume such persons could never be a Sunday-school teacher or an elder. We have a wrong understanding of I Timothy 3 and Titus 1. Those are descriptions of what we now are by the grace of God, not what we have always been. We must re-think some things that we practice in the light of grace.

Transformed by the power of Christ — Because you are

transformed by the power of Christ, you are included in the reign of Christ (2:7-10). "We are his workmanship, created in Christ Jesus." Now the word "workmanship" is a Greek word — poema. You are God's poems. Your life was all messed up. It didn't make any sense. God put it in order — prose. But he did a better job than that. He made it poetry. He made it beautiful. But the next word is very humbling. He says you are created in Christ Jesus. Now to create means to make out of absolutely nothing. So when God started to make something out of you, He had nothing to work with. But this is the grace of God.

Helpful in the service of Christ — You are created in Christ Jesus for good works (v. 10). We are saved by works — the works of God. All the works we do after forgiveness are expressions of gratitude. We do not work in order to earn merit. We merit, earn, and deserve damnation. We are given salvation upon our obedience. But then we spend the rest of our life happily serving the one who is so gracious to us.

Do you believe that faith moves mountains? Let me assure you that God's grace moves mountains. Mountains of sins. Not only are you saved by grace, if you will be helpful in the service of Christ, others will be saved by grace.

A long time ago, you were taught to pray as you went to bed: "Now I lay me down to sleep." I pray you have grown up and are ready now when you start the day to say,

Now I get me up to wake.
I pray thee, Lord, my soul to shake.
If I should die before tonight,

339

I hope I've told somebody of the grace of God
And done it right. Amen.

NOTES

1. *Christian Standard*, Feb. 22, 1981, pp. 164-166. Used by permission.

19

"Jesus, the Crucified God"

CHARLES R. GRESHAM

In Lloyd Douglas' intriguing story, *The Robe*, Marcellus the centurion has been given charge of a crucifixion detail in Jerusalem. It is that fateful day when Jesus, the prophet of Galilee, is led out to the place of the Skull and executed. Marcellus wins the Galilean's seamless robe. The impact of this episode is so traumatic that Marcellus becomes half-crazed, and, blaming it on the robe which he believes is cursed, he tries to rid himself of it. But, he finds no peace of mind, no release. Often he awakens after a nightmare, trembling and afraid. Frequently he slips into some strange trance, and when friends would attempt to help him, he would seize them roughly and cry out in a strange eerie voice — "Were you out there?"

That is the question of that sorrowful, yet victorious,

Negro spiritual, "Were you there when they crucified my Lord? Were you there when they nailed Him to the tree?"

And that beloved disciple, John, can answer in the affirmative. "Yes, I was there. I was there through all the trials. I was there when vacillating Pilate washed his hands and gave Him over to be crucified. I was there as they laid that cross on His bruised and bleeding back and made Him carry it to the place of execution. I was there when they stripped Him of His clothing and laid His naked body along that rugged bark and drove those nails through His hands and feet. I heard His groans; and I heard His plea to the Father for forgiveness for those who treated Him so shamefully. I was there! Weeping unashamedly as were those women who loved Him so — His mother, His aunt, Mary Magdalene. Yes! Yes! I was there!"

John relates that poignant story in the nineteenth chapter of his gospel. It had lived so vividly in his memory. Its poignancy is matched by its paradoxical truth. Here is Jesus, the Crucified God. The One who had said, without batting an eye, "Before Abraham was, I am," and "I and the Father are one," is crucified — treated as a common criminal. What paradox! And yet, what marvelous grace!

We, too, must be "out there," if we are ever to know and experience the benefits of this crucified God. Like Abraham Cowley, we must also say

> Methinks I hear of murdered men the voice
> Mixed with the murderers' confused noise
> Sound from the top of Calvary;
> My greedy eyes fly up the hill and see
> Who 'tis hangs there, the midmost of the three;
> O! how unlike the others he;

Look! how he bends his gentle head
  with blessing from the tree,
 His gracious hands, ne'er stretched but to do good,
 Are nailed to the infamous wood!
 And sinful man does fondly bind
 The arms which he extends to embrace all humankind.

"John, you were there. You were out there on that
wind-swept crag of rock where those crosses were raised.
What did you see?" John, tears streaming down his
cheeks, a sob in his voice, says

"I Saw the Crucified Son"

John recalls: "There they crucified him" (verse 18).
He also tells of those soldiers in the crucifixion detail,
taking his garments and dividing them among themselves,
gambling for his seamless robe since they did not want to
tear it (verses 23-25). He then adds: "And standing by
the cross of Jesus was Mary."

There they were — mother and Son. They had been
together like this 30 or so years before. Their ways had
parted just three short years before. Each had walked a
lonely way, but their paths had drawn together and the
end had come. Now Mary knew what Simeon's words
had meant, "Yea, a sword shall pierce through thy own
soul also" (Luke 2:35a). No sword could be so cruel as
that pain piercing her heart now.

She was in the city when the shadow fell, haunting the
outskirts of the angry throng as they cried for his life. She
saw him standing, crowned with thorns, beaten, condemned. She had wept uncontrollably as she followed

along the "way of sorrows," groping her way in the twilight of tragedy. Now, of all those figures gathered at the foot of the cross, she was the most forlorn and forsaken.

For the religious politicians, this One was a dangerous agitator; for the High Priest, a fanatic; for the disciples, a beloved Teacher; but for Mary — He was still her son! Richard Crashaw says:

> She sees her son, her God
> Bow with a load
> Of borrow'd sins; and swim
> In woes that were not made for Him.
> Ah, hard command
> Of love! Here must she stand
> Charg'd to look on, and with a steadfast eye
> See her life die:
> Leaving her only so much breath
> As served to keep alive her death.

Through a sea of misting tears, she saw her son crucified, and through a sea of pain; causing His head to swim, the Crucified Son saw His mother. He also saw that beloved disciple nearby, supporting her, comforting her. Through parched, dry lips He speaks: "Woman behold your son! Son, behold your mother!" (verses 26-27).

Even to the end the human and divine are in perfect balance, in creative tension. The human son speaks to a human mother; the divine, compassionate Son of God arranged for her care.

"Were you there, John?" "Yes, I was there. I heard Him. I took Mary to my home. I cared for her as my own mother throughout her days."

Were we there? If so, the Crucified Son speaks to us of motherhood, familial responsibility, concern for parents, sympathy and sharing for those who gave us life. Are we out there ?!!!

John continues his recollection. "I was out there and ...

"I Saw the Crucified Sufferer."

The awful struggle with sin and evil and death is almost over; and Jesus knowing that all was now finished, said, "I thirst" (verse 28). They had offered Him a soothing draught of drugged wine at the beginning, but He had refused. He would not meet the Last Enemy of man with senses stupefied. As someone has said:

Thou wilt feel all, that Thou may'st pity all;
And rather would'st Thou wrestle with strong pain,
Than overcloud Thy soul
So clear in agony.

"I thirst" — that cry from parched, cracked lips, hoarse, hardly understood, is the only cry of physical weakness and the only vocal expression of physical suffering that he utters. Now, He accepts that bit of moisture raised to His lips — moisture made not by drugged wine but by sour vinegar, the common drink of the Roman legion.

He suffered, but not just physical pain (that is apparent in the very process of crucifixion), He suffered for our sins. "He bore our own sins in His body on the tree," Peter declares (I Peter 2:24). Thus, He seals the fulfilled truth of that great passage in Isaiah that speaks of a Suffering Servant "wounded for our transgressions...bruised for our iniquities" (Isa. 53:5).

But the Crucified Sufferer may well ask us: "Were you

345

there? Were you out there when I suffered for you? Did you hear my parched cry, 'I thirst?'" "Why do you thirst?" asks St. Bernard, "surely for the redemption of mankind and the joy of man's salvation."

"For what dost thou thirst, Lord Jesus," cries Augustine, "for wine from the vine or water from the river? Nay. Thy thirst was my salvation. Thy food my redemption."

Christina Rosetti writes:

> I lift my eyes and I see
> Thee, tender Lord, in pain upon the tree,
> Athirst for my sake and athirst for me.

Is not this the motive of our service? Should we not rush to Him and hold that sponge to His lips? Miss Rosetti adds:

> Thou sayest this sad day, 'I thirst' again,
> And I, remembering how, to ease Thy pain
> Some harsh-faced Roman, stained and seared with war,
> Gave Thee his vinegar
> (And earned a fuller comfort than he gave),
> Go forth to see for Thee at Thy behest
> Not only such suave souls as please me best,
> But rough, sour souls that Thou didst parch to save!

"Were you there, John?" "Ah, yes, I was there to the bitter end and...."

"I SAW THE CRUCIFIED SAVIOR"

" When Jesus had received the sour wine, He said, 'It is

finished;' and He bowed His head and gave up His spirit" (verse 30). "It is finished!" Those three words, translating just one longer word in the original, speak volumes. Certainly that could be said of any life, for every life closes — is finished — in death. One could even see here that such a statement could well mean: "This is the end; all is over."

But Jesus' life was not a common life. His life was complete as no life had ever been or would ever be. The meaning of this pregnant phrase is larger and more glorious than might be understood at first hearing. "It is finished" is the triumphant word of the Savior, crucified for us.

We may well ask, in light of those interpretations of this great event given by His apostles, what was finished? Everything the Father had given Him to do was finished. Ever since He had asked His mother, when a boy of twelve, "Did you not know that I must be about my Father's business?" (Luke 2:49), even until this crucial moment, He had perfectly accomplished the Father's will. "I must work the works of Him who sent me," He reminded His adversaries (John 9:4). He had prayed in the garden: "Not my will, Thine be done" (Luke 22:42).

What was finished? All that was necessary to the accomplishment of human redemption was finished. "He died unto sin once," Paul will say (Romans 6:10). "While we were yet sinners, Christ died for us" (Romans 5:8). In His ministry, He had anticipated the Cross. This was the "hour" that He had awaited. He had announced this to His disciples. He had clearly indicated that He would "give his life a ransom for many" (Mark 10:45).

"It is finished" is the victorious cry of the Redeemer;

and the perpetual anthem of the Redeemed runs parallel to that. "Worthy art Thou....for Thou wast slain, and hath redeemed us to God by thy blood out of every kindred, and tongue, and people and nation" (Rev. 5:9).

So we speak of the "finished work of Christ" and see its culmination at the Cross. But, though this is the consummation of the work of Christ, it is only the beginning of the work of His church. He cries: "It is finished." We answer: "It now begins!" The work He must do is ended; the work He calls us to do begins and continues.

John was there when hateful, vengeful men crucified their God. John was there! He reports what he saw and heard. We understand that such an act — so despicable, so unworthy — by divine grace has become for us saving power.

But we were there, too! When He died "to sin and for sin, once" it was not only the sin of the rough, foul-mouthed soldiers who drove the nails; not only the sins of those self-righteous Pharisees and priests; it was my sin and yours. We were there, too.

When the Bolsheviks had murdered the Czar of Russia and exterminated all others of royal blood, they printed a cartoon representing one of their number with a blood-dripping axe in hand, climbing a ladder to heaven. The caption of this coarse picture was "And now for God." How foolish! That was done so long ago. Yet it continues again and again as the "Son of God is crucified afresh" by indifference, worldliness and unbelief.

The poet underscores that truth:

Lord, I have joined in the hateful cry, —
Slay Him, away with Him, crucify!

348

Lord, I have done it, ask me not how,
Woven the thorns of Thy tortured brow;
Yet in His pity so boundless and free,
Jesus the crucified pleads for me!

John recalls that the Lord's side was pierced by the soldier (verse 34ff) and he is reminded of that prophetic verse in Zechariah: "They shall look on him whom they have pierced" (12:11). The "they" includes us as well as those hostile hordes gathered there at Calvary. We were there! We drove the nails! We pierced His side!

But, we can realize this and come to Him, the crucified, now risen Lord. In faith, we can say in the words of Christina Rosetti:

Ah Lord, we all have pierced Thee: will Thou be
Wroth with us all to slay us all?
Nay, Lord, be this thing far from Thee and Me;
By whom should we arise, for we are small,
By whom if not by Thee?

Lord, if of us who pierced Thee, Thou spare one,
Spare yet one more to love Thy Face,
And yet another of poor souls undone,
Another and another — God of grace,
Let mercy overrun.

CONTRIBUTORS

Raymond L. Alber

Raymond Alber, growing up in a minister's home, is a native of Nebraska. He graduated from Phillips University in Enid, Oklahoma and did post-graduate study at Butler University's School of Religion, Indianapolis. He also participated in special studies in Psychology and Pastoral Counseling at Cotner College on the campus of the University of Nebraska. In 1972 he was granted the Honorary Doctorate of Divinity degree from Kentucky Christian College.

Alber was in general evangelism for several years, heading the Alber Evangelistic Party which held meetings in 32 of the continental United States and on the island of Hawaii. Over 5,000 came to Christ as a result of these meetings.

Following this period in general evangelism, Dr. Alber ministered to outstanding congregations in Nebraska, Florida, West Virginia and California. All of these churches grew rapidly under his leadership.

Prior to his retirement in 1980, Alber served thirteen years as Vice President for Development of the Emmanuel School of Religion, a graduate seminary of the Christian Churches and Churches of Christ, located in Johnson City, Tennessee.

Dr. Alber has been a familiar figure on state and national platforms. He served two years as president of the National Evangelistic Association and has served on numerous boards and committees. He has written and lectured extensively in the areas of evangelism and steward-ship.

Since retirement, Dr. Alber has been busy in evange-lism, holding Stewardship Seminars, leading churches in financial campaigns, serving in interim capacities with churches and working as a consultant in development with ESR. He has also had more time to devote to wood craftsmanship, particularly in making beautiful clocks and various items of furniture from hardwoods.

Dr. Alber is married to the former Elizabeth Cheathan of Paris, Illinois. They have two children: Gary, a CPA in Ventura, California, and Ann, a Director of Medical Social Work in Asheville, North Carolina.

Jesse Bader

Jesse M. Bader was born in Bader, Illinois, April 15, 1886. He studied at the University of Kansas from 1905-07 and completed an A.B. degree at Drake University in 1911. (Later, 1930, Drake University would confer the honorary D.D. upon him for his contributions in ministry and evangelism). Dr. Bader held outstanding evangelistic ministries in Atchison, Kansas (1911- 1918) and Kansas City, Missouri (1919-20) before being called to become Secretary for Evangelism of the newly-merged United Christian Missionary Society, headquartered in Indianapo-lis. For eleven years he guided the Disciples in evangelistic strategy and with Charles Reign Scoville and others founded the National Evangelistic Association as an adjunct of the International Convention. During this time he was instrumental in founding the World Convention of the Churches of Christ and served as this body's general secretary until his retirement.

In 1932, Dr. Bader was called to head up the department of evangelism of the Federal Council (later National Council) of Churches of Christ in America, a post he held until his retirement in 1954. During these years he moved across America breathing the evangelistic spirit of life into churches. Few men in this century have done more in proclaiming salvation and establishing the convert. His reputation was so well known that when Billy Graham launched his crusades, Dr. Bader was one of the key people with whom Graham consulted.

In 1957, Bethany Press, published his book, *Evangelism in A Changing America,* which sets out his conception of the evangelistic motive and task. He had written widely on the subject in various journals, but this book sets out clearly his deep commitment.

Dr. Bader was married to Golda Maude Elan in August, 1910. Mrs. Bader was a supportive helpmate in his labors through the years.

Dr. Bader died August 19, 1963 in New York City having given his life to two great concerns of the Restoration Movement — Evangelism and Christian unity.

Harvey C. Bream Jr.

Harvey C. Bream, Jr. is from a family of preachers. His father was a minister of the gospel as is his brother. He has two brothers-in-law and two nephews who are ministers and had an uncle who was a minister.

He was born in Champaign, Illinois, but grew up in

Kentucky, Pennsylvania, New York, Ohio, and West Virginia.

He was graduated from The Cincinnati Bible Seminary with an A.B. degree in 1944. He completed three years of postgraduate resident work in the same institution. He received the honorary Doctor of Divinity degree from Kentucky Christian College in 1979.

He had student ministries with the Chatham and Kentontown, Kentucky, Churches of Christ. He served for several years during this period as the editor of several college and mission publications. He served the Montgomery Road Church of Christ, Cincinnati, Ohio, from 1948-1952. He is listed in the second edition of *Who's Who in Religion*.

From 1952-1957 he served as an evangelist with The Christian Restoration Association. During this time he led in the establishment of three churches and aided seven other new churches in their establishment. Through the years he has served on faculties in 69 weeks of Christian service camps and held 374 weeks of revival meetings. In 1957, working in conjunction with the Christian Evangelizing Fellowship of Greater Cincinnati, Ohio, and The Christian Restoration Association, he served as evangelist in establishing the Forest Dale Church of Christ in Cincinnati, Ohio. During this period he also served as the CRA director of evangelism and associate editor of its monthly publication, *The Restoration Herald*. He was called to the editorial post of this publication in 1961 and served in this capacity through July 1970. On August 1, 1970, Mr. Bream assumed his duties as president of The Cincinnati Bible Seminary and continued in this position until 1989 when he became Chancellor. In 1989, he began a second

354

ministry with Forest Dale Church of Christ in Cincinnati, Ohio.

Mr. Bream has served as president of the Greater Cincinnati Christian Ministers' Association; on the Executive Committee of the Cincinnati Christian Evangelizing Fellowship; has served on the North American Christian Convention Committee; serves as lecturer and speaker for many churches, conventions, faith-promise rallies, men's meetings, and youth rallies.

In 1949 he married Mary Ann Work of Cincinnati, Ohio. They have four adult children: two girls and two boys.

J. V. Coombs

J.V. Coombs was born in Indiana, spending his early years on a farm in the Eel River Valley. Completing the usual elementary education at New Brunswick (Boone County), he entered the Ladoga, Indiana Academy. Following this collegiate preparation he enrolled and graduated from Central Indiana Normal School in 1877. Later, in 1882, he completed the Classical course at the University of Chicago. Following this formal education he was selected as president of Central Indiana Normal, serving two years and moved to the presidency of East Illinois College where he served for two years. In 1883 he became professor of History and Literature at Eureka College, a position he held for six years.

In 1889, Coombs entered general evangelism, giving himself unstintingly to this strenuous task. He often preached six or seven times on Sunday and on one occasion he preached 192 successive nights without a break. His preaching was simple, centering around the great themes of the Gospel.

Coombs was one of the first of the Restoration Movement's evangelists to develop a manual of procedures of preparation for a campaign. His book, *Campaigning For Christ*, sets these procedures out carefully. He believed that with such preparation and the involvement of many workers, more could be accomplished in a shorter meeting than had been true in the past.

For more than thirty years Coombs continued in general evangelism. Before his death in Danville, Indiana on December 19, 1920, he preached throughout the United States, lectured in the chautauqua circuit; wrote books and tracts (his *Religious Delusions, The Christ and the Church* and *Christian Evangelism* had a wide readership), and was instrumental in leading 18,000 people to Christ. He was also able to encourage at least 100 to enter full-time Christian ministry.

Alger Fitch

Dr. Alger Fitch is Professor of Bible at Pacific Christian College, Fullerton, California, where he specializes in New Testament Studies.

Dr. Fitch is often called upon to hold evangelistic meetings and lectureships in churches and Bible colleges across the nation. Because of his unique ability to communicate the Word and his interest in the unity of Christians, he is welcomed throughout the brotherhood in its various expressions, and interdenominationally as well. His scholarly treatment of New Testament material combined with a preaching style that uses visuals (charts, posters, and worksheets) gets the message across.

The interest Dr. Fitch has in the roots of the Restoration Movement is reflected in his Master's thesis for U.S.C., *Alexander Campbell and His Psalms, Hymns and Spiritual Songs Hymnal*, and his Doctoral Dissertation for the School of Theology, Claremont, *Alexander Campbell: Reformer of Preaching and Preaching of Reform* (published by Sweet Publishing Co., Austin, Texas, 1970, reprinted by College Press, 1988).

He authored a survey of the New Testament, *Afterglow of Christ's Resurrection* (Standard Publishing Co., Cincinnati, Ohio, 1975), and writes often for the Christian Standard.

Two other books, soon to be released from Standard, will be *Claiming God's Promises* and *The Book of Revelation in the Missionary Prospective*.

Dr. Fitch has held several pastorates in Oregon and California. These churches began with but a small nucleus but soon grew into strong congregations. In order to multiply his efforts, he chose to teach in Bible Colleges, spending ten years at Northwest Christian College, Eugene, Oregon, and since 1978 has served at Pacific Christian College, Fullerton, California.

The Fitches have traveled and preached extensively. They have visited 32 different countries and made comparative study of the methods employed by missionaries going out independently or under the auspices of missionary organizations. Their more recent trips have been to Brazil and behind the Iron Curtain where they strengthened those who labor there.

Benjamin Franklin

Benjamin Franklin was born in Belmont County, Ohio, February 1, 1812. Later his family moved to Indiana and here near Middletown, Henry County, Indiana, he was immersed by Samuel Rogers. Franklin was 24 years old at the time and though he had little formal education he began almost immediately to engage in Christian work and soon was preaching extensively. His first twelve years were spent in Indiana where he was instrumental in starting many local congregations. Later he extended his sphere of operation to include Ohio and Kentucky and other states. Within thirty years he had been instrumental in seeing more than 8,000 baptized into Christ.

Franklin's forte was in general evangelism not in pastoral work. Frequently his evangelistic labors would catapult him into debates in which he comported himself well.

Franklin began his editorial work in January, 1843, taking charge of the *Reformer*, a monthly published at Centerville, Indiana. Later, he relocated in Cincinnati and entered into partnership with D.S. Burnett, publishing jointly *The Reformer and the Christian Age*. This partnership lasted only a brief time. In 1856 Franklin began *The American Christian Review* and continued to edit this paper until his death in 1878.

In 1864 Franklin moved his family to Anderson, Indiana (even though the *Review* would continue to be published in Cincinnati). From here he continued his editorial work, participated in extensive evangelistic labors, and published two volumes of sermons, *The Gospel Preacher*, Volumes I and II. Perhaps his most lasting work is his evangelistic tract, *Sincerity Seeking the Way to*

Heaven, which had wide circulation and was reprinted many times after his death.

The extensive labors of Franklin took their toll and the last few years of Franklin's life were spent in virtual invalidism. He is still considered one of the prime evangelists of the Restoration Movement.

Charles R. Gresham

Charles R. Gresham is the son of a Christian minister, Fred Gresham. He is a graduate of Hope High School, Hope, Kansas, and received his A.B. degree from Manhattan Bible College, Manhattan, Kansas in 1949. He was a graduate student at Phillips University Seminary, Enid, Oklahoma, in 1949-1950, and attended Perkins School of Theology, Southern Methodist University, Dallas, Texas, in 1953 to take further graduate work. He received his Master's degree in Religious Education from Southwestern Baptist Theological Seminary in 1956, and his Doctor's degree in Religious Education from the same seminary in Ft. Worth, Texas, in 1958. He received the Ed. D. from Southwestern in 1970. He has also done advanced work in education at Central State College, Edmond, Oklahoma, and completed residence work for a Master's degree at Kansas State University, Manhattan, Kansas in History and Philosophy. Recently, he completed a M.A. in Church History at Cincinnati Christian Seminary.

Dr. Gresham's major work has been in the College and Seminary classroom, having taught at Dallas Christian College; Midwest Christian College, Oklahoma City; Manhattan Christian College, Manhattan, Kansas; Emmanuel School of Religion, Johnson City, Tennessee and Kentucky Christian College, Grayson, Kentucky, where he presently is Professor of Bible and Christian Education.

Dr. Gresham is the author, co-author, or editor of a number of books. His most recent are *What the Bible Says About Resurrection* and *Preach the Word* (which he edited and to which he contributed several sections).

Dr. Gresham has served several Midwest, Southwest and Southeast churches in both part-time and full-time capacity. He has also held numerous evangelistic meetings and seminars in various phases of Church life.

Dr. Gresham has contributed to the Christian Churches and Churches of Christ at large through his work in the Chaplaincy Endorsement Commission, the Convention platform, and his participation and leadership of various Unity Forums.

Dr. Gresham married Ruth Smith of Urbana, Illinois, and they have four grown children.

Keith P. Keeran

Keith (or "Pete", as he would prefer to be called) Keeran was born in Ohio, June 21, 1943. After finishing public school in Marion, Ohio, he enrolled at Kentucky Christian College, receiving the A.B. degree in 1968. After additional academic work in Speech and Communications at Morehead State University, Morehead, Kentucky, he earned a M.A. in Homiletics and Speech from Abilene Christian University. In 1971 he began teaching Speech and Homiletics at Great Lakes Bible College in

Lansing, Michigan, continuing in this position for twelve years. While at Great Lakes Bible College, Dr. Keeran received the Ph.D. degree from Michigan State University in an interdisciplinary program in Communications, Religion and History. In the fall of 1982 he joined the faculty of Kentucky Christian College and was selected as president in the summer of 1987.

Dr. Keeran has had several located ministries through the years. He has held a large number of evangelistic meetings and is in constant demand in this field. In recent years he has combined leadership in evangelism with seminars for leadership training in local churches. He has also lectured on preaching at various colleges, ministerial retreats and Conventions.

Dr. Keeran is not only a teacher of preachers but has served as an ideal model of what evangelistic preaching ought to be.

James Earl Ladd, Sr.

James Earl Ladd, Sr. was born at Amity, Oregon, December 17, 1901. After finishing high school he decided to be a physician and enrolled in the University of Oregon where he spent two years in pre-med study. While involved in his pre-med work, Carroll Roberts, minister of First Christian Church, Eugene, Oregon, influenced him to enter full-time Christian service. In telling of his decision for the ministry, Mr. Ladd would later say, "Why study medicine to patch up a body for seventy years when I can preach the gospel and patch up men's souls for seventy billion years — yea, forever and ever."

Ladd enrolled in Eugene Bible University (now Northwest Christian College) and received both B.Th. and B.D. degrees. For seventeen years (from 1927 to 1943) he was in the general evangelistic field with the exception of two years which were spent in a located ministry at Grants Pass, Oregon. In May, 1943, he became minister of the Central Christian Church, Portland, Oregon. Here he labored for seven and one-half years. His years were cut tragically short by his untimely death on February 27, 1951.

Evangelism was Ladd's strong emphasis. Thousands came to Christ during his years as a general evangelist. During his ministry at Central Christian in Portland there were more than 1200 additions. An added feature of Ladd's evangelistic influence was the many young people that he encouraged to enter specialized Christian service. More than 300 were so influenced, forty of these coming from the Portland Church during his last years there.

Ladd's influence has been perpetuated not only by the many who came to Christ, or by those who made special commitments for ministry, but by his own family. James Earl Ladd II has followed in his father's footsteps and is an outstanding preacher, evangelist, and teacher of preachers (serving now at Puget Sound College of the Bible, Edmonds, Washington). His daughter, Beth Alice, prior to her untimely death, served with her husband as a missionary in Ethiopia.

A.B. McReynolds

A.B. McReynolds was born in Jamestown, Indiana,

November 21, 1899. He left home at the age of fourteen, traveling westward. Two years later he began teaching school in Oregon, although he had only a grade school education himself. After teaching school for sometime, he decided that he would study law, but three months later he changed his mind and made his decision to become a preacher of the gospel.

McReynolds enrolled in Texas Christian University in the fall of 1917 and received both bachelors and masters degrees. In 1923, he became minister of the church at Athens, Texas. After two years of ministry, he was called to become state evangelist for the Churches of Texas, holding the position for three years. In 1928, he entered the general evangelistic field and continued in this field until his health broke some ten years later. He moved to the Kiamichi Mountains of southeast Oklahoma, hoping to regain his health. Here in this unevangelized, needy area, in spite of poor health, he launched that work now known as the Kiamichi Mountain Christian Mission which has planted two dozen churches in the area and annually conducts camps and clinics attended by hundreds. At the time of his death, A.B. McReynolds was probably known more for the Kiamichi Men's Clinic than his fruitful labors as evangelist.

McReynold's evangelistic campaigns were fruitful. For several years he had the distinction of having the most additions in a single church meeting than any man in America. It was not unusual for 100 to 500 people to be added in some of his evangelistic meetings. It is estimated that some 10,000 people were brought to Christ during his eight and one-half years in the general evangelistic field.

An added feature of McReynold's evangelism was his emphasis upon tithing. Not only did he have many converts, he also had many lukewarm church members accepting the tithing plan of church finance. As a result, many congregations were strengthened financially as well as spiritually and numerically.

Charles Reign Scoville

Charles Reign Scoville was born in DeKalb County, Indiana, October 14, 1869. His early life on an Indiana farm prepared him well for the severe labors of the evangelistic field. After graduating from high school, he farmed with his father until financial reverses caused them to lose the farm. On his own Scoville succeeded in securing a college education, graduating from Tri-State Normal College at Angola, Indiana in 1882. For some time he taught school but after 1891 when he united with the Church of Christ at Angola his destiny as a preacher was set. In 1892 he preached his first sermon and accepted the ministry of his first church (South Scott in Steuben County, Indiana). That fall he held his first evangelistic meeting resulting in forty-two additions. Soon he was receiving numerous calls for evangelistic meetings. Realizing that he needed further education, he entered Hiram College in the fall of 1894, completing a seven year course in five years and leading, through evangelistic labors, 1000 people into Christ. Following his graduation from Hiram he entered full-time evangelism. His work ended in death, January 23, 1938 at Garden City, Kansas while engaged in an evangelistic meeting in the church at that place.

It would be impossible to give a complete survey of Scoville's success as an evangelist. There were perhaps as many as 30,000 additions to the church during those many years of his evangelistic labors. His crowning victories were the meetings held in Allegheny and Pittsburgh, Pa., where 667 were added in 82 days, and the great meeting in Des Moines, Iowa, where there 1114 added in 100 days. Certainly, Scoville stands as the prince of Restoration evangelists as far as length of service and statistics are concerned.

Robert C. Shannon

Robert Calvin Shannon was born on a farm near Corinth, Kentucky, that was, he says "so poor they had two rocks to one dirt." Following his high school education, he enrolled at Cincinnati Bible Seminary earning the A.B. degree at that institution. Other formal education included work at Georgetown (KY) College, Tusculum College (Greenville, TN), and Lutheran Theological Seminary (Columbus, OH).

Shannon began preaching at age 17 while still in High School and has preached regularly since that time. Significant ministries have been held in Lancaster, Ohio, and Greenville, Tennessee. In 1966 he became Senior Minister of First Christian Church, Largo, Florida, the second largest congregation in the state. In 1984, he resigned this fruitful ministry to work with TCM Mission in preaching and teaching behind the Iron Curtain. His base of operation is in Vienna, Austria. In addition to his local ministry, Brother Shannon has been active in the Restoration

Movement at large. He is a past president of the Southern Christian Convention; past president of the North American Christian Convention; a member of the Book Publishing Committee of Standard Publishing; and a member of the Board of Trustees of Atlanta Christian College. He has preached numerous evangelistic meetings and lectured in a number of our colleges on the subject of preaching.

Shannon has also been active in the civic affairs of Largo, having served on the Personnel Advisory Board of the city and he has been a member of the Board of the Largo Public Library and the Lake Seminole Hospital.

Shannon is married to the former Barbara Jean Adams. They have two children: J. Michael, who is a professor of Ministries at Cincinnati Bible College, Cincinnati, and Beth Ann, a public school teacher.

Shannon is a prolific writer, having written *The New Testament Church* (1964), *Broken Symbols* (1970), and co-authored *Expository Preaching* (1982) with his son, Mike. He has been a regular contributor to several religious journals and has had a regular column as Contributing Editor to the prestigious *Pulpit Digest* since 1976.

Shannon's preaching ministry has taken him all across the United States, Canada, Great Britain, Eastern Europe, New Zealand, and the Caribbean. He is, indeed, a master at the art of preaching and an exciting model of the expository preacher.

O. George Stansberry

George Stansberry is one of the outstanding evangelists among Christian Churches and Churches of Christ. He is a native of Johnson City, Tennessee. Here he attended public school and at First Christian Church, he made his decision for Christ, being baptized by George Mark Elliot. It was First Christian, Johnson City, that later ordained him to the Christian ministry with J.H. Dampier officiating.

Brother Stansberry attended Cincinnati Bible Seminary earning the A.B. degree in 1947 and the M.A. in 1949. After a student ministry with the Garden City Church of Christ, Columbus, Indiana, and a full-time ministry with the Brookville, Indiana, Church of Christ, he entered full-time evangelism in 1955.

During these years, Brother Stansberry has conducted nearly 700 evangelistic meetings, averaging nearly 25 meetings per year. He is the one general evangelist who has been in the field the longest and has been the most active through these years. Thousands have been baptized as a result of his evangelistic efforts.

Brother Stansberry serves as the Chairman of the Board of Trustees of his alma mater, Cincinnati Bible Seminary. He also serves as a member of the Convention Committee of the North American Christian Convention.

Brother Stansberry married Marjorie Graham of Erlange, Kentucky, in 1948. They have four adult children, three sons, and one daughter.